My Rock and Roll Fantasy

Richard M. Adler

Dedication

To my grandfather, Max Grover (whom I called "Poppy"), who opened my ears and heart to the magic of music. His steady belief in me helped shape my passions.

To my grandmother, Rose Grover, (whom I called "Nana"), my protector and champion, whose love and support helped me buy my first electric guitar and amp, and begin the journey I call *My Rock and Roll Fantasy*.

To my parents, Shirley and Joseph Adler, thank you for your unwavering love and support and for giving me the freedom to follow my dream.

To my wife, Cathy, and our children, Jennifer, Ryan and Jonathan, your unwavering support, kindness, and faith in my ability to write this book made these pages possible and filled every moment of this journey with purpose.

To my cherished grandchildren, Liam, Owen, Aiden, Maddie and Colin, who fill my life with laughter, inspiration, and a love that knows no bounds. You are the shining light that makes every note sweeter and every day more meaningful. As you read this book, I hope you not only discover your Poppy's passion for music but also gain a deeper understanding of who I am, the dreams I chased, the songs that shaped me, and the moments that defined my journey.

Author's Note

The events recounted in these pages are drawn from memories spanning more than half a century. While I have endeavored to portray people, places and experiences as faithfully as possible, the passage of time inevitably shapes and softens the edges of recollection. Certain details, such as names, dates, dialogue, or specific sequences, may differ from others' recollections or historical records, and for this, I take full responsibility.

This memoir reflects my personal perspective, colored by emotion, reflection, and the imperfect nature of human memory. It is not a documentary record, but rather a mosaic of moments as I remember them. Where the heart of the story resides, I have prioritized emotional truth over rigid precision.

I extend my gratitude to you, the reader and to those who shared this journey, for understanding that these pages are, above all, an offering of the past as it lives within me.

All vintage posters, flyers, and advertisements appearing in this book are reproduced for historical and educational purposes in the context of commentary and personal memoir. They are presented as part of my firsthand recollections of events and are not used for commercial promotion of the artists, venues, or events. No sponsorship or endorsement by the original creators, performers, or rights holders is implied.

Table Of Contents

Foreword

On February 9, 1964, history was made. The Beatles, a band from Liverpool, England, appeared on *The Ed Sullivan Show* for the first time, and 73 million people tuned in to watch. It was the moment America fully embraced Beatlemania. That night, everything changed, not just in music, but in culture, fashion, and even the way young people saw the world.

Before The Beatles, rock and roll was dominated by American artists. But these four young men brought something fresh, exciting, and completely different. Their sound was electric, their harmonies were tight, and their energy was contagious. It wasn't just their music, though, it was their whole attitude. They had long hair, sharp suits, and a sense of humor that made them seem cooler than anyone else.

Like millions of other kids, I was glued to my family's television in Forest Hills that night. But for me, this wasn't just entertainment it was life-changing. I had first heard The Beatles a few months earlier, on a car ride home from a Boy Scout camping trip. The song was *I Want to Hold Your Hand*, and I had never heard anything like it. It was new, it was exciting, and it made me feel something no other song ever had. I needed to know who this band was. I needed to hear more.

I wasn't alone. Millions of kids just like me rushed out to buy Beatles records. *Meet the Beatles* became my prized possession. I played it over and over until I was sure the needle would wear through the vinyl. Every new song, every new album just made me love them more.

Before that night, *The Ed Sullivan Show* was mostly for my parents' generation, Sinatra, Dean Martin, Perry Como, Broadway acts, and comedians. But when The Beatles took the stage, it felt like a whole new world had opened up. The girls in the studio screamed so loud you could barely hear the music. Every time they shook their heads and sang "Woooo!" the crowd went wild. Watching them command that stage, I knew exactly what I wanted to do, I wanted to play music. I wanted to be in a band. I wanted my own *Rock and Roll Fantasy*.

Just three days later, I attended my first rock concert, The Beatles at Carnegie Hall on February 12, 1964. The walls shook with excitement, and I knew I was in the right place. That night, my dream was set in motion.

And so begins *My Rock and Roll Fantasy!*

Richard M. Adler

Chapter 1

Brooklyn

We lived at 962 Mongomery Street Brooklyn, NY. from 1950 - 1957

I was born in Brooklyn, NY on May 6, 1950, to Shirley and Joseph "Sonny" Adler. My dad was a World War II veteran who came home almost broke from the Army and regretted it his entire life. He was a First Lieutenant and Quartermaster stationed in Italy, a role that gave him access to supplies that others might have used to make a fortune on the black market. But he saw himself as GI Joseph, honest to the core. He played by the rules and guarded his inventory like a mother hen. Even so, he still managed to land in hot water after winning $10,000 in a craps game. How do you win $10,000.00 in a crap game with soldiers making Army pay? The next day, he put the money in an envelope and sent it home. All mail was opened by the Army and inspected before it could be mailed. Of course, the Army, when they saw this sum of money, thought my dad was selling supplies on the black market and called him in to find out how he got the money. When they asked him, he said he won it in a crap game.

"Yeah right," the MP said. They asked him where the game was, but Dad only knew the division that hosted it. They asked if he had any witnesses who could attest to his winnings, but he couldn't produce any. So they put him in a jeep and drove him to the division that hosted the game. During the drive, Dad was afraid they wouldn't be able to find anyone who could act as a witness. Fortunately, someone from the game recognized him and told the investigators he had won a lot of money. All was forgiven, but Dad was afraid to do anything illegal for fear of getting caught. Other family members came home from the war with their pockets full, but not Dad. He was a gambler who was desperately in need of Gamblers Anonymous, but I digress.

I grew up playing with all my dad's Army gear that he brought home from the war. I loved his canteen, utility belt, mess kit holster, and all his medals. Dad raced on ice skates in high school, and I played with and lost all of his skating medals along with his Army medals, which he regretted much later in life.

I grew up a Brooklyn Dodger fan. Poppy, my mom's dad, Max, would take me on weekends to Ebbets Field to watch the Dodgers play. I still remember the first ball game I went to. It was a night game. Walking through the portal and seeing the field for the first time was burned into my memory. It was so green, and the dirt was so brown. It is an image I will never forget. I was fortunate to see Jackie Robinson play his last year for the Brooklyn Dodgers.

My maternal grandparents, Rose and Max Grover, lived in the same apartment building as we did at 962 Montgomery Street in Brooklyn, NY. They lived on the first floor, and we lived on the second. My grandfather, who I called Poppy, took me everywhere. He took me to the roller-skating rink, where I entered races. I got so good they wouldn't let me race in my age group. I had to race with the 8- and 9-year-old boys. I was only six years old, but I still won a good number of races, which really pissed off the older boys. I had my own skates, thanks to Poppy, with a blue carrying case that I decorated with stickers from the different skating rinks I raced at. I thought one day I would grow up and be a Roller Derby star, but that was not in the cards.

My family lived on a street where the residents of each house came from a different ethnic background and religion. My friends were Latino, Irish, Italian, Polish, German, and probably many other origins. In Brooklyn in the 1950s, people from different religious and ethnic backgrounds thought of themselves as quite different, though all felt thoroughly and completely American. The public schools instilled patriotism and a common national identity. If the older generation of that era were alive today, they would marvel at the fact that the Irish, Italians, Eastern European Jews, Germans, Scandinavians, and others are now described in the U.S. Census as simply "white."

Brooklyn was a different world back then. There, you didn't have just one mother, you had fifty. We all played outside with no real parent supervision, or so we thought, until we did something wrong. Then you would hear screams coming from different windows, "Richard Adler, you better stop that or I will call your mother." Really? You could not get away with much being a kid in Brooklyn without someone seeing you.

My earliest memory is around three years old. My dad bought me a toy cap gun with a holster and a cowboy hat. Back then, toy guns were made of metal, not some cheap plastic. I remember strapping on that gun, putting on the hat, and going with my mother to visit a friend down the block. When we got to my friend's building and entered the lobby, a kid my age asked to see my gun. I drew my weapon and whacked him on the top of his head with the back of it, like I saw on some western on TV. His mother had to take him to the hospital for stitches. That kid used to run the other way when he saw me coming. I was getting a reputation as a badass at three years old. Every parent on the block knew about this incident and tried to keep their kids away from me.

When I was about six, my Nana sent me to the corner grocery store with a note and some money. The store was on the other side of Montgomery Street, so I had to wait for an adult to cross me. Inside, I would hand the note and the money to the grocer, and he would fill the order, which always included pot cheese. What the heck was pot cheese? The grocer would hand me the bag with my change, and I would wait for an adult to cross me again, then deliver the bag to Nana. Can you imagine doing that today? Who sends a six-year-old to cross a street by asking a stranger for help? Different times.

The best thing about living in the same building as my grandparents was protection. Whenever I got into trouble and my mom or dad started yelling at me and threatening me with a beating, I would run out of the apartment, down the stairs, and Nana would protect me. "Don't you ever lay a finger on this boy," she would yell. For me, beating avoided.

I never went on vacation with my parents. I always stayed home with my grandparents while they went away. I swore back then that if I had kids, I would always take them with me on vacation.

One year, I got a kid's golf set for my birthday. My parents were on vacation in the Berkshires, and I was home with my grandparents. I brought the golf set outside, and some of the other kids wanted to play. Someone rolled the ball, another used the club to hit it, and I was the catcher. I guess I stood too close and got hit in the eyebrow with the club. I had a nasty gash, and blood covered my face. Nana heard me crying and came out to see what was wrong. When she saw me, she let out such a scream that she actually scared me. Nana rushed me to the hospital for stitches.

A year later, I went to watch the older kids play baseball behind the grocery store. Of course, I still needed an adult to cross me. For some reason, maybe they were short players, they asked me to be their catcher. I was so excited. The very first pitch, the batter swung and hit me in the mouth. I bled profusely from a big gash in my lip. I ran home bleeding, but had to wait for an adult to cross me. There I was, bleeding all over my shirt and pants, asking strangers for help. I finally got across and ran home. This time, it was my mother's turn to scream and take me to the hospital for stitches.

That same year, I got a new bike for my birthday, with training wheels. I took it out for my first ride when a group of big kids, about eight or nine years old, told me that only babies used training wheels. They said they would take them off and teach me to ride a two-wheeler. We went to the backyard, which was mostly concrete and away from cars and pedestrians. This seemed like a good place to learn. I got on my bike, one of the big kids pushed me slowly at first, then faster, and then he let go. Wow, I was riding! The only problem was, no one taught me how to stop. I kept going until I hit a brick wall. I slammed my pelvis into the handlebars and then fell off. It would have gone viral if YouTube had existed. Once again, my mother had to take her bleeding son to the hospital for stitches.

At seven years old, I got married to Carol Meshberg, who was also seven. We dressed up, and one of the kids on the block officiated the ceremony. She had bridesmaids, and I had a best man. When the kid said, "I now pronounce you man and wife," I got my first kiss from Carol. I believe there were wedding pictures, but they have been lost over the years. We took the wedding very seriously. We were boyfriend and girlfriend until I moved away the following year. Needless to say, she was heartbroken.

The only thing I remember about first grade in Brooklyn was the smell of PS 221, a combination of body odor, school lunches, and paint. They were always painting that school. The big memory was the windows, which had to be opened from the top using a pole. I guess they didn't want any kids falling out. Another odd thing was that the playground was on the roof. It was gated for our protection, and the fence covered the top as well as the sides, so I guess basketballs and kickballs wouldn't fly off the roof to the sidewalk below.

Chapter 2

Bethpage

I followed the record charts like they were the stock market. I analyzed which songs were on their way up and which were on the way down.

My introduction to pop music was *"Davy Crockett"*. I played that record every chance I got on my parents' record player. I would sing along and pretend that I was Davy Crockett, king of the wild frontier. My mother loved Julius LaRosa and would play "Eh Cumpari" for me. I loved that record, and as a five-year-old in Brooklyn, I would dance around the house and make believe I was playing the instruments in the song. My mom got a big kick out of it, and I put on a show for her every time she put that record on.

My sister Mindy and me

On November 29, 1957, my sister Mindy was born. I was seven years old. I had been an only child up to that point, and now I had a sister. I wondered what that would be like. Would Mom and Dad love her more than me? What about Nana and Poppy, would they now direct their attention to my sister and forget about me? But she was also someone to play with in the apartment. I was conflicted.

We moved to Bethpage, NY, from Brooklyn when I was seven years old. My parents bought the house at 22 Barnum Avenue for $19,990. It was a new house in a new housing development called Barnum Estates, which had been farmland just before the houses were built.

It was mid-July 1959, and I was nine years old, visiting the Bataglias' house, our next-door neighbors. I was spending time with Darlene, who was my age. She had a sister, Nancy, who must have been eleven or twelve. Nancy was listening to the radio, and I heard "Lipstick on Your Collar" by Connie Francis coming out of her room. I don't remember exactly what it was about the music that grabbed me, but Nancy was dancing around the house and singing along with the song. It was magical. I wanted to feel like that. I wanted to dance around the house and sing, just like I did back in Brooklyn for my mother. Darlene, Nancy, and I listened to the radio for a good two hours before I had to go home for dinner. When I got home, I asked my parents for a radio, and my dad bought one for me. I was hooked. I listened to that radio as much as I could. I must have known the words to every song they played.

Richard M. Adler

When I was ten years old, Poppy took me to a record store for the first time. He told me he was going to buy me the top ten 45s for that week. Every week, we would return to the record store, and he would buy me any new records that entered the top ten on the charts. This wasn't such a great feat, since they played the same twenty songs over and over until the words were embedded in your brain forever.

He bought me a black-and-white carrying case to hold my new record collection. I was so happy and so appreciative that Poppy did this for me. The first records he bought me that year were "*Only the Lonely*" by Roy Orbison, "*Itsy Bitsy Teenie Weenie Yellow Polka Dot Bikini*" by Bryan Hyland, "*Cathy's Clown*" by The Everly Brothers, "*It's Now or Never*" by Elvis Presley, "*The Twist*" by Chubby Checker, "*Everybody's Somebody's Foo'l* by Connie Francis, "*Alley Oop*" by Hollywood Argyles, "*Mr. Custer*" by Larry Verne, "*Sink the Bismarck*" by Johnny Horton, "*Walk Don't Run*" by The Ventures, "*Wild One*" by Bobby Rydell, "*Save the Last Dance for Me*" by The Drifters, "*I'm Sorry*" by Brenda Lee, and the list goes on and on. Needless to say, I had the best record collection of any ten-year-old kid in Bethpage, Long Island. Thanks, Poppy.

With these great records, I decided to have a dance party and invite the neighborhood kids over. My parents had a new patio built with a brick wall around it. I thought it would be the perfect place to hold the party. Like a good DJ, I planned every song I was going to play and the order in which I would play them. I also made a list of food for the party: chips, pretzels, popcorn, and soda.

Soda would not be a big deal, because my father worked next door to the Canada Dry factory in Maspeth, NY. One day, he did a huge favor for an executive at Canada Dry. He allowed their trucks to unload in his loading dock because the Canada Dry dock was closed for repair. This executive told my father that to thank him, he would leave a case of soda every week for my dad to pick up free of charge. This went on for many years. Needless to say, we always had soda in the house.

I was so excited about my dance party. It was just two days away when I was riding my bike to my friend's house. A girl named Cindy, who lived two houses away, stopped me to talk about the party. I was in a rush. I stopped just long enough to tell her that I didn't have time to talk, I was late and really had to run. She held on to the back of my bike and wouldn't let go. I got so angry that I turned around and slapped her in the face. She let go, and I went to my friend's house.

When I got home, my parents were furious. Apparently, Cindy told her mother that I slapped her, and Cindy's mom called mine. My parents sat me down and explained that a boy should never hit a girl. My punishment was to cancel the dance party. Not only did I not get to have the party, but I had to call all my friends and tell them it was canceled. I was devastated, but from that day until now, I have never hit another girl or woman in anger. I guess it was a small price to pay for a life lesson.

My parents waited a month and told me that I could have the party if I still wanted to. The party was great, and all my friends couldn't believe I had all those records. I was the only one of my friends who actually owned a record collection that didn't include things like *Davy Crockett* or *Disney's Greatest Hits*. It was a collection better than even their teenage brothers or sisters had.

Across the street from our house was a boarding house. In that house lived a college girl named Vivian, who took me swimming at an indoor pool once a week. I guess my parents hired her to teach me to swim, but back then, I thought of her as a friend who I went swimming with. Vivian would come to the house to pick me up, and she would ask if she could see my record collection. Even this college girl thought I had the coolest record collection.

Chapter 3

Forest Hills

In 1961, we moved from Bethpage to Forest Hills, NY.

Forest Hills is a neighborhood in Queens, New York City, adjacent to Corona, Rego Park, Glendale, Forest Park, Kew Gardens, and Flushing Meadows–Corona Park. The area was originally referred to as "Whitepot." The current name comes from the Cord Meyer Development Company, which bought land in 1906 and named it Forest Hills after Forest Park. Forest Hills has a long history of tennis and was home to the US Open until 1978. The West Side Tennis Club moved there in 1914 and built the Forest Hills Tennis Stadium with approximately 13,000 seats.

The Forest Hills Stadium hosted the U.S. Open until 1978, making Forest Hills synonymous with tennis for generations. The U.S. Open tennis tournament was held at the West Side Tennis Club before it moved to the USTA Billie Jean King National Tennis Center in Flushing Meadows Park, about four miles away. When the Open was played at the tennis stadium, the tournament was commonly referred to merely as Forest Hills, just as the All-England Lawn Tennis Association Championships are referred to simply as Wimbledon.

The Tennis Stadium hosted numerous music concerts including The Beatles, Simon & Garfunkel, The Who, Rolling Stones, Bob Dylan, Creedence Clearwater Revival, The Monkees, and Jimi Hendrix during the 1960s and 1970s, those are just the ones that I attended. I was fortunate to live within walking distance of the stadium and attended all of these great concerts right in my backyard.

Mr. Brodsky's 6th Grade Class PS 175

In the photo on the previous page, I am standing next to Mr. Brodsky, who is on the left. Steve Feinberg is directly below me. Jeff Lane is directly above me, Michael Hanowitz is in the 3rd row 4th from the left, and Richie Stern (who was in the Ramones for about 15 minutes) is in the 2nd row 2nd from right. All good friends in the 6th grade.

Three of my sixth-grade girlfriends are in the 1st row. Mindy Goldstein, 1st on the left, Barbara Cooper, 2nd from right, and Leslie Beatus, 1st on right.

I was in Mr. Brodsky's 6th grade class at PS 175. I was the new kid in school and Mr. Brodsky started calling me "The Bethpage Commando" because I had just moved to Forest Hills from Bethpage. I guess I was getting in trouble a lot because he was always saying, "The Bethpage Commando strikes again."

Mr. Brodsky's favorite saying was "The pen is mightier than the sword." My parents did not react well to my first report card, which Mr. Brodsky filled out with his mighty pen.

In 6th grade I started going steady with girls, which meant that you gave her your ID bracelet, which had your name on it, and she would wear it to show everyone she was your steady girl.

For me, going steady with a girl only lasted a few weeks or a few months depending on the girl. We used to have parties where kids played spin the bottle and seven minutes in heaven, but guys who were going steady just "made out" with their girlfriends. I believe I went steady with 6 different girls in 6th grade. I was like a kid in a candy store. Before 6th grade, I never thought about girls, but now I thought about them a lot.

Steve Feinberg and Me

My 6th grade friend was Steve Feinberg. Steve lived in the same apartment complex as I did, and we formed a friendship when I first moved to Forest Hills. Steve was also in Mr. Brodsky's 6th grade class. Steve was one of the good guys, always smiling and joking around.

I remember Steve came to my Bar Mitzvah. We were walking home from Temple with my sister Mindy, who was 6 years old at the time, when she fell into a puddle of dirty water.

Her dress was ruined and we had to rush her home to get changed for the big party. My mother expected Mindy to wear that dress to the party but now she would have to find something else. My mother didn't have another nice dress for her. She kept saying that she wanted Mindy to look nice for the pictures. Well, she didn't have to worry about the pictures!

My parents did not own a camera and really didn't have the money to hire a photographer, so they asked my cousin Bob, who owned a camera, to take pictures at the party. Bob had to work that day, so he arrived at the party straight from work. Bob forgot his camera, so there are no pictures from my Bar Mitzvah party. I guess my mother didn't have to worry about Mindy's dress after all.

Topps Baseball Cards: A Very Sad Story

My father once did a favor for an executive at Topps. They were the company that made the baseball cards. Topps was a client of the corrugated box company that my father worked for.

After doing that favor, the Topps executive started sending 2 complete sets of baseball cards to my dad from 1955 to 1965. He also did the same with football cards. He told my dad to give them to me and said I should play with one box and leave the second box sealed and unopened. He even sent my dad 2 sets of Beatles cards.

I was flipping baseball cards and putting them on my bike wheels with clothespins so they made a noise as the wheels turned. I had all the boxes of cards on the top shelf of my closet. Imagine all the rookie cards I had of many great players during that time.

In 1968, I left for the University of Oklahoma. When I returned home for Thanksgiving, I noticed my mother had cleaned out my closet. I asked her what she did with my baseball cards and she said, "I hope you didn't want them. I threw them out. You never even opened them and they were taking up the entire top shelf of your closet." Thanks, Mom.

I can't imagine what those boxes of cards would be worth today.

Richard M. Adler

Bullying

When I was in 9th grade, like many other kids, I was being bullied by some of the tough kids in the neighborhood. Nick, Mike, Ivan, and Marty. When they got together, they made my life a living hell. They would walk down the halls of Halsey Jr. High School and when they saw me they would crash into me, knock me over, or knock the books out of my hands. They would collectively push me around and call me names for no apparent reason. I was much smaller than they were and they knew I wouldn't fight back.

It was embarrassing to be knocked around by these morons. I didn't like looking weak in front of my classmates, especially the girls. It got so bad that I couldn't take it anymore. I was about to explode.

My dad went up to the school to complain that I was being bullied on school grounds and demanded that the school do something about it. I guess the school called their parents and told them to control their kids. Mike, one of the kids whose parents were called, must have gotten a beating from his parents because he was so mad at my father that he told some kids he had a knife and was going to kill my father. Word got back to me, and I told my dad. My dad stormed out of the house and headed right for the playground where these kids hung out.

Dad walked up and asked, "Which one of you is Mike? I am Richard's father and I heard that you are looking for me." As soon as my dad finished his sentence, Mike got up and ran away.

One day, I was walking down Yellowstone Blvd and saw Marty coming down the street. The very sight of him made my blood boil. I decided that here is where I would make my stand.

Marty was alone, so as he approached me, I just snapped. I started punching and wrestling with him. I actually flipped him off his feet onto his back. I got on top of him, grabbed him by the hair, and started bashing his head into the pavement.

I didn't realize it, but we were in the middle of Yellowstone Blvd. which was a very busy two-lane road with cars traveling in both directions. With Marty and me in the middle of the road, cars stopped on both sides. A man jumped out of his car and pulled me off of Marty and put me in his car. He said that if that guy ever got up, he would kill me. So, this kind man drove me home.

Two days later, Ivan was walking alone in front of my apartment building. I saw Ivan and the same thing happened. I exploded. I started fighting with Ivan, who was not only much taller than I was, but if he was a heavyweight, I was a lightweight. Once again, I was able to throw Ivan to the ground. I jumped on top of him and this time I just started punching him in the face.

Then I felt a hand on my shoulder and a voice yelling at me to stop. It was my mom. She was afraid I was really going to hurt Ivan. What? I was afraid he would get up and hurt me. Well, I let Ivan up. He was so humiliated that he ran away.

From that day on, no one ever bullied me again. Bullies hate guys that fight back. They prefer the weak guys who are afraid and refuse to fight back. They are all so brave and tough when they are together, but apparently not so much when they are alone. Not me. I was ready to take a beating as long as they would stop bugging me. I think that Marty and Ivan were both shocked when I decided to fight back.

Richard M. Adler

Chapter 4

The Beatles

Photo by William Warby on Unsplash

The Week that Changed My Life began on February 7, 1964, when I was glued to my radio, listening to the biggest event that had taken place in my short 13 years on this planet. The Beatles were coming to America, and the DJs on New York Top 40 radio were all over this story. We were receiving reports every 30 minutes about the arrival of The Beatles at New York's John F. Kennedy Airport. The excitement was building; we all knew that this was going to be a momentous event.

On the morning of February 7, 1964, a Boeing 707 operated by Pan Am, flight 101, took off from London Airport carrying The Beatles. The flight was bound for New York City, and its details, including flight number and arrival time, were announced by Murray the K, a DJ at the 1010 WINS radio station. This information was then picked up by other radio stations like WABC and WMCA, which only added to the excitement surrounding the band's arrival.

When The Beatles' plane arrived at JFK Airport at 1:20 P.M., the scene was unlike anything that had been seen before. Around 5,000 excited fans, mostly young girls, had gathered on the upper balcony of the airport's arrivals building, holding signs and banners to greet the band. Additionally, about 200 journalists, photographers, and videographers from various media outlets were eager to get a glimpse of The Beatles and capture their arrival. Before The Beatles' first American tour, Brian Epstein faced challenges in handling the rising demand for the group's merchandise. As a solution, he approached his lawyer, David Jacobs, who suggested that Nicky Byrne, a seasoned professional in the field, should take over the management of the merchandising division. Byrne agreed to take on the responsibility but requested a 90 percent commission for himself, leaving only a 10 percent share for The Beatles and NEMS combined. Despite his lack of understanding of the magnitude of the market, particularly in America, Epstein approved the agreement. However, this decision resulted in an estimated loss of 100 million dollars in potential income for The Beatles.

Byrne had struck a deal with the WMCA and WINS radio stations in which every fan who turned up at JFK would be given one dollar and a free Beatles t-shirt. Unbeknown to Byrne, Capitol had also arranged for posters and car stickers bearing the legend 'The Beatles are coming' to be distributed throughout New York City. The Beatles held their first press conference in the United States at JFK Airport.

After I saw so many kids turn out for The Beatles' arrival at JFK, I heard they were staying at the Plaza Hotel in NYC. I got on the subway and went down to the Plaza to see what was going on. It was crazy. Hundreds of kids were hanging out in front of the hotel. I thought it was going to be easy to meet one of the girls who were screaming for The Beatles that day. I actually met a few really nice girls and we exchanged phone numbers. I dated two of them a couple of times, but one lived in Brooklyn and one in the Bronx, which wasn't very convenient for a 13-year-old boy from Queens whose only mode of transportation was the subway.

Prior to The Beatles' debut in the United States, Brian Epstein had reserved rooms at the Plaza Hotel for the group. However, the management of the Plaza was under the impression that they would be hosting British business travelers. Upon The Beatles' arrival, the hotel staff were caught off guard by the overwhelming reaction from fans. During their subsequent tours, The Beatles opted to stay at the Warwick Hotel instead. While there, they occupied an entire wing, and as a keepsake, took all of the hangers from the closet before departing.

While staying at the Plaza, numerous fans attempted to gain access to see The Beatles. Some even tried to pass themselves off as reporters, and some may have succeeded. Departing from the hotel was chaotic too, but the group managed to get out successfully.

The Beatles had the entire 12th floor to themselves at the Plaza. The girls on the street found out what floor The Beatles were staying on, and every time they saw a curtain move on the 12th floor, they started to scream. Everyone listened to their transistor radios and followed the comings and goings of The Beatles, thanks to Murray the K and Cousin Brucie reporting their every move.

Some girls I was talking to found a car with open windows, and inside were maid uniforms for the Plaza. They rolled up their pants and put on the uniforms, hoping to sneak in through the employee entrance, but the security guard caught them, made them take off the uniforms, and kicked them out.

Another girl rented a limo and tried to sneak into the hotel. She was all dressed up and tried to look older, but she was caught and not allowed to enter the Plaza.

February 12, 1964, was Lincoln's Birthday and I was off from school. I heard that The Beatles were returning to New York from Washington, D.C., by train. I decided to head to Penn Station to see The Beatles. When I arrived, it appeared that 10,000 other kids had the same idea. The place was mobbed. It was insane. Everyone was singing Beatles songs and "We Love You Beatles." The Beatles were traveling to New York from Washington, D.C., by train, where they had performed their first U.S. concert the night before. The train ride took two hours. At the last minute, the police detached the car The Beatles were in from the rest of the train and diverted it to an isolated platform. A plan to take them up a special elevator was spoiled by fans, so The Beatles charged up the closest set of stairs. Their limo was unable to get through the mob of kids, so they jumped into a taxi idling on Seventh Avenue, which took them back to the Plaza Hotel, where they got ready for the night's concerts. The police smuggled them out through the kitchen to their waiting limos. They were late for their sound check at Carnegie Hall.

That night, I was lucky enough to get a ticket to Carnegie Hall to see The Beatles and attend my first rock concert. Tickets for the concerts had gone on sale at the box office on January 27 and had completely sold out by the following day. Two thousand nine hundred people saw each of the two shows, which were promoted by New York impresario Sid Bernstein. I attended the early show, which was scheduled to start at 7:45 p.m. The warm-up act for both performances was The Briarwoods.

I met a girl named Carol at Penn Station. She was going to see The Beatles that night at Carnegie Hall with her friend Sue. While we were at Penn Station, Carol called her mom to check in, and her mom told her that Sue was sick and would not be able to go to the concert. Carol came back and told me what happened, then asked if I wanted to go with her. This was my lucky day. I called my mom and told her I would be home late because I was going to see The Beatles at Carnegie Hall. I also told her not to worry because Carol's father was going to pick us up and drive us home.

This was the first time a rock act performed at Carnegie Hall. Sid Bernstein negotiated with Carnegie Hall before anyone in the United States knew who The Beatles were. The folks at Carnegie Hall thought The Beatles were a string quartet from England. They were livid when they discovered The Beatles' true identity.

"Carnegie Hall didn't have to worry about its sacred property or paintings on the wall. They shook a little bit, and they asked me never to come back again!" said Sid Bernstein.

George Martin had wanted to record The Beatles' Carnegie Hall performances, and although Capitol Records agreed, he was denied permission by the American Federation of Musicians.

"Carnegie Hall was terrible! The acoustics were terrible, and they had all these people sitting on the stage with us. It was just like Rockefeller's children backstage, and it all got out of hand. It wasn't a rock show; it was just a sort of circus where we were in cages. We were being pawed, talked at, met, and touched, both backstage and onstage. We were just like animals," said John Lennon.

The Beatles played the following songs at the concert:

- Roll Over Beethoven

Richard M. Adler

- From Me to You

- I Saw Her Standing There

- This Boy

- All My Loving

- I Wanna Be Your Man

- Please Please Me

- Till There Was You

- She Loves You

- I Want to Hold Your Hand

- Twist and Shout

- Long Tall Sally

When The Beatles were announced, the crowd went berserk. It was mayhem and pandemonium. After the seventh song, John Lennon yelled "SHUT UP" into the microphone. That request fell on deaf ears. The crowd kept screaming and never let up. For the entire 34 minutes The Beatles were on stage, the screaming stayed at the same loud level. We really had to struggle to identify the songs they were playing because the noise was deafening!

Since this was my first rock concert, I assumed all concerts had seating on the stage. I wondered how you got to be lucky enough to score seats right on the stage. It turns out there were so many celebrities and politicians asking Sid Bernstein for tickets that he had to add seats on the stage to accommodate the demand. Even with all the added seats, Sid Bernstein still had to deny many requests from celebrities and politicians because there was not a single seat left for either show. They were completely sold out.

Richard M. Adler

Chapter 5

Guitar Lessons

Me with my Gretsch Firebird and Tommy with his Gretsch Tennessean

I had many opportunities in school to learn an instrument. I took trumpet lessons, but I never practiced. I really wasn't into "Cherry Pink and Apple Blossom White." Then I took drum lessons, but all they gave me were two sticks and a practice pad. How boring! Neither of those instruments captured my interest or imagination.

Richard M. Adler

After seeing The Beatles on the Ed Sullivan Show and at Carnegie Hall, I knew I had to learn to play guitar so I could form a band and have all the girls scream when I went on stage.

I asked my mother to let me take guitar lessons, and she arranged for me to go to a neighborhood music store, where I took weekly lessons. I was not very happy with them because the teacher started me off with "Twinkle, Twinkle Little Star." How boring! I wanted to rock, and he was teaching me "Twinkle, Twinkle." Not exactly what would get the girls to scream. So, I bought a Beatles music book, and while the teacher was teaching me "Twinkle, Twinkle," I was teaching myself "All My Loving."

I had learned Every Good Boy Does Fine, which are the notes on the lines of the music staff (EGBDF), and FACE, which are the notes on the spaces. Armed with that information, I was able to figure out the notes to the melody. I asked my music teacher what the difference was between the lead guitar and the rhythm guitar in a band, and he told me that the lead guitar played the melody and the rhythm guitar played the chords. That wasn't exactly correct, but I did learn the melody line. I practiced every chance I got.

Once I started playing guitar, I stopped playing football and baseball. I was the quarterback for the Green Hornets, a Pop Warner football team. We played on the field at Fleet Street in Forest Hills. During one of my last Pop Warner games, I was running a naked bootleg around the right end. Alex "Bugsy" Garfield was just about to tackle me when I gave him a stiff arm to his helmet. Bugsy, who was a good player and much bigger than me, grabbed my arm and threw me to the ground, dislocating my left shoulder.

I was down on the ground screaming when my coach, Dick Gottesman, ran out on the field, put his foot in my armpit, grabbed my left hand, and pulled my shoulder back into its socket. Man, that hurt. I had to wear a sling for a couple of weeks, and that was the end of my Pop Warner football season. I know Bugsy was really upset that he hurt me, but I just want him to know it was not his fault. It was all part of the game.

I was the pitcher and catcher for Michael C. Fina's Little League team, but not at the same time. We also played our Little League games at Fleet Street, which had both baseball and football fields. I had dreams of being a professional ballplayer, as every boy does, but that dream changed on February 9, 1964.

My mother had rented me an acoustic guitar, but I wanted an electric guitar and was very disappointed when the clerk at the music store handed me the acoustic. Oh well. My mom told me to learn to play the acoustic, and then we would talk about an electric guitar. I guess she remembered paying to rent that trumpet. I had a newspaper route where I delivered the New York Post. I was determined to buy an electric guitar, so I saved my money one tip at a time. One day on my route, I was collecting money owed for the week. I entered an apartment building and was followed in by a tough-looking kid who was much older than me and didn't look like he was from Forest Hills. I pressed the elevator button and waited for it to come down. When the doors opened, this kid got on with me. He had a knife in his hand and said, "Hand over your money," then grabbed my book of accounts out of my hands.

Thinking fast, I told him I had just started making my collections. The woman in apartment 5F owed me for four weeks. I told him I would give him that money if he waited behind the wall so she couldn't see him through the peephole. I said she might get scared if she saw a Black kid standing outside her door, especially in this neighborhood. He agreed and hid behind the wall as I rang her bell. When she opened the peephole and saw it was me, she opened the door, and I almost knocked her over as I ran into her apartment, slammed the door, and locked it.

I lied. It was my final collection of the day, and there was no way this kid was getting my money. I called my father, and he came to pick me up. The funny part was that the kid who tried to rob me rang the woman's doorbell and asked if his friend was still inside. She started screaming at him to leave and said she was calling the police. By the time my father got there, the kid was long gone, and my money was safe to put toward my new electric guitar.

My 14th birthday was coming up, and when anyone asked me what I wanted as a birthday present, I told them I wanted money toward my electric guitar and amp. My parents and my aunt gave me money, but my Nana asked how much I had saved. She said that if I gave her what I had, she would add whatever was needed, and we could go buy an electric guitar and amp for my birthday.

We went to Manny's Music Store on 48th Street in Manhattan and purchased a sunburst-colored Kent guitar with a strap, a case, and a small amplifier. I was smiling from ear to ear. I was so happy. I wanted to plug that guitar in right there and play "All My Loving," but what would I play for an encore, and then maybe "Twinkle, Twinkle Little Star"? I didn't think so.

We hopped on the subway and went home to Forest Hills. I couldn't wait to plug it in and start playing. I practiced for hours and hours until my fingers began to bleed. At my next lesson at the music store, I brought my electric guitar. My teacher told me it was a good one and that if I practiced really hard, I could make it sound great. On my way out of the store, I looked in the window and saw this beautiful red Hagstrom guitar. I wished I had bought that one, but I didn't have enough money, and it was out of my Nana's budget.

Every week, I would look at that guitar and drool. It was almost three times the price of my Kent guitar, but I wanted it. It had a tremolo bar, which mine didn't have. It also had lots of knobs and switches. It looked like it could play itself. If I could only afford that guitar, I thought, it would make me a star.

On my way home from my lesson, this kid Tommy stopped me as I was walking up the stairs to my apartment building. I had seen him before but we never spoke. He was a little older than me and we weren't in any classes together. He didn't participate in any of our stickball games, Ring-a-leveo or any of the games the kids in the neighborhood played. In fact, I don't remember him ever coming down to hang out with us. While I was walking up the stairs, he asked me if I played guitar. I wanted to give him a wise-ass answer like "No I just carry it around to look cool" but instead I just said "yeah, I'm taking lessons". Tommy asked me if I wanted to jam". I asked "What's that?" he told me that we could get together and play songs together. Oh! Ok. That sounded cool and scary at the same time. I didn't know many songs and I never played in front of anyone but my teacher, my sister and my parents. Tommy told me to come to his apartment with my guitar and amp that afternoon.

I lived on the second floor and Tommy lived on the third floor of my building. I went to Tommy's apartment feeling a little nervous. What if he was really good? What if I suck? Wait, I did suck! Oh well, I rang his doorbell and he answered the door. Tommy invited me in. He said that his parents would be home in about an hour and a half so we had to stop once they got home. Tommy didn't have an electric guitar. He had a nylon string classical guitar which he began to strum. He was pretty good. He knew the chords to a few Beatles songs which I knew the melody to. We played those songs then we played them again. By that time, he said that his parents would be home soon and we would have to stop. He asked me if I knew any other kids that played instruments so that we could start a band? I told him that I would ask around in school. I had a friend Ira Nagel who I would talk about music with. He seemed to like music as much as I did so I asked him if he played an instrument but, he told me that he didn't. I told Ira that I was starting a band with my friend Tommy and we needed a bass player. I encouraged Ira to go to the same Music Store as me for lessons but he didn't have a bass or an amp. Good news, Ira just got some money for his Bar Mitzvah and I encouraged him to use that money to buy a bass and amp. I didn't need to push Ira too hard because he wanted to be in the band.

Ira bought a Bass Guitar and Amp before even taking a lesson. Ira learned to play and became a very good bass player and we asked him to join our band. Ira would come over to my apartment and jam with Tommy and me. We needed a drummer but I didn't know anyone who played the drums. Ira said that he met a kid that went to private school who played the drums and had a drum set. Ira took me over to this drummer's house. Howie Segal lived only a block and a half down the street from me. I never saw him before. He lived in a private house. Everyone I knew in Forest Hills lived in an apartment house. This was perfect. A drummer and a private house. Lucky us. We asked Howie if we could watch him play the drums. Howie was happy to have someone to show off to so down his basement we went. Howie got behind the drums and began playing Wipeout. Wow, he was good. Much better on drums than we were on guitar. We told Howie that we had a band and wanted him to join up with us. Howie said that we should bring Tommy and our guitars to his house the next day and we could jam. We did just that and played all the songs we knew, which were not many, but it sounded great to me. We didn't have microphones so we couldn't hear the singing over the music. But we were having a great time. My friend Roy came down to hear us play and wanted to be in the band. He played a little piano and wanted to play keyboards in the band. Only one problem, where does a 14-year-old kid get a portable organ? They cost way too much money. Janet, my girlfriend at the time had a pump organ that was sort of portable but the problem was that it wasn't electric. That means that we could not plug it into an amplifier. We tried to put a mic near the organ to pick up the sound but Roy's keyboard was never really audible. Due to the fact that he didn't have an instrument that could be used in the band, Roy never became a member of the band. A few years later, Roy bought a Vox organ and became a pretty good musician. So, the band was back to Tommy, Ira, Howie and me. We practiced a lot in Howie's basement but Howie's mother most probably needed a break because one day we came over to practice and she said, "Howie can't practice today, he needs to go out and get some sun". What? Sun? We were playing music, who needed sun. I couldn't understand how this could happen until later years when I grew up and realized that the basement was not soundproof and she most probably couldn't hear herself think when we were playing.

Most of us in the band went to Halsey Junior High School all but Howie who went to private school. Every Friday night, the school had a dance party in the gym. They played records so that the kids could have somewhere to hangout and not get into trouble. I had asked one of the teachers who was a chaperon at the dance if our band could play for one of the dances. We would play for free just so people could hear us and we could play in front of a real audience. The teacher agreed and asked if we wanted to play the following week. I was so excited. I ran home and went upstairs to Tommy's apartment. He lived on the 3rd floor of the building and I lived on the second floor. Tommy always came out to the hall when his parents were home. So, we stood in the hall and I gave him the good news. "We have a gig". No money but an audience and there will be girls there to watch us play. We went out and bought a microphone and stand which we plugged into one of the guitar amps. Tommy and I shared the vocals on the same mic. I really couldn't play the melody and sing at the same time so Tommy did most of the singing. We didn't have enough songs to fill the entire night so we just kept playing the songs we knew over and over again. The funny part was, no one complained that we played the same songs 4 times that night. It was thrilling that the kids actually applauded after each song. Looking back, I wonder if they even knew what songs we played.

We continued playing Friday nights at the Halsey Gym using the name Tommy and The Tigers. One night another band showed up. They were worse than we were. Their lead singer played maracas and sometimes the tambourine.

During a song that he played the maracas on, he would bang them together keeping time to the music. I guess he really got into it because midway thru the song, he banged them just a little too hard and both maracas broke open and all the little balls inside spilled all over the dance floor. We sat there watching this and laughing our asses off. Then on the very next song, after spending about 10 minutes cleaning up all the little balls that spilled onto the dance floor, they started another song. This time the lead singer didn't play the maracas or the tambourine but during a guitar solo, he began swinging the microphone like Roger Daltry of the Who. He was really getting into it when the mic hit the Basketball Backboard and bounced down hitting the lead singer on the head. Again, we laughed our asses off. Although the band wasn't very good, the lead singer was really good. He had a great voice and gave us a couple of good laughs that night.

After the show, when the bands were packing up to leave, Tommy and I walked over and began talking to the lead singer. We found out his name was Bob Rowland. We talked a lot about our influences and found out that Bob was from England, that magical land across the sea, home of The Beatles, The Stones, The Who and all of the British Invasion bands. Bob told us that he loved Doo Wop music and sang with his friends in the bathroom at school. Funny, we did that too. Bob told us that his band sucked but thought we were pretty good. He asked if we needed a lead singer. Tommy called me outside for a conference. Howie and Ira came outside as well to join our little band meeting. We took a vote and just like that, Bob was now the lead singer of our band. We invited him to our next band practice which was the next day at Howie's house.

At band practice we changed our name from Tommy and The Tigers to The Tiger 5.

We played a lot of parties and school dances. One day Ira came to us and told us of a gig he got us in Rockaway Beach. It was at a boarding house playing on the front porch facing the street. It was for a street fair with lots of people. This is the first time we got to play outside of Forest Hills. Rockaway Beach was the closest beach to Forest Hills. Tommy and I would hitchhike to Rockaway Beach in the summer. We would have our girlfriends stick out their thumbs and we would hide. When a car stopped to pick up the girls, we would jump in. I can't believe no one objected or pulled us out of the car. We never thought that it was dangerous to hitch to the beach but guys must have gotten very pissed off thinking that they were picking up 2 unattached girls and then got duped. I always thought that Tommy wrote the song Rockaway Beach about our summer adventures and was disappointed to find out that Dee Dee actually wrote it.

The Rockaway Beach gig was very satisfying for the band. We got to play for new people and received a warm reception.

Richard M. Adler

One day, Ira called me up and told me that his uncle owns Wetson's, which was like a McDonald's before McDonald's came to New York. Wetson's was an American fast food hamburger chain that existed from 1959 to 1975. At its peak, Wetson's had approximately 70 locations in the greater New York metropolitan area. The chain was known for its signature burger, the "Big W", 15-cent burgers, 10-cent fries, and the slogans "Look for the Orange Circles" and "Buy them by the bagful".

Wetson's was founded in 1959 by Harold Norbitz and Carl Wetanson. The pair had visited a McDonald's during a trip to Chicago's suburbs in the mid-50s and were impressed by the concept, cheap food and fast service. They "basically duplicated" the McDonald's concept at a time when there were no McDonald's in the metropolitan New York area.

Errol Wetanson, who was Ira's cousin and son of Carl Wetanson the owner of Wetson's, married actress Margaux Hemingway which was very impressive to the members of our band.

Ira told me that he was talking with his cousin about the band. He told Ira that they were opening a new Wetson's somewhere in Queens and he wanted to know if we would play at the Grand opening. He also told Ira that Gary Stevens, who was a Disk Jockey on WMCA radio was going to be there to introduce us. WOW! now that is very cool. We were all excited about playing this grand opening. A big time DJ would get to hear us play. We felt like we were on the verge of making it. We were sure that once Gary Stevens heard us play, he would help us get a recording contract.

Gary Stevens and his "Wooley burger" bear, aimed at teenagers listening on small transistor radios in their rooms. (7pm-11pm - First show was in April, 1965)

The day finally came; we went to Wetson's and set up our equipment in the parking lot. We were so nervous. We didn't know that there was an all-girls Catholic high school across the street from Wetson's. When it came time to perform, the parking lot was filled with high school girls. The girls outnumbered the boys in the audience by 5 to 1. The parking lot was jammed with kids. There was no stage, just a roped off area in the parking lot.

Gary Stevens was signing autographs and giving out Good Guys Tee Shirts and some records.

WMCA was a radio station in New York City featuring a lineup of DJs known as the "Good Guys." WMCA is credited with having been the first New York radio station to broadcast a recording by The Beatles .

I remember a few names of the Good Guys. There was Joe O'Brien, Harry Harrison, Jack Spector, Dandy Dan Daniels, B. Mitchell Reed and Gary Stevens. The WMCA Good Guys logo which was printed on Tee Shirts and Sweatshirts were very popular back then and lots of kids were wearing them that day. The logo on the shirts was a Smiley Face with the text WMCA Good Guys.

It was time for us to go on Stage. We left our dressing room, which was the kitchen of Wetson's, with guitars in hand and waited at the door for Gary Stevens to introduce us. Gary Stevens was at the microphone doing a promo for WMCA radio and for his show. He kept going on and on until finally he shouted "Ladies and Gentlemen, The Tiger 5". The parking lot erupted with thunderous screams and we opened the back door of Wetson's and ran across the parking lot to the stage. The kids were going crazy, screaming and applauding like we were The Beatles. We were amazed. The only thing I could think of was that since we were with Gary Stevens, the crowd thought that we must be a famous band. So, we could hardly hear ourselves think as we plugged in our guitars. We started playing our set. We began with Twist and Shout then Hang on Sloopy. We started playing Shout when all hell broke loose. The girls started charging the stage like a pack of wild dogs. They were pulling our hair and trying to rip our shirts off our backs. They went nuts; all I could see is a sea of screaming faces. There was no security provided and the crowd was out of control. I thought to myself, this is how The Beatles must feel during their concerts. The workers inside Wetson's were watching us perform and they saw the dangerous situation developing in the parking lot. They raced out and started pulling the girls off of us and somehow got us back inside Wetson's. They went back and retrieved our amplifiers and drums. They locked all the doors and didn't allow anyone to enter. I had a scratch on my face, my hair was pulled so hard that my scalp hurt and my sweater was ripped from where a girl tried to rip my sleeve off. The girls were banging on the door and windows. I was afraid that someone was going to get hurt if the glass broke. The manager of Wetson's had to call the Police to control the crowd. After a few minutes the crowd calmed down but the girls who were at the door. that we were hiding behind, began passing notes under the door with their phone numbers on them. It was a teenage boy's dream come true. I was 15 years old at the time and had enough phone numbers to ensure that I would have a date on Friday and Saturday night for a couple of years.

We were actually very lucky that we got out of that parking lot alive. I guess I always wanted to have girls screaming for me playing guitar. You need to be careful what you wish for.

Chapter 6

Forest Hills Goes Crazy for The Beatles

In the summer of 1964, a miracle happened. The Beatles were scheduled to perform two shows in Forest Hills on Friday and Saturday, August 28 and 29. What were the chances? The Tiger 5 had to go see the Beatles.

We anxiously waited for the tickets to go on sale at 11 a.m. on May 1, 1964, at Limelight Products, located at 118-30 Queens Blvd. in Forest Hills, next door to the Kew Tavern bar. Tickets were priced from $1.95 to $4.95. The 15,983 available tickets quickly sold out. Rather than turn fans away, the promoters added more seats up close on the tennis green for the premium price of $6.50.

We stood in line and got our prized tickets to the first show on Friday night. Sixteen thousand lucky kids each night got a chance to see the Beatles, and we were part of that lucky group.

It was surreal being in the Forest Hills Tennis Stadium and seeing the Beatles arrive by helicopter and land on the tennis courts behind the stadium. I had never seen any performers arrive at a concert by helicopter. It definitely added to the mystique. It was like watching gods descend from the heavens. The Beatles arrived late because the helicopter pilot did not have permission to take off and had to wait for clearance. They took to the stage at 9:50 p.m., much later than expected, and We could hardly hear the Beatles over the screaming, so the best we could do was try to identify which song they were playing. The Beatles performed their standard 12-song set for the U.S. tour: "Twist and Shout," "You Can't Do That," "All My Loving," "She Loves You," "Things We Said Today," "Roll Over Beethoven," "Can't Buy Me Love," "If I Fell," "I Want to Hold Your Hand," "Boys," "A Hard Day's Night," and "Long Tall Sally."

Saturday night, we wanted to go to the second show, but we didn't have tickets. Ira, I think, knew one of the ticket takers. Ira had us all give him $1.00 and bribed the ticket taker to let us in. To my amazement, it worked. So we got to see both Forest Hills shows.

For security, an eight-foot fence was erected around the stage with barbed wire on top. At one of the shows, a girl managed to get on stage and grab George Harrison. An alert security guard had to wrestle her away, but she held on until a second security guard managed to free George from her clutches.

Another incident occurred when a boy jumped on stage and approached George. This time, a security guard stopped the boy before he could grab him. There was a rumor that the boy had a knife and was going to stab George because his girlfriend was so in love with him. I have never been able to confirm whether that rumor was true.

It is almost impossible to explain the feeling we were all collectively experiencing before, during, and after seeing the Beatles live. For us 14-year-old kids, it was life-changing. We wanted to experience those incredible feelings again by going to many more rock concerts, but I was never able to feel that way again, except at Shea Stadium in 1965 and 1966.

I was 15 years old and enjoying playing in the Tiger 5 when Tommy came to me and said we needed to take the band to the next level. We wondered how to do that. Being just 15 years old, what did we know?

I met a guy named Philip Edwards, who was a record producer, and asked him if he would be interested in recording my band. He asked when he could come see us at a live show. I told him we usually performed at junior high school dances and parties and invited him to one of our rehearsals at Howie Segal's house.

Phil Edwards was an adult, and I never asked Howie or his mother if they would mind having an African American record producer come down to their basement to audition the band.

Phil showed up at Howie's house at the prearranged date and time. Of course, Howie's mother answered the door and saw Phil Edwards standing there. She was a little apprehensive about letting him in. I went upstairs and assured her that he was a record producer coming to audition the band. Mrs. Segal opened the door and let him in.

Phil came down to the basement and took a seat on the couch. He asked if we had any original songs. Fortunately, Tommy had recently written "Come Dry Your Tears." We played it, and Phil loved the song. We played a few cover songs by the Beatles and the Stones, and Phil got up and left. He said he would be in touch.

A few days later, Phil called and asked if we could be at the recording studio the next day. I said yes and called the other guys. Everyone was excited.

The next day, we all hopped on the subway and went to the recording studio. Phil had us set up, and before we knew it, he asked us to do a run-through so they could get the settings on the soundboard right.

We did the song, and Phil said, "Okay, boys, we're ready to record."

We all got so nervous. We recorded the song live, which meant we did the music and the singing at the same time. Most bands record the music first and then the vocals. I guess Phil wasn't willing to pay for all that studio time.

Then he told us that for the flip side, he wanted us to do the song "He's Got the Whole World in His Hands." Phil already had the backing track and asked us to gather around one microphone to sing the vocals. We did one rehearsal and one take, and our day in the recording studio was over.

The following week, I got a call from Phil Edwards telling me that he had gotten a radio station in Connecticut to play the record. He gave me the date and time.

What luck. That was the day my school was taking us on a field trip to the Shakespeare Theater in Stratford, Connecticut, to see *Hamlet*. I brought my transistor radio with an earphone and waited for the approximate time Phil gave me to turn it on. At first, there was another song on the radio, not the Tiger 5. Then another song came on, and again it wasn't us. Then, it happened. The DJ said, "Here is a new band from New York City, the Tiger 5 with their new song 'Come Dry Your Tears.'"

I yelled out in a very quiet theater, "My record is on the radio!" and the entire audience turned around and looked at me. I didn't care. I was hearing our song on the radio for the very first time.

Unbeknownst to me, that would be the first and only time I ever heard a record I had recorded on the radio.

I couldn't wait to get home to tell the other guys in the band that I had heard our record played on the radio. When they found out, they all thought we were going to be stars, but that was not to be.

Richard M. Adler
Malibu Dude Ranch

We needed a paying gig. Up to that point, most of our performances had been free. I opened the newspaper and started reading the ads to see which hotels might be hiring bands. I circled a number of ads and began making phone calls. I called a few hotels in the Catskills, but they had already booked all their bands for the summer. I then called Malibu Dude Ranch in Milford, Pennsylvania.

The man on the phone asked me where our band had played. I told him that we had played at junior high school dances and parties. Thinking fast, I told him that we had played at two other dude ranches and that they had asked us back. I also told him that we had just recorded a record for Phil Edwards, and the guy seemed impressed.

He asked me how much the band charged for a weekend. I wasn't ready for that question. I thought he would tell me how much they paid, and I would simply say yes. Now I had to make up a number. I told him we got $200 for a weekend, plus expenses. He told me they usually didn't pay that much, so we settled on $150 for the weekend, and the dude ranch would provide round-trip transportation, hotel rooms, and food.

It was all agreed, and he gave us an open date. Without speaking to the other band members, I accepted the date. Fortunately, everyone was available that weekend, and just like that, we had our first paying gig.

It was now time to go to Malibu Dude Ranch. We were to meet the bus at 8th Avenue and 42nd Street, but how would we get there? We decided to take the subway. We walked a block, carrying as much equipment as we could, leaving one guy with the rest of our gear in front of my apartment building. After walking one block, we left one guy with the equipment we had just carried, and three of us went back to where we had left the rest. We kept doing this for the five blocks to the subway station.

Somehow, we dragged all of our equipment to the 67th Avenue subway station in Forest Hills. It was unbelievable, carrying guitars, amplifiers, drums, and our suitcases. We had two guys stand on the subway platform while the other three carried everything down two flights of stairs. We had to make many trips, so the two on the platform guarded the equipment.

The GG train, which was a local, pulled into the station. When the train doors opened, we had one guy stand by the door to hold it open, because we couldn't load everything onto the train in the short time the doors remained open. We finally got all of our equipment on the train and headed to Roosevelt Avenue, where we had to switch to the E train. Again, we had to unload all of our equipment and repeat the process.

We finally made it to 42nd Street, dragged everything up the stairs, and then to the corner of 8th Avenue. When the bus pulled up, it was a school bus. We had to carry all the equipment to the back of the bus. We were exhausted, but we were ready to make the trip to Pennsylvania for our first real gig.

Malibu Dude Ranch holds the title of the oldest dude ranch on the East Coast. Activities on the ranch ran the gamut, offering everything from horseback riding and archery to rowboats, hayrides, bonfires, and dancing to live music. And that's just scratching the surface.

After a two-hour drive, we finally arrived. We dragged all our equipment off the bus and into the hotel. We checked in at the front desk, and the girl behind the counter showed us where to set up our equipment. So, now we had to drag everything into the saloon and set it all up. Too bad we didn't know about roadies back then.

Malibu Dude Ranch gave the band first-class accommodations in the Bunkhouse. The Bunkhouse was where you'd expect cowboys to live, but we were from Forest Hills, and this was a far cry from the Plaza Hotel.

What I loved most about Malibu Dude Ranch was that we were allowed to go horseback riding whenever we wanted. We made friends with the wranglers, and they let us ride out on the trails without a guide.

I had been horseback riding a few times in Forest Hills, but this was special. We could ride wherever we wanted and for as long as we liked on wooded trails. We even played tag on horseback in an open field. The problem with the Malibu horses was that they always wanted to turn around and run back to the barn, so you had to fight them to get them to go where you wanted.

Once, we were riding in an open field, and I decided to try to make the horse gallop. We were off to the races when the saddle slipped, and I was suddenly riding on the side of the horse. I had to throw my arms around the horse's neck and hold on for dear life. The horse slowed down, and I fell off. I had to try to re-saddle the horse, which I knew nothing about. I figured it out, got back on, and rode the horse back to the barn, where I asked the wrangler to give me a lesson on how to properly saddle a horse and put on the bit. He also taught me how to groom and care for the horse. We returned to Malibu Dude Ranch a number of times over the years, and those skills came in handy.

It was now dinnertime. We were having a Texas BBQ, and I was hungry and looking forward to it. Once dinner was over, it was time for the Tiger 5 to perform their first set in the saloon.

We played a lot of Beatles songs, as well as "Wipeout," "Shout," and "Walk, Don't Run." By the end of the second set, we ran out of songs. I had forgotten to ask how many sets we had to perform each night, so we repeated our first two sets, and no one complained.

The best part of Malibu Dude Ranch was the teenage girls. We became the popular guys at the ranch, and all the girls wanted to hang out with us. This provided phone numbers for future dates, since most of these girls lived in NYC.

We had a bunkhouse and teenage girls. What could possibly happen? Between sets, I always found time to sneak back to the bunkhouse for a quick make-out session with one of the female guests. I don't think the guys ever caught on to where I was going on my breaks.

Richard M. Adler

Malibu Dude Ranch was the first time I went away with friends and **without** parental supervision. We were 15 or 16 years old and were loving our newfound freedom.

We performed at Malibu Dude Ranch a number of times over the years. On one trip, we invited a few of our Forest Hills friends up for the weekend. We had a bunkhouse with extra beds, and no one ever checked how many people were staying with us.

One night, we had a party in the bunkhouse. We were all smoking weed and drinking Boone's Farm apple wine. Bob Rowland, our lead singer and resident comedian, kept us in stitches. Bob is the funniest and nicest guy I have ever known, and I'm glad that after all these years, we **have** remained close friends.

Bob's hobby was learning the routines of famous comedians and telling us jokes all night before bed. One night, I laughed so hard that my sides ached. It was uncontrollable laughter. Bob would say the first line of a joke, and everyone would crack up. When we finally calmed down, he'd start again, only for us to burst into laughter after the first line. This went on for what seemed like an hour.

Once again, Bob tried to tell the joke: "Two camels were walking in the desert," and again, uncontrollable laughter followed. By now, everyone was in pain from laughing. Finally, Bob continued, "Two camels walking in the desert. One camel says to the other, 'I don't care what anyone says, I'm thirsty.'" That was the punchline. Everyone just groaned.

After all that pain, we started throwing things at Bob, but no one would ever forget that night.

Chapter 7

Hullabaloo

In early December 1965, my friend Tommy Erdelyi and I went to Rockefeller Center to try to see the taping of the Hullabaloo TV show. When we got there, no tickets were available. Tommy and I were both 15 years old and desperately wanted to see the show.

We saw someone come out from a door that led to a stairway. We knew what floor the show was on, so we decided to have an adventure. We walked up the stairs, opened a door, and suddenly we were standing backstage at Hullabaloo. That episode featured the following guests:

1. Frankie Avalon – "Do I Hear a Waltz?"
2. The Hollies – "Look Through Any Window"
3. Nancy Sinatra – "So Long Babe"

Richard M. Adler

4. The Ronettes – "You Baby"
5. Lola Falana – "Wouldn't It Be Loverly"
6. TV Theme Song Medley
7. The Yardbirds – "I'm a Man"

The first band we saw backstage was The Hollies. Graham Nash had a strangely shaped 12-string guitar, which I later learned was a VOX Phantom 12. I asked him about it. He asked me if I played, then offered to let me try it. I took the guitar, strapped it on, and started playing. Paul Samwell-Smith from The Yardbirds asked if I could play "For Your Love." I told him I didn't know the chords. He told me they were Em, G, A, Am. As I started playing, Alan Clarke, Graham Nash, and Paul Samwell-Smith began singing "For Your Love" to my guitar playing.

I thought I had died and gone to heaven. I was so concerned because we didn't belong backstage, and I didn't want to call attention to Tommy and me, but there I was in the middle of this amazing impromptu jam session, a real Hullabaloo at Hullabaloo.

Just then, a security guard walked in and asked Tommy and me if we had backstage passes. Graham Nash stood up and said, "What's your name?" The guard said, "Matt." Then Graham said, "Matt, please meet Richie, the producer's son," and turned to me and winked. The guard apologized and said if I needed anything, I should let him know.

Tommy and I laughed so hard when the guard left. Then Tommy punched me in the arm and said, "I can't believe you didn't let me play it." I said, "Tommy, I was in another place." All I kept repeating to myself was, "This isn't really happening."

We stayed through rehearsal and started talking with The Ronettes. They said they were going to the NBC commissary for some food and asked if we wanted to join them. What? Who, me? I couldn't believe it. We went with them and had burgers and fries together, with The Ronettes! Unreal.

We all went back and watched the filming of the show. Tommy and I were amazed that no one threw us out even though we didn't have backstage passes. Then something strange happened. The security guard came over. We thought he was going to ask us to leave. Instead, he asked if everything was okay and if we needed anything. I told him everything was great. He said,

"Say hi to your dad for me after the show. Tell him Matt took good care of you."

Later, one of the crew members came over and said, "Your dad is one of the best producers I've ever worked with." For weeks, we went back to the show using the same staircase. The security guards always said hello.

Hullabaloo was an American musical variety series that ran on NBC from January 12, 1965, through April 11, 1966, with repeats airing through August of that year. Similar to ABC's Shindig! and in contrast to American Bandstand, it aired in prime time.

Hullabaloo served as a big-budget showcase for the leading pop acts of the day and competed with Shindig!. A different host presided each week, including stars like Sammy Davis Jr., Jerry Lewis, Gary Lewis, Petula Clark, Paul Anka, Liza Minnelli, Jack Jones, David McCallum, and Frankie Avalon, who would perform a couple of hits and introduce the other acts.

Many early episodes included black-and-white segments taped in the UK and hosted by Beatles manager Brian Epstein. Sid Bernstein

Richard M. Adler

was the booking agent. Some episodes were taped at NBC Studios in Burbank, California, but most were filmed in New York City, either at Studio 8H in the RCA Building (later home to Saturday Night Live) or NBC's color studio in Brooklyn.

The series began as a one-hour show airing from 8:30 to 9:30 p.m. on Tuesdays. Its first season ran 18 new episodes from January through May 1965, followed by summer repeats from 10:00 to 11:00 p.m. The second season of 30 new episodes aired from September 1965 to April 1966 in a shortened half-hour format on Mondays from 7:30 to 8:00 p.m. From May to August 1966, repeats aired before the series was replaced by The Monkees in September.

Hullabaloo was even referenced in the Ramones song "Do You Remember Rock 'n' Roll Radio?" I like to think Tommy included it as a nod to our incredible Hullabaloo adventures.

Chapter 8

Murray the K Shows

Murray the K's Christmas Show 1964

Throughout his New York radio career, Murray the K, a New York radio DJ, produced multi-racial rock 'n' roll shows three or four times a year, usually during the Easter school recess, the week before Labor Day, and between Christmas and New Year at the Brooklyn Fox Theater. Those shows featured the top performers of the era and introduced new acts such as Dionne Warwick, The Shirelles, Chuck Jackson, The Zombies, Little Anthony and the Imperials, The Ronettes, The Shangri-Las, Gene Pitney, Ben E. King, and many more.

The week-long, four to five shows-a-day presentations continued throughout the most explosive periods of civil rights unrest in the mid-60s, culminating in Murray the K's final show at the RKO Theater with a lineup that included The Who and Cream in their American debuts.

On December 29, 1964, my friend Roy Appel and I went to Murray the K's Christmas Show at the Brooklyn Fox Theater.

This show starred: Chuck Jackson, Ben E. King, The Drifters, The Shirelles, Dick & Dee Dee, The Shangri-Las, Patti LaBelle & The Bluebelles, The Vibrations, Dionne Warwick, The Zombies, The Nashville Teens, and The Hullabaloos.

When we arrived, we went to the stage door and told the guard that my uncle was Murray the K and he was expecting me. The guard thought about it and said to come in and wait for Murray in the first room on the right that was on the second floor. Could it really be that easy? We ran up the stairs to the room, which was where all the food was waiting for the performers. We hung out in the room for a few minutes, knowing that we were going to get kicked out once the security guard found out that I was not related to Murray.

Then we saw Rod Argent from The Zombies walk into the room and call us over. He asked if we could help him carry his Vox organ down the stairs to the stage. What? Roy and I jumped at the chance to carry Rod Argent's Vox organ. That is when Roy's love affair started with the Vox organ. He saved his money, and he finally bought one. We had a band, and the first song he learned to play on that organ was "She's Not There." I know this doesn't seem like a great story, but two 14-year-old rock and roll crazies thought it was the coolest thing that ever happened.

Well, I guess that Murray the K was busy when the security guard went to look for him because we stayed the entire show and watched it from the wings and even ate upstairs in the room with all the stars. How was I to know that 10 years later, I would be booking shows for The Drifters and The Shirelles, two groups we met backstage that day? Another cool fact about one of the groups from this show: Mary Weiss of The Shangri-Las lived across the street from me when I lived on 99th Street and 63rd Drive in Rego Park.

After the show, The Zombies decided to go for a walk outside the theater, and Roy and I tagged along with our new friends. But as soon as we got outside the theater, they were mobbed by a horde of crazed teenage girls screaming and trying to grab hold of them. I was getting pushed and pulled, and one girl pulled my hair and ripped my shirt. The police had to come and save the members of The

Zombies, Roy, and me from bodily harm and escorted us back into the theater with a stern warning to stay inside.

Murray the K's Easter Show 1967

Murray the K attempted to capitalize on the new sound of rock music by presenting a show called *Music In The 5th Dimension*. This show, which ran from Saturday, March 25th to Sunday, April 2nd, at the RKO 58th Street Theatre in Manhattan, marked the end of an era for Murray's solo act and vocal group presentations. The show featured five performances a day, starting at 10 in the morning and lasting until after midnight. Kids would line up early to get into the concert. Tickets could only be bought at the door, as advance tickets were not sold. Once all the seats were filled, they stopped the line, and the rest of the kids had to wait until the next show. This process continued for five shows a day.

It was Easter of 1967, and I was buzzing with anticipation. My younger sister, Mindy, was about to experience her first real rock concert. We were going to Murray the K's Easter Show. Murray the K, the legendary New York DJ, was putting on his annual holiday show, and this one was supposed to be something special. This wasn't just another show; it was a showcase of the new sounds emerging in rock music. We got there early, as any serious fans would, and were thrilled to find ourselves with great seats in the front of the orchestra, only about 25 feet from the stage.

The show started with Murray the K, who was kind of a big deal in New York City, coming out to introduce the bands. He was wearing a Beatles-style wig, which was kind of funny.

The first act was a band called Mandala. Mandala was a Canadian R&B and soul band from the 1960s. The band was formed in 1965 in Toronto, Ontario, as The Rogues and changed their name prior to their first Canadian Top 40 hit, *Opportunity*. The band is best known for containing well-known Canadian guitarist Domenic Troiano, who recorded with The James Gang and The Guess Who in the seventies, and drummer Pentti Glan, who later played with Alice Cooper and Lou Reed (Glan was the drummer on Reed's 1974 live album *Rock n Roll Animal*). The band also featured Roy Kenner, who later became the lead singer with the James Gang, both during and after the period when Troiano was lead guitarist with that band.

Then it was one band after another.

Next came a comedy act called the Hardly Worth It Players, a short-lived 1960s comedy troupe primarily centered around the work of Bill Minkin and Dennis Wholey. They gained notoriety for producing satirical musical recordings that spoofed contemporary politics, often by impersonating well-known politicians of the era.

Following them was The Blues Project, an American band formed in New York City's Greenwich Village neighborhood in 1965. The group's original lineup broke up in 1967. Their songs drew from a wide array of musical styles. They are most remembered as one of the most artful practitioners of pop music, influenced by folk, blues, rhythm and blues, jazz, and the pop music of the day. I remember seeing them at the Café Au Go Go in Greenwich Village. I met Al Kooper and Steve Katz backstage at The Doors concert, and he told me about their new band, Blood, Sweat and Tears. And now I got to see them again at the Easter show.

Some of my favorite songs by The Blues Project were:

- *No Time Like the Right Time* – Often considered their most notable single, this track showcased the band's experimental approach to blending rock and blues. It received some national radio play and helped define their distinctive sound.

- *Flute Thing* – A well-known instrumental penned by band member Al Kooper, *Flute Thing* stood out for its innovative jazz and psychedelic flourishes. It remains one of their signature tracks.

- *I Can't Keep from Crying Sometimes* – Originally written by Blind Willie Johnson, their adaptation became a live staple, highlighting the band's roots in the blues tradition

71

while incorporating their electrified and improvisational style.

- *Wake Me, Shake Me* – Although a cover of a traditional gospel tune, The Blues Project's version featured extended improvisations and jam-band tendencies, presaging the improvisational rock scene that would flourish later in the decade.

- *Steve's Song* – A more introspective track, this demonstrated the band's softer, folk-influenced side and served as an example of their eclecticism.

I guess you could say I was a big fan.

In between the bands, Murray's wife, Jackie, had her "K" girls doing dance numbers and a "Wild Fashion Show." We could have used more bands and less of this crap!

The real excitement, for me anyway, came when the two bands from England hit the stage. This was their first time ever playing in the United States. First up was The Who. As soon as they started playing, the whole place went wild. It was like nothing I had ever seen. Pete Townshend was smashing his guitar, and Keith Moon was a maniac on the drums. At the end of their set, they started smashing all of their equipment. The smoke was billowing around the stage, and Keith Moon kicked his drum set over, which was just crazy. I'd never seen anything like it before. It was like the music was coming to life on stage. It was a total explosion of sound and energy. They played two songs: *My Generation* and *Substitute*.

Then, during the chaos, I saw something fly into the air. It was a drumstick, spinning end over end, which was apparently launched from Keith Moon's drum set. It landed not too far away from us in the aisle. Almost immediately, kids jumped up, trying to get to the stick. Mindy went to get up too, but I pulled her back down. It just wasn't safe. It was complete mayhem. I was genuinely worried that she was going to get hurt. It was just too dangerous to try and grab the drumstick as a souvenir with all the kids fighting for the prize.

Pete Townshend of The Who noted, "We were smashing our instruments up five times a day. We did two songs, the act was twelve minutes long, and we used to play *Substitute* and *My Generation* with the gear smashing it at the end, and then we'd spend the twenty minutes between shows trying to rebuild everything so we could smash it up again."

According to Don Lehnoff, The Who's gear was set up on a raised platform on wheels, and at the end of "My Generation," Keith Moon would flip over his drums and cymbals. Their roadie would then quickly piece everything back together in time for the next show.

On the final performance, The Who used smoke pots to create explosions and almost blew up their amps. According to Pete Townshend, "(Murray) used to complain because he had what he called his personal microphones, which used to come in for a bit of bashin'. And so, we used to actually get daily lectures from him about abusing his personal microphone, which we thought was pretty funny." Roger Daltrey broke a total of 18 microphones during the run of the show. Townshend said, "We didn't really know what was going on and we didn't take it very seriously. And when it got to the last day, we all put funny masks on and went in and sat and listened to (Murray the K) with these masks on. I remember he asked us to take them off, demanded we remove them." They did not remove their masks.

Richard M. Adler

The Who, formed in London in 1964, emerged as a prominent English rock group whose original lineup spanned from 1964 to 1978. During these years, Roger Daltrey led on vocals, Pete Townshend handled guitar, John Entwistle played bass, and Keith Moon was on drums. Widely regarded as one of the 20th century's most groundbreaking rock bands, their impact on the genre included pioneering the use of the Marshall stack and large-scale sound systems, incorporating synthesizers into rock, introducing distinct playing techniques from Entwistle and Moon, employing Townshend's hallmark guitar feedback and power chords, and defining the rock opera format.

Their influence resonated with numerous hard rock, punk, power pop, and mod groups. In recognition of their achievements, they entered the Rock and Roll Hall of Fame in 1990.

Their first release as The Who, "I Can't Explain" (1965), broke into the UK top ten and paved the way for more hit singles, among them "My Generation" (1965), "Substitute" (1966), and "Happy Jack" (1966).

In 1967, they played at the Monterey Pop Festival and launched "I Can See for Miles," which became their only American top-ten hit. Two years later, in 1969, they produced the concept album Tommy, featuring the track "Pinball Wizard," to both critical and commercial acclaim.

Their standing as a revered live act was further cemented by performances at Woodstock and the Isle of Wight festivals, along with the release of the concert recording Live at Leeds in 1970. By then, expectations weighed heavily on Townshend, and the ambitious follow-up concept to Tommy, titled Lifehouse, had to be abandoned. Its intended material was reshaped into the 1971 album

Who's Next, which delivered enduring favorites like "Won't Get Fooled Again," "Baba O'Riley," and "Behind Blue Eyes."

In 1973, they produced another concept album, Quadrophenia, which paid homage to their mod heritage, and later took charge of adapting Tommy into a film in 1975.

The band continued drawing large crowds on tour until stepping back from regular live performances at the close of 1976. Although they released Who Are You in 1978, its reception was overshadowed by Moon's passing shortly afterward.

After that, Cream took the stage. They were incredible as well. They were also making their US debut, and, like the Who, they played like they were trying to bring the whole building down with them. They played two songs: "I Feel Free" and "I'm So Glad." It was other-worldly.

In 1966, a groundbreaking British rock supergroup known as Cream took shape in London, its lineup featuring bassist Jack Bruce, guitarist Eric Clapton, and drummer Ginger Baker. Although all three contributed to the writing process, Bruce served as the main vocalist and principal songwriter, while Clapton and Baker added their own material as well. Each member was already established from previous notable acts, and this collective pedigree helped Cream earn recognition as the first true supergroup. Their playing skills were widely admired, with all three musicians displaying exceptional instrumental mastery.

Cream's career lasted a short three years, yet they managed to produce four albums during that time. Their debut, Fresh Cream (1966), was followed by Disraeli Gears (1967), Wheels of Fire (1968), and Goodbye (1969). Starting with Disraeli Gears, producer and multi-instrumentalist Felix Pappalardi joined them in the studio, guiding the band's fusion of blues rock, psychedelic sounds, and hard rock textures. Over the course of their run, Cream sold in excess of 15 million records globally. Their third release, Wheels of Fire, achieved a historic milestone as the first double album to reach platinum status. Along the way, they found international success with singles like "Sunshine of Your Love" (1967) and "White Room" (1968).

Despite their achievements, mounting friction between Bruce and Baker led the group to a decision in May 1968 to disband. Still, the band agreed to record a final album, Goodbye, and embark on one last tour. This farewell culminated in two final concerts held at the Royal Albert Hall on November 25 and 26, 1968. The performances were filmed for theatrical showings and, by 1977, were made available as a home video called Farewell Concert. Bruce passed away in 2014, and Baker died in 2019, leaving Clapton as the only surviving member.

Cream's influence and status were formally acknowledged in 1993 when they were inducted into the Rock and Roll Hall of Fame. They also received accolades on several "100 Greatest Artists of All Time" lists, earning a place at number 67 in Rolling Stone and number 61 in VH1's rankings. Additionally, they were acknowledged by VH1 as the 16th greatest hard rock artist of all time.

After the two English bands, Wilson Pickett came on stage and tore the place up. He performed two of his hits: "Land of a Thousand Dances" and "Mustang Sally."

By 1967, Pickett had already solidified his place as a powerhouse in soul, boasting hits such as "In the Midnight Hour," "Land of 1000 Dances," and "Mustang Sally." Live audiences knew him for his dynamic vocal style, raw emotional delivery, and commanding stage presence. His appearance at the Easter Show brought these qualities to a diverse crowd who had come to witness a broad spectrum of popular sounds, an experience that mirrored the changing landscape of the music industry itself. In the midst of British rock bands experimenting with their amps turned high and Motown groups perfecting their silky harmonies, Pickett stood out as an emissary of pure, unfiltered soul.

Stepping onto a stage shared by rising rock superstars and established R&B icons, Pickett delivered a set that had people dancing in their seats. Where rock acts pushed sonic boundaries with guitar distortion and heavy backbeats, Pickett kept the audience riveted with driving rhythms drawn from the deep well of Southern soul. His backing ensemble, razor-sharp and impeccably rehearsed, complemented the singer's fervent vocals with the kind of tight, horn-infused grooves that had become a hallmark of his records at Atlantic and Stax studios. Every number crackled with energy, as though the recordings that fans knew so well had sprung to life, magnified and intensified for a live crowd that could hardly contain its excitement.

One of the most remarkable aspects of the Murray the K Easter Show was its cultural cross-pollination. While The Who smashed instruments and Cream offered up their heavy blues-rock jams, Pickett's performance acted as a bridge. His music drew on the gritty intensity of gospel, the universal appeal of the R&B charts, and the immediacy of a live band that knew how to incite a frenzy of call-and-response from the audience. The show's variety format allowed fans to witness a collision of genres and styles, but it was Pickett's set that cut through the noise, reminding everyone that soul music, stirring, heartfelt, and deeply rooted in African American tradition, would remain a powerful force in the evolving soundscape of the late '60s.

Richard M. Adler

By the time the Easter Show had concluded, attendees left with vivid memories of Wilson Pickett's stage presence: that trademark rasp, the sweat-soaked suits, the crescendos that seemed to lift the crowd off their feet. Indeed, his contribution to that legendary bill helped set a standard for high-energy live performance. Decades later, it remains a touchstone moment, representing not only a highlight in Pickett's illustrious career, but also a snapshot of a pivotal era in which soul, rock, and pop music converged under one roof. In many ways, the Murray the K Easter Show of 1967 captured the musical spirit of the time, and Wilson Pickett stood at its center, reminding everyone why he was one of soul's most indomitable voices.

Murray had booked two soul acts for the show: Wilson Pickett and Smokey Robinson. However, Smokey Robinson never appeared. Don Lehnoff stated, "Smokey Robinson was hired for the show as advertised, but at the first rehearsal, I sat in the audience seats and watched Robinson, still wearing his trench coat, arguing on stage with Murray the K. At one point, Smokey stormed off the stage and up the aisle to the exit, not to return." Lehnoff understood that Robinson walked out because Mitch Ryder was billed above him. I was really bummed that Smokey Robinson did not perform. Despite Robinson's absence, the show went on.

The contrast of Cream and The Who doing their rock thing and Wilson Pickett with his soul music was just fantastic.

The final act of the show was the headliner, Mitch Ryder, who had a number-one hit at the time. It was clear that a new generation of rock had arrived. Mitch Ryder was the headliner of the show.

Mitch Ryder is an American rock vocalist whose vigorous sound and energetic stage persona helped shape the gritty R&B-rock fusion coming out of Detroit. Over the course of more than forty years, he has recorded upwards of 25 albums, each release reflecting his trademark blend of soulful passion and no-holds-barred intensity. His greatest achievements came alongside his band, Mitch Ryder and the Detroit Wheels, who enjoyed a string of hits during the mid-to-late 1960s. Among their most celebrated tracks were the 1966 smash "Devil with a Blue Dress On," which soared to the number four spot on the charts, as well as "Jenny Take a Ride!" peaking at number ten in 1965, and "Sock It to Me, Baby!" reaching number six in 1967. These songs became emblematic of Detroit's raw, blues-infused rock 'n' roll spirit and cemented Ryder's status as a dynamic force in American music. In 1966, Mitch Ryder went solo and left the Detroit Wheels behind.

According to Don Lehnoff, who was part of the band backing Mitch Ryder, it was billed as the "Mitch Ryder Show" because Ryder was embarking on a solo career at the time. Lehnoff explained, "At the insistence of his producer, Bob Crewe, Mitch was embarking on a solo career and we appeared as the Mitch Ryder Show. I was part of a ten-piece band hired to back Mitch up, five guys from Baltimore, three from the Chicago Loop who opened the Ryder shows, plus a trumpet from Florida and guitar from New York." The Wheels declined the opportunity to be augmented with horns and parted company.

Backstage, there was chaos. Ginger Baker was drunk, and there were LSD trips, flour fights, and flooded dressing rooms. Wilson Pickett, who was a model for the new Ryder band, called a meeting because The Who were using smoke bombs and he felt they were unprofessional. According to Don Lehnoff, "Wilson Pickett was more or less the model for the new Ryder band, with Ryder being marketed as the 'blue-eyed soul' version. We even covered some Pickett tunes in our show. They even took Mitch down to the Apollo one night to sit in with Pickett on a later show. Pickett's drummer at that time was Buddy Miles."

Despite the chaos, the show was a success on stage. While Murray's young fans enjoyed the show, the new rock stars thought Murray was a joke. Al Aronowitz noted that "Everybody hated Murray, hated him for his power and success, hated him because he screamed and hollered and wore tight pants, hated him because he forced his ego down your throat like a hard-sell used car dealer who makes it seem like you're going to buy the car anyway, but you've also got to take him along as part of the deal." Ronnie Spector observed, "The Beatles were only putting up with him because he was a big New York disc jockey, but they thought it sucked that he called himself the Fifth Beatle and they couldn't wait to get rid of him."

The Murray the K show had a different guest act every day. The rotating guest acts were The Young Rascals, Simon and Garfunkel, Phil Ochs, and the Blues Magoos.

The Chicago Loop and the act Jim and Jean also performed, but I don't remember anything about their performance.

That night, Mindy and I witnessed the end of one era of music and the birth of another. It was more than just a concert; it was an experience. The energy, the chaos, the pure rock and roll power, it was all so intoxicating. Even though we didn't get the drumstick, the image of it flying through the air and the pandemonium that followed is something I'll never forget. It was a night that cemented my love for rock and roll, and it was all thanks to Murray the K and, more importantly, a handful of incredible musicians who showed us what the future of music sounded like. It was, without a doubt, a rock and roll fantasy come to life.

Murray Kaufman, professionally known as Murray the K, was a highly influential figure in the New York City rock and roll scene as an impresario and disc jockey during the 1950s, '60s, and '70s. Born on February 14, 1922, Murray had a background in show business: his mother was a vaudeville pianist, and his aunt was a character actress. Murray himself worked as a child actor in Hollywood films in the 1930s. After serving in the Army, he organized shows in the Catskills and worked in public relations, promoting songs. He also gained experience as a radio producer and co-host at WMCA, working with personalities like Laraine Day and Eva Gabor. Additionally, he promoted baseball players such as Mickey Mantle and Willie Mays.

Murray the K's career took off in 1958 when he moved to WINS/1010 to host the all-night show, "The Swingin' Soiree." He was later moved to the 7 to 11 p.m. time slot, where he remained for seven years. His show was known for its innovative segues, jingles, sound effects, and creative programming, always opening with Sinatra. Tom Wolfe described him as "the original hysterical disk jockey." By the mid-1960s, Murray was the top-rated radio host in New York City. He left WINS in 1965 when the station changed to an all-news format. In 1966, he became program director and primetime DJ at WOR-FM, one of the first FM rock stations. There, he played long album cuts and thematically linked songs without commercial interruption. He championed artists like Bob Dylan and Janis Ian, and defended Dylan's move to electric. He later worked at other stations, including CHUM in Toronto, WHFS in Maryland, and WNBC in New York.

Murray the K was an early and ardent supporter of The Beatles, and he famously called himself "the Fifth Beatle." He was the first DJ to welcome the Beatles when they arrived in New York in 1964. Murray broadcast his show from the Beatles' hotel suite and accompanied them to their first U.S. concert in Washington, D.C. He was also backstage at their Ed Sullivan Show premiere and even roomed with George Harrison in Miami, broadcasting his radio shows from his hotel room. Although he claimed that Harrison or Ringo Starr gave

81

him the moniker "Fifth Beatle," he is seen calling himself that in a phone conversation with the Beatles upon their arrival in New York.

Throughout his radio career, Murray produced rock and roll shows at the Brooklyn Fox Theater. In 1967, his show moved to the RKO 58th Street Theater in Manhattan, featuring both traditional and progressive rock acts.

Murray also released numerous LP record albums, often compilations of hits by the acts that appeared in his Brooklyn Fox shows. He produced and hosted television variety shows featuring rock performers, including It's What's Happening, Baby. In addition, he collaborated on a psychedelic multimedia event called The World. He also authored a book titled Murray the K Tells It Like It Is, Baby. Murray the K was inducted into the National Radio Hall of Fame in 1997.

Murray the K was known for his innovative and energetic style and is remembered for his significant contributions to rock and roll radio and his support of many popular artists of the 1960s.

Chapter 9

Tangerine Puppets

"We thought the guys in the Tangerine Puppets were the coolest in the world" – Mickey Leigh (Joey Ramone's brother), from his book I Slept with Joey Ramone.

The Tangerine Puppets (from left to right) Tommy Erdelyi, Richard Adler, Bob Rowland, Scott Roberts, John Cummings

In 1966, Tommy Erdelyi met John Cummings in the Forest Hills High School cafeteria. He told me that John was very cool, knew a lot about music, and played bass. Tommy then told me that John wanted to form a band with him and asked if I would join. I was torn. This would break up the Tiger 5, and I would have to leave my friends Bob, Ira, and Howie out of the band. Tommy and I went over to John's parents' apartment in Birchwood Towers to meet him for the first time.

John was tall, skinny, and his dirty blonde hair was cut like a Beatle, but one side was longer than the other and covered his left eye. I assumed that he didn't have his hair cut that way, but that he combed it forward to look cool. When his father was home, he combed it the way it was cut, with a part.

John had the same issue I did, our fathers. My dad believed that a man should be well-groomed. When I started growing my hair, he would tell me to go to the barber and get it cut. I rebelled and told him no. My father got enraged, grabbed me by the arm, and escorted me to the barbershop where I received my father's requested haircut – short. This was a constant battle in my house during my high school years. It was frustrating not to be able to present yourself the way you wanted. My father didn't understand how important it was for me to look like a rock star. It was very depressing, to say the least.

John, Tommy, and I talked music, and I found out that John was a big Rolling Stones fan and worshipped Brian Jones. John also liked many of the same British bands that Tommy and I liked: The Rolling Stones, The Who, The Yardbirds, The Animals, Them, and The Kinks. But there was one glaring exception – The Beatles. John hated The Beatles and refused to play their music in his new band.

John had a friend, Scott Roberts, who was a drummer, and he wanted him in the band. We needed a lead singer, and John didn't know one, so I recommended my good friend Bob Rowland, who was the lead singer in the Tiger 5.

The Tangerine Puppets

Richard M. Adler

Do these faces look familiar?

Who?

NEW YORK — The band pictured in the photo above (1966) never made it to the top, but the individual musicians did alright for themselves. From left to right are Richard Adler, owner of Somerset Talent; Tommy Ramone, drummer in the Ramones; Scott Roberts, singer-songwriter now playing New York area clubs; Johnny Ramone, guitar player in the Ramones; and Bob Rowland, agent with Supreme Talent. The name of the group was Tangerine Puppets.

John agreed to give it a try. He liked the fact that we had the same format as the Rolling Stones, with John on bass, Tommy on lead guitar, Scott Roberts on drums, Bob Rowland as lead singer, and me on rhythm guitar.

We agreed to have our first band practice in the basement of John's friend George's house. We all lived in apartment buildings, so it was difficult to practice at full volume in an apartment. We wrote out a list of songs that we all needed to learn. The list included Rolling Stones songs: "Empty Heart," "It's All Over Now," "Around and Around," "Route 66," "The Last Time," "Satisfaction," "Heart of Stone," "Not Fade Away," "I Just Want to Make Love to You," and "Walking the Dog." Kinks songs: "Well Respected Man," "You Really Got Me," and "All Day and All of the Night." Yardbirds songs: "Smokestack Lightning" and "For Your Love." And by Them: "Gloria," just to name a few.

Our first band practice went well, but John never told us that he had first asked George to be in the band. When Scott showed up, it was very awkward. So, we let George play a couple of songs, and then Scott played a couple of songs. Scott was definitely the better drummer, and he was a really good singer. After the band practice, John decided that he wanted Scott in the band, but we would lose George's house to practice in. John said we would work it out.

My parents both worked, so my apartment was available for band practice in the afternoon. We had to be done before my parents got home. We set up in our living room and had our band practice. It went well, and everyone left before my parents got home. No problem. So, we had a couple of band practices in my parents' apartment. I had to bribe my sister Mindy, who was 10 years old, not to tell our parents that the band was practicing. She kept our secret, but my mother's friend Marilyn, who lived in the apartment above us, complained to my mother. She said the first two times she left the apartment because it was so loud it hurt her ears, but after the third time, she had to put her foot down. My parents were livid. Needless to say, we never practiced at my apartment again.

We were now in need of a place to practice. One of our girlfriends offered us her parents' basement, which worked for a while. But her parents finally threw us out.

Bob Rowland mentioned that his parents were away next weekend. We could practice in his parents' apartment in Parker Towers. Well, this did not end well. We had our band practice, and we were in the middle of a song when Bob's parents walked in the front door. We didn't see them at first, but Bob's father was so mad that he went after Bob. He started yelling and smacking Bob around. We grabbed our guitars and left. We rang for the elevator. When it arrived, we got in, and there was a guy in the elevator. When he saw that we were carrying guitars, he asked if we were in a band. He told us he had just gotten back from California where he auditioned for a TV show about a rock band. He said he thought he got the part. It was Davy Jones, who lived in Parker Towers at the time. Davy was starring in Oliver! on Broadway and lived in Bob's building.

Strange how things work out. Ten years later, I was booking shows for Dolenz, Jones, Boyce & Hart, and The Monkees.

The Dirt Bomb Fight

The summer of 1966 in Forest Hills always comes back to me in sun-soaked flashes and the kind of mischief only teenagers can dream up. We were hanging around the Howard Apartments, restless and looking for any excuse to break out of our doldrums. By "we," I mean the crew: John Cummings, later known to the world as Johnny Ramone, Jeff Lane, Marc Lester, Ira Nagel, and a few others who'd gladly leap in to remind me they were there too, given half a chance. We were all just kids then, not fully aware of who we would become, only that we had big personalities, big opinions, and an unquenchable thirst for excitement.

That afternoon felt like every other: the sun hammered down on the concrete, making the pavement shimmer with heat. The chatter was about music, always music. The British Invasion had everyone talking. The Beatles or The Rolling Stones? It was a constant debate. The Beatles were typically the crowd favorite, but John was already forging his own path, one contrary opinion at a time.

As we passed around a piece of chalk and scribbled nonsense on the building walls for fun, someone (to this day, I'm not entirely sure who) decided to write "The Beatles" in big, blocky letters. It was a harmless piece of teenage graffiti, but John couldn't stand the sight of it. He was a die-hard Rolling Stones fan, relishing the raw, rebellious energy they brought. Without a second thought, he snatched the chalk from whoever had it last and scrawled "Rolling Stones" on an adjacent wall.

We should've realized trouble was brewing when John glowered at the word "Beatles," like it was an insult aimed directly at him. He was never one to keep his opinions under wraps. In a flash, he grabbed a dirt bomb near the sidewalk, a clump of earth mixed with pebbles, twigs, and the grit that accumulated along the apartment foundations, and hurled it at the fresh Beatles graffiti. A little mushroom cloud of dust exploded on impact, leaving a faint smear of dirt over "The Beatles."

Of course, the rest of us couldn't just let that stand. It became this unspoken dare: pick a side and defend your band. Before I knew it, most of us, fans of The Beatles, were launching dirt bombs at John's "Rolling Stones" words, while John threw every clump of dirt he could find back at "The Beatles." Jeff was ducking and weaving behind a trash can, popping up to fire a dirt missile every now and then. A few other kids dove behind parked cars, yelling battle cries that were more comedic than intimidating. It was chaos, but the best kind of youthful chaos. Nobody was really out to hurt anyone. We were just being wild kids, immersed in a swirling dust cloud of our own making.

Every so often, we'd hear a neighbor yelling out a window to knock it off, but that only made us fight harder, like we needed to prove we could keep this ridiculous conflict going without adult interference.

Dirt bombs whizzed through the air, smacking against walls, ricocheting off trash cans, and sometimes splattering across unsuspecting passersby who didn't know what in the world was happening. A few onlookers laughed at the spectacle, while others looked downright annoyed.

The ringleader, of course, was John. He acted like throwing these dirt bombs was an art form, mixing them just right for maximum impact. Every time he nailed the Beatles name, a self-satisfied smirk spread across his face. We were all howling and shrieking, half in delight, half in that nervous excitement that only teeters a hair's breadth away from danger.

And then, as if by fate, real danger struck. Marc Lester had been staunchly on The Beatles' side, determined to land a perfect shot on the "Rolling Stones" graffiti John had just refreshed. He stood on a low ledge, shouting something about how The Beatles were the true kings of rock, then leaped off to lob a particularly hefty dirt bomb. In mid-jump, his left leg caught on a metal pipe protruding from the building.

It happened so fast, yet I saw every split second: Marc's leg snaring on the pipe, his face contorting from triumph to shock, his body twisting in midair. He crashed to the ground with a bone-chilling thud, the kind that leaves a hush in its wake. For a heartbeat, none of us moved. Then Marc let out a yell I'll never forget. Blood was everywhere, soaking his jeans and pooling on the ground. A girl nearby screamed. Jeff and I rushed forward, and John dropped his latest dirt missile instantly. Everything else, the laughter, the bravado, stopped cold.

I remember hearing, "You can see his bone!" from someone in the group. I looked at Marc's leg and nearly retched. An eight-inch-long gash ran from below his knee down his calf. The torn skin gaped open in a ragged wound so deep it seemed unreal. The color drained from Marc's face, and he groaned, his voice ragged with pain. In that moment, the dirt bomb war was over. The only thing that mattered was getting Marc help.

We sprang into action, adrenaline fueling our panic. Jeff supported Marc's shoulders, John scooped his legs, and I hovered anxiously, making sure we didn't accidentally bump the injury. A couple of us took turns carrying him, and others raced ahead to alert the hospital. Thankfully, we were only a few blocks from the local emergency room, an advantage we didn't fully appreciate until we were trudging through those streets with Marc bleeding all over us.

Neighbors and strangers gawked at the sight, some shaking their heads in disapproval, others stepping aside with expressions of sympathy. By the time we got to the hospital, Marc was nearly unconscious from the pain and shock. A nurse took one look at his blood-soaked pants and ushered him through the swinging doors. The rest of us just stood there, breathing heavily and still covered in dust, not sure if we'd be chased out or if we should follow. A doctor eventually emerged, scowling at our obvious handiwork, but too busy to lecture a bunch of shell-shocked kids.

They stitched Marc up. Who knows how many stitches that wound took, and told him to keep off the leg for a while. When he was finally discharged later that day, we helped him hobble home. He had a hefty bandage wrapped around his calf, and he looked pale as a ghost. We all breathed a collective sigh of relief.

Naturally, that was the end of our so-called war between The Beatles and The Rolling Stones. The chalk on the walls was hosed off, and none of us dared mention dirt bombs for a long time. Even John looked ashamed, and that was quite a sight, considering how headstrong he usually was. It was like we'd all grown up a bit in those frantic few hours. One moment we were carefree, slinging dirt bombs, and the next, we were confronted with real pain, real consequences.

In the weeks that followed, Marc's scar became a thing of neighborhood lore. People retold the story like some kind of epic battle wound, always embellishing the details: "I heard it was a foot-long gash!" or "They said the bone stuck out two inches!" But the truth was unsettling enough. For a while, Marc wore that bandage like a badge of honor and a cautionary tale rolled into one.

Then, a year later, The Beatles released their groundbreaking album *Sgt. Pepper's Lonely Hearts Club Band*. The music scene shifted on its axis, and we all felt it. Suddenly, the world was buzzing about this astonishing new record, filled with experimental sounds and boundless creativity. Even John, who had been The Beatles' harshest critic just that summer, couldn't help but be impressed. When he finally admitted, "You know, *Sgt. Pepper* isn't half bad," we teased him mercilessly but also realized it meant something more. Music was bigger than just taking sides. It was about being open to what might come next, because in rock and roll, something new was always around the corner.

Looking back, I still laugh at the sheer ridiculousness of that afternoon. It was a sweet slice of teenage madness, a moment of pure anarchy set to a rock and roll soundtrack. But I also remember the coppery smell of blood, Marc's trembling lip, and the knowledge that we'd stared down real injury in the midst of our silly game. In a strange way, that day foreshadowed the path we'd all take. We'd keep flirting with trouble, pushing the boundaries, and charging into the unknown, sometimes recklessly, sometimes with brilliance, always looking for that moment of raw energy that made us feel alive.

Richard M. Adler

Because if there's one thing I learned from that dirt bomb fight, it's that rock and roll, like life, can pivot on a dime, unpredictable, messy, thrilling, and sometimes a little dangerous. You can't erase that thrill any more than you can wash the dust off your clothes. And I guess that's the beauty of it all. The Beatles and The Rolling Stones might have seemed like enemies that day, but in the end, they both wrote chapters in our hearts, shaping who we were and who we'd become. And John, as time would reveal, would play his own major part in rock history, though none of us knew just how big that part would be when we were just kids chucking handfuls of dirt at the Howard Apartments.

Palisades Amusement Park

The Tangerine Puppets had the good fortune to perform at Palisades Amusement Park in Cliffside Park, New Jersey, as the opening act for Vito and the Salutations, who had a hit record with "Unchained Melody."

The day before the first show, I realized we didn't have transportation to Palisades Park. I wondered how we were going to get there. It seemed like we'd need two subway trains to the Port Authority Bus Terminal and then a bus to Palisades Park.

Fortunately, I was hanging out with my friend Suzy Weishoff that day. Suzy offered to ask her father if he could drive us. Miraculously, he agreed. We loaded all our equipment into Suzy's dad's station wagon, but after packing in the guitars, amplifiers, and drums, there was no room left for all the band members. There were five band members, Suzy, and her dad. Seven people crammed into the car, but there was no space for two of Scott's tom-toms. I sat in the backseat on one side, and Scott sat on the other. We each held one of Scott's tom-toms out the open window as we drove to Palisades Amusement Park. Needless to say, it was an uncomfortable ride.

The MC for the show was Dandy Dan Daniels, one of the WMCA Good Guys. Halfway through our last song, "Satisfaction," Bob, our lead singer, and Scott, our drummer, swapped places. Bob took over the drums, and Scott finished singing "Satisfaction" and danced around the stage like Mick Jagger. But during the mic exchange, Dandy Dan intercepted the mic and said, "Let's give a big hand to The Tangerine Puppets." Our performance came to an abrupt halt, and we just waved and walked off the stage to thunderous applause. Apparently, our set had run too long, and Dandy Dan needed to stop us to make room for the headliner. Afterward, we piled back into Suzy's dad's station wagon for the uncomfortable ride home.

Palisades Amusement Park was a 38-acre amusement park located in Bergen County, New Jersey, across the Hudson River from New York City. It was situated atop the New Jersey Palisades, partly in Cliffside Park and partly in Fort Lee. The park was home to the famous Cyclone roller coaster, the Tunnel of Love, and the world's largest saltwater pool.

The park operated from 1898 until 1971, remaining one of the most visited amusement parks in the country until its closure. In 1962, Chuck Barris composed and Freddy Cannon recorded a song about the park titled "Palisades Park." The song was an upbeat rock and roll tune, featuring a distinctive organ part and incorporating amusement park sound effects. "Palisades Park" received nationwide radio play and increased the park's fame even more, drawing in a surge of visitors.– *Wikipedia*

Zacherley TV Show Disc-O-Teen

In 1966, the Tangerine Puppets were booked on the TV show *Disc-O-Teen*, starring Zacherley, on WNJU-TV in Newark. Zacherley was an American television host, radio personality, singer, and voice actor. He was best known for his long career as a television horror host, often broadcasting horror films in Philadelphia and New York City in the 1950s and 1960s. He was one of the first late-night television horror movie hosts, playing a crypt-dwelling undertaker with a booming graveyard laugh.

We were thrilled to be booked on a show with our favorite TV ghoul. We had one problem: transportation, again. This time, I went to my father and told him about our issue. My dad, who was a dispatcher for a corrugated box company, said he might be able to help. He checked and found out that he had a tractor-trailer going to Newark around the time we needed to get there. He arranged for the driver to first stop at my apartment in Forest Hills so we could load all of our equipment into the trailer. The band rode inside the trailer with the equipment, and I rode in the cab with the driver.

We arrived at the TV station and schlepped our equipment up to the stage. Then, we went to our assigned dressing room to change into our stage clothes, which didn't look much different from our street clothes. After we finished changing, we walked around the studio and stumbled upon Zacherley's dressing room. Zacherley saw us and asked us to come in. He was busy putting on his ghoul makeup when John said, "Hey Zacherley, I didn't know you wore makeup."

Zacherley replied, "Did you think I looked this beautiful all the time?"

We all cracked up.

We played one song, then waited for the show to end. We packed up our equipment and loaded it back onto the tractor-trailer for the ride home. The show was taped for a later airing, so my family and I got to watch it together on UHF. UHF required an additional round antenna that attached to the back of the TV set. There weren't many English-speaking shows on UHF, so we had to set it up for the first time just to watch the show. Unfortunately, there was no DVR back then, so I believe I was the only one in the band who got to see it on TV.

Just Jamming at Manny's

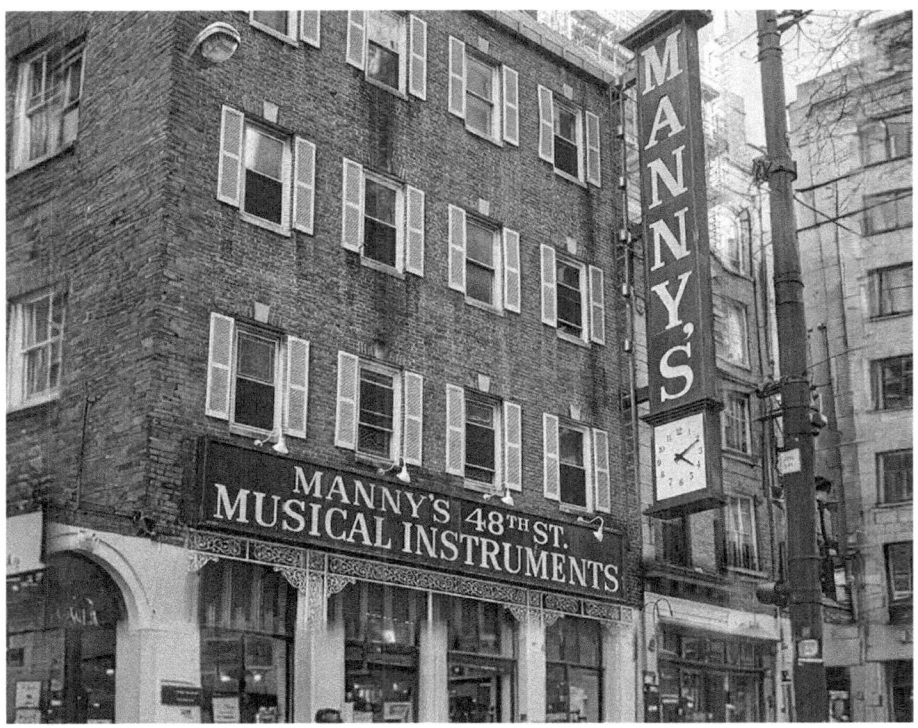

When I was 16, my favorite place in the world was Manny's Music Store on 48th Street in New York City. If you were a musician in the 1960s, Manny's was the place to be. It was like Disneyland for musicians.

Every weekend, I would walk into Manny's, eager to try out the latest guitars. I must have driven Henry, the salesman, absolutely crazy. Every time he saw me, he'd shake his head, let out a deep sigh, and say,

"Richie, what guitar would you like to try today? Are you ever going to make up your mind and actually buy one?"

I'd just smile, grab a guitar off the wall, and start playing. I wasn't ready to buy yet, but I was determined to find the perfect guitar. In the meantime, I tried them all.

One Saturday afternoon, I was sitting on a stool in Manny's, playing a slow blues tune through an amplifier. I was completely lost in the music when suddenly, I heard someone next to me start playing along. He had a great feel, matching my rhythm and adding his own lead parts. It felt completely natural, like we had played together before. We jammed for about ten minutes, locked into a groove, trading licks back and forth.

I started to notice that people had gathered around us, listening. A lot of people. For a moment, I thought, wow, am I really drawing this big of a crowd? When we finally finished playing, everyone clapped, and I turned to my jam partner to introduce myself. "Hey, I'm Richie," I said.

"Nice to meet you, Richie," he replied. "I'm Lek."

I paused for a second. That name sounded familiar

"Lek?" I asked.

He nodded.

"Yeah, Lek Leckenby. I play guitar for Herman's Hermits."

I couldn't believe it. I had just been jamming with the lead guitarist of one of the biggest bands in the world!

We started talking, and he was a really down-to-earth guy. We chatted about guitars, music, and life on the road. Then Lek looked at his watch and said,

"I've got to get back to the hotel. We have a show tonight."

Then he turned to me and asked,

"Want to keep talking while I walk back?"

Of course, I said yes.

As we approached the hotel, I noticed a huge crowd of screaming girls outside. Lek laughed and said,

"We better go through the side entrance. Too many fans out front."

I followed him inside, and before I knew it, I was riding the elevator up to the band's floor. When we got there, Lek knocked on a few doors, introducing me to the rest of Herman's Hermits. They were friendly, joking around, and totally relaxed.

Then, out of nowhere, Lek asked,

"Want to come to the show tonight?"

I didn't have to think twice.

"Absolutely!"

And that's how I first met Lek Leckenby and Herman's Hermits, just another afternoon of jamming at Manny's. Little did I know that less than eight years later, I'd be booking them for clubs and concerts and even producing their final album. Life has a funny way of working out.

Richard M. Adler

Another Jam at Manny's

Now, here's where things get really interesting.

When I was in Forest Hills High School, I was in two bands with Randy California, who was still Randy Wolfe at the time. One was called The Tangerine Puppets, and the other was Newport News, with Walter Becker, who later went on to form Steely Dan. One of my closest friends back then was Randy Wolfe. We spent hours jamming together, dreaming about making it big. Like me, Randy loved hanging out at Manny's. One day, when he was just 15 years old, he went to Manny's to try out some guitars, which was our favorite pastime. He was sitting on a stool, lost in his playing, when another guitarist sat down next to him and started jamming along. Now, this might sound familiar, two musicians, just meeting by chance, jamming in the middle of the store, but this time, something incredible happened. After they finished, the guitarist turned to Randy and said,

"Man, you've got a great feel. Want to come sit in with my band?"

Randy was thrilled. Of course, he said yes. That guitarist? Jimmy James. His band? Jimmy James and the Blue Flames. And if you haven't figured it out yet, Jimmy James was Jimi Hendrix.

Jimi took a liking to Randy and gave him a new nickname: Randy California, because he was from California. The bass player in the band was also named Randy, so Jimi called him Randy Texas. And just like that, my friend Randy went from jamming at Manny's to playing alongside one of the greatest guitarists of all time.

My Rock and Roll Fantasy

It's funny how music works. Sometimes, all it takes is being in the right place at the right time, with the right guitar in your hands. Just jamming at Manny's.

Fun fact: Randy Wolfe and Walter Becker lived in the same apartment building in Forest Hills. Randy taught Walter how to play guitar.

Richard M. Adler

Chapter 10

Café Wha?

Photo by Ajay Suresh from New York, NY, USA - Cafe Wha?

Cafe Wha? is a club at the corner of MacDougal Street and Minetta Lane in the Greenwich Village neighborhood of Manhattan, New York City. The club has presented numerous musicians and comedians. Bob Dylan, Jimi Hendrix, Andre Alves, Bruce Springsteen, The Velvet Underground, Cat Mother & the All Night Newsboys, Kool & the Gang, Peter, Paul and Mary, Woody Allen, Lenny Bruce, Joan Rivers, Bill Cosby, Richard Pryor, and many others all began their careers at the Wha.

Although Cafe Wha? was sold by its owner, Manny Roth, in 1968, the club remains at its original location, 115 MacDougal Street, between Bleecker and West 3rd Streets, in the basement of The Players Theatre. Roth was the uncle of David Lee Roth.

We were 15 years old and loved hanging out in Greenwich Village. It was the center of the music scene, and Tommy and I wanted to be part of it. We used to take the E train to West 4th Street and hang out in Washington Square Park with other music enthusiasts. There were always people playing guitars and singing, and we started meeting a lot of fellow musicians.

We would go to the afternoon shows at Cafe Wha?, where they let teenagers in to listen to the music and buy non-alcoholic juice drinks. It made us feel very grown up and involved in the Village music scene.

Cafe Wha? was down a steep flight of stairs, which every rock musician cursed having to carry their amps and drums down and back up.

I remember the floor was made of broken pieces of marble, and the walls were painted black. The club crammed 325 people sitting next to each other on long benches with a very small table in front, which held your drink.

Bob Dylan, in 1961, played at the club. He performed Woody Guthrie songs, but after being late for his set three times, Manny Roth fired him.

The one band I remember seeing the most at Cafe Wha? was The Ravens. I wonder whatever happened to them

My bands, The Tiger 5 and The Tangerine Puppets, played afternoon sets at Cafe Wha?. After one of our first sets, Tommy and I went over to the Nite Owl Cafe and watched The Lovin' Spoonful. They were rehearsing a new song, "Do You Believe in Magic." They played it over and over. After the fifth time, John Sebastian asked us, since we were the only other people in the club that afternoon, what we thought. I said I liked it, it had a good beat, and you could dance to it, which is something kids always said on American Bandstand when they did "Rate A Record." We all laughed, and they played it again. That night, they recorded the song, and the rest is history. "Do You Believe in Magic" is a song written by John Sebastian. In a 2007 DVD entitled *The Lovin' Spoonful with John Sebastian: Do You Believe in Magic*, Sebastian illustrates how, in 1965, his group The Lovin' Spoonful released the song as the first single from their debut studio album, *Do You Believe in Magic*. The single was well received by the public and became a top ten hit on the Billboard Hot 100, peaking at number 9. According to the lyrics, the magic referenced in the title is the power of music to supply happiness and freedom to both those who make it and those who listen to it. The Lovin' Spoonful's version was ranked number 216 on Rolling Stone's list of the 500 Greatest Songs of All Time. Billboard said of the original single release that the "pulsating folk-flavored rhythm number serves as a strong and exciting debut for a new group in the Byrds vein." He sped up the three-chord intro from Martha and the Vandellas' "Heat Wave" to come up with the intro to "Do You Believe in Magic."

In 1966, The Tangerine Puppets faced a problem. Bob Rowland, our lead singer, failed one of his subjects in school, and his father forbade him from playing in the band until he got his grades back up. We now had to find a lead singer to replace Bob.

I had a musician friend in school named Randy Wolfe. Randy was a talented guitar player and singer. He also played the harmonica. We already had two guitars in the band, Tommy and me, so Randy agreed to become our lead singer. Randy was a new kid in school. He came from California to New York because his stepfather, Ed

Cassidy, who was a drummer, had gigs set up in clubs in NYC. Ed moved the entire family to Forest Hills. We told Randy that being the lead singer of our band was only temporary until Bob was able to return. Randy was happy just to be playing with us.

Randy and I used to jam together after school. One day, Randy pulled a sawed-off neck of a wine bottle out of his guitar case and started playing the blues. I had never seen anyone actually use a bottle neck to play bottleneck guitar. Most people used a metal cylinder that you stuck your finger into. Randy told me that this is how the old blues men played bottleneck guitar, using an actual glass bottle neck.

The Living Room and Phone Booth

The Tangerine Puppets were the house band at the Living Room and the Phone Booth, both well-known nightclubs in NYC.

I had a friend in Forest Hills High School whose parents owned both clubs. One day, he approached me and asked if we would be interested in playing for Sweet 16 parties. We jumped at the chance. A club filled with teenage girls and we would be the only boys? "Hell yes." He also said that we would get paid. I actually expected him to ask us for money. Needless to say, we were thrilled to have a steady gig every Saturday and Sunday afternoon. This would still permit us to play gigs at night.

Since Randy was joining a working band, he put away his guitar and just came with his harmonica. Randy did a great job filling in for Bob, but once Bob returned, we had to ask Randy to leave. Randy asked me if I would be interested in joining a blues band he was forming with Walter Becker. I knew Walter from Halsey Junior High School, which we attended together, but he then went to Stuyvesant High School, so we kind of lost touch. I knew Randy was an incredible musician and Walter was a nice kid, so I agreed to play in the band as a side project. But I believe they were looking for a full-time commitment, which I couldn't give them. We practiced a few times, then Randy called and said that they had a gig in a club in Greenwich Village next Saturday night. I had a Sweet 16 to play during the day, so I told Randy that I would meet them at the club. The band was called Newport News after a blues tune that Randy taught us. We were a blues band and Walter was the lead singer and harmonica player. We had only practiced about five tunes, so we faked our way through the rest of the set. I was watching Randy's hands on his guitar to try to pick up the chords, but Randy was playing shapes I had never seen before. Needless to say, I was messing up badly. The gig was fun because it was the first time I played at night in a Greenwich Village club.

Randy spent a lot of time teaching Walter to play guitar

Randy was such a nice guy and a good friend, but the kids in Forest Hills High School were cruel. Randy didn't bathe as often as he should and had a distinct odor. He received the nickname of "Pig," which I thought was a bit harsh. My mother always knew when Randy was in my apartment. When she came home from work, she would run around the house opening the windows in the middle of winter, but she never said anything. Still, I knew why she was doing it.

Randy California, when he was in my band the Tangerine Puppets, was still known as Randy Wolfe. When Randy left the Puppets and Newport News didn't work out, he had a gig playing at the Cafe Wha? with Jimmy James and the Blue Flames. Randy invited me down one night to see the show. I went down to the Village on the subway with Randy. I guess I was 16 and Randy was 15 years old. During the show, I noticed that Chas Chandler, the bass player for the Animals, was seated two tables away from me. After the show, I went back to the dressing room to hang out with Randy when Chas Chandler came in asking to see the two guitarists. Chas asked Randy and Jimmy James if they would come to England and form a band, and Chas would manage and produce them. Randy told Chas that he was only 15 years old, so he would need to call his mother and ask her. Chas called her from the club's pay phone, but Randy's mom told Chas that Randy needed to finish high school, then he could have him. So, Jimmy James, who changed his name back to Jimi Hendrix, went to England and formed the Jimi Hendrix Experience, and Randy went to California after leaving Forest Hills High School and formed the band, Spirit.

Jimi Hendrix changed Randy Wolfe's name to Randy California while they were playing together in the band Jimmy James and the Blue Flames. Jimi already had a member of his band named Randy Palmer, so he named them based on the state of their birth: Randy California and Randy Texas.

Walter Becker went on to form a band with Donald Fagen at Bard College, where they both were students. Their drummer was Chevy Chase, who went on to be one of the original cast members of Saturday Night Live and star in movies. I personally like the Vacation movies he did. Walter and Donald went on to play in a band backing Jay and the Americans. I guess Randy did a good job teaching Walter to play guitar. Walter and Donald Fagen formed Steely Dan, with Walter on guitar and bass.

Spirit

Spirit was an American rock band that formed in 1967 in Los Angeles, California. They had a unique sound that mixed rock, jazz, and psychedelic music, making them stand out from other bands of the time. While they never became as famous as some of the biggest rock bands of the era, they developed a loyal fan base and influenced many musicians who came after them. Their most famous song in the United States was "I Got a Line on You."

This song was written by Spirit's lead guitarist and singer, Randy California, who was only in his late teens when the band started. He was a talented musician who had even played with Jimi Hendrix when he was younger. The band recorded "I Got a Line on You" between March and September of 1968 while working on their second album, *The Family That Plays Together*.

Richard M. Adler

The song was produced by Lou Adler, a well-known producer who had worked with famous artists like The Mamas & the Papas and Carole King. The recording sessions were intense, as the band wanted to create something that truly captured their energetic and unique style. They mixed bluesy guitar riffs with powerful drumming and catchy melodies, creating a song that was exciting and memorable. The band worked hard to perfect the sound, and when the final version was ready, they felt they had something special.

Spirit's record label, Ode Records, released "I Got a Line on You" as a single in October 1968, a few months before the album came out. At first, it didn't get much attention, and it seemed like it might go unnoticed. But by late November, college radio stations started playing it, and word began to spread. Fans were drawn to its upbeat rhythm, powerful guitar work, and catchy lyrics. Soon, it was climbing the music charts.

By March 15, 1969, the song had reached No. 25 on the U.S. Top 100 chart, making it Spirit's biggest hit. It also became popular in Canada, where it peaked at No. 28 on March 24, 1969. The song's B-side, "She Smiles," didn't become as well-known, but it still contributed to the band's growing reputation.

Although "I Got a Line on You" was their biggest hit, Spirit had several other great songs that fans loved. Some of their most memorable tracks included:

- "Mr. Skin"—A song named after drummer Ed Cassidy, who was known for his bald head and powerful drumming style.

- "Fresh Garbage"—A psychedelic rock song with a deep message about pollution and waste.

- "Animal Zoo"—A song that mixed humor and social commentary, describing the craziness of modern society.

- "Nature's Way"—A haunting and beautiful song about environmental issues, which became one of Spirit's most enduring tracks.

Spirit's story began with a small band in Los Angeles called The Red Roosters. This early group included Randy California (guitar and vocals), Mark Andes (bass), and Jay Ferguson (vocals and percussion). They played in local clubs and small venues, slowly building their musical skills.

Things changed when Randy's stepfather, Ed Cassidy, joined the band as their drummer. He was much older than the other members, but his experience made a huge difference. He had already played jazz and rock music with several famous musicians, and his powerful drumming gave the band a strong backbone. The final piece of the puzzle was keyboardist John Locke, who added a smooth, jazzy feel to their sound.

Originally, they called themselves The Spirits Rebellious, after a book by Kahlil Gibran. However, they later decided to shorten the name to just Spirit, which was easier to remember and fit their mysterious, free-spirited vibe.

Spirit never became as famous as bands like Led Zeppelin or The Doors, but their music had a big influence on many rock musicians. Their mix of rock, jazz, blues, and psychedelic sounds made them stand out, and their songs still have a special place in the hearts of their fans. Even though they didn't dominate the charts, their music inspired future generations, proving that sometimes, great music doesn't need to be the biggest hit to leave a lasting impact.

Steely Dan

Steely Dan is one of the most distinctive and respected rock bands in American music history. Formed in 1971 by Walter Becker and Donald Fagen, the band fused rock, jazz, Latin, blues, R&B, and pop influences. Their music featured witty lyrics, dry humor, and a smooth, sophisticated sound. Unlike the louder rock acts of their era, Steely Dan focused on smart, cool, and often mysterious compositions.

Rolling Stone once called them "the perfect musical antiheroes for the Seventies," highlighting how their sound stood apart from the mainstream.

Becker and Fagen met in the late 1960s as students at Bard College in New York. They bonded over a shared love of music and a desire to explore new sounds. After college, they moved to Los Angeles and began writing songs professionally.

In 1971, they formed Steely Dan. The name, taken from a steam-powered device in William S. Burroughs' novel *Naked Lunch*, reflected their offbeat sensibility. Rather than emulate popular hard rock bands, they focused on intricate compositions with jazz-like harmonies, complex rhythms, and layered, cryptic lyrics.

Initially, Steely Dan had a full touring band. Their early albums, *Can't Buy a Thrill* (1972) and *Countdown to Ecstasy* (1973), featured radio hits like "Do It Again" and "Reelin' in the Years."

Their blend of catchy hooks and refined arrangements earned both commercial success and critical praise.

However, Becker and Fagen were perfectionists. They disliked the rigors of touring and preferred studio work. In 1974, they stopped performing live and concentrated on studio recording.

Steely Dan evolved into a studio-focused project. Becker and Fagen hired top-tier session musicians, professionals brought in to record specific parts to execute their musical vision. Known for their meticulous process, they often recorded the same track multiple times using different lineups to achieve the desired sound.

This perfectionism led to a string of acclaimed albums:

- *Pretzel Logic* (1974) – Featuring "Rikki Don't Lose That Number"

- *Katy Lied* (1975) – Includes "Black Friday" and "Doctor Wu"

- *The Royal Scam* (1976) – Noted for its darker, funkier tone

- *Aja* (1977) – Their most successful album, featuring "Peg," "Deacon Blues," and "Josie"

Aja became a critical and commercial triumph. Its polished production, jazz-influenced solos, and futuristic sheen helped establish it as a landmark record.

In 1980, they released *Gaucho*, another highly produced album that took years to complete. But rising tension between the bandmates led to Steely Dan disbanding in 1981.

In the 1980s, Becker and Fagen mostly stayed out of the spotlight. Fagen's solo debut, *The Nightfly*, received praise, but Steely Dan remained inactive.

Still, their music continued to attract a devoted fan base. Listeners poured over every lyric and chord change, keeping the band's legacy alive. In 1993, Becker and Fagen reunited and began touring again.

In 2000, they released *Two Against Nature*, their first new studio album in nearly 20 years. It won four Grammy Awards, including Album of the Year, proving their relevance decades after their debut.

Steely Dan continued to tour and gain new fans while delighting long-time followers. In 2001, they were inducted into the Rock and Roll Hall of Fame. VH1 ranked them No. 82 among the 100 Greatest Musical Artists, and Rolling Stone placed them No. 15 on its list of the 20 Greatest Duos.

Walter Becker passed away on September 3, 2017, leaving Donald Fagen as the last original member. Fagen has continued performing under the Steely Dan name, keeping their music alive for new generations.

Steely Dan remains beloved because of their unique style. Their songs combined sharp lyrics, emotional depth, and remarkable musical craftsmanship. They showed that rock could be subtle, intelligent, and smooth, proving that originality can be just as powerful as volume.

Chapter 11

Forest Hills High School Talent Show

Forest Hills High School, the original Rock and Roll High School, where rebellion was an elective and attitude was always in tune.

Forest Hills High School, man, I feel so incredibly lucky to have gone there. It wasn't just that I got a solid education, but the place was a total hotbed for rock bands back in the 60s and 70s.

Forest Hills High School, often called the original "Rock and Roll High School," is located at 110th Street and 66th Road. The school first opened in 1937 and is well known for its strong academic programs.

All four original Ramones, Joey, Johnny, Tommy, and Dee Dee, were students here. But they weren't the only famous names to walk the halls. Burt Bacharach, Art Buchwald, Jerry Springer, Leslie West, Randy California, Paul Simon, and Art Garfunkel also went to Forest Hills High School.

Richard M. Adler

To honor the Ramones and their connection to the neighborhood, the New York City Council put up a street sign in front of the school, naming the street "Ramones Way."

Walking around the halls of Forest Hills, it was like whenever you bumped into someone and said hello, the next thing out of their mouth was usually, "How's your band doin'?" There were so many bands kicking around. My band, The Tangerine Puppets, considered ourselves super lucky to be the only rock band in the whole school picked to play at our in-school talent show, and it was by popular demand.

Our school was seriously overcrowded, so they split it into three sections: Forest, Park, and Hill. I was in the Forest section. Each section had its own assembly in the auditorium on different days. That's how they dealt with the massive student body. There weren't enough seats for one or even two assemblies. They needed three. I think there were over 1,250 kids in my graduating class. It was insane.

One day, I got called down to Mr. Sirota's office. Mr. Sirota was one of the deans and also my gym teacher. He asked me if The Tangerine Puppets would play at the school talent show. He explained that the talent show was going to be on three separate days, one for each section: Forest, Hill, and Park. I was totally psyched and said yes right away without even checking with the other guys in the band first.

Turns out, we had a problem. All of The Tangerine Puppets went to Forest Hills High, except for our drummer, Scott Roberts. Scott was only in 9th grade and went to Halsey Junior High. He asked Halsey for permission to play at Forest Hills for the three shows, but his school said no way. They thought he would miss too many classes. So now we were stuck. What were we going to do about a drummer?

I was taking guitar lessons from Freddie Lefkowitz, who was a friend and lived in the apartment building across the street from me. During my lesson, I told Freddie about our big drummer problem. Freddie told me he didn't just play guitar, he also played drums, and he said he would be happy to play with us since he also went to Forest Hills High. I called the other guys in the band to let them know Freddie was in on drums. Everyone was so relieved that we had a drummer and the show was back on track. Well, not exactly as planned.

The day before the first show, I got called down to Mr. Sirota's office again. Uncle Miltie, that's what we called him because his first name was Milton, told me they were going to let us play three songs during the talent show. The first song would start as the students were coming into the auditorium and finding their seats. The second song would be during the actual show, and the third song would be at the end when everyone was leaving for their next class.

The next day, we played our first song as all the students were walking in and supposedly finding their seats. We were rocking out to "You Really Got Me" by The Kinks. But instead of finding their seats, everyone ran up to the front of the stage and started dancing in the aisles. It was an amazing scene, especially since it was during school hours. The teachers were freaking out. When we finished the song, the audience went wild, cheering and giving us a huge round of applause. Once the applause died down, everyone actually had to find a seat.

The talent show started, and then it was our turn again. We got on stage, the lights came up, and we launched into "Satisfaction" by the Rolling Stones. During the song, I looked out into the audience and saw Jeff Hyman, who would later be known to everyone as Joey Ramone, standing by the exit door. He had one foot propped up behind him on the door, and his head and long hair were hanging down low. Jeff was also wearing a chain with a medallion on it that dangled at the end of his hair. All I could think, as I was playing guitar, was that Jeff looked exactly like a question mark.

Meanwhile, John, our bass player, was running all over the stage with his bass held way up high, like he was carrying a machine gun. The vice president of the G.O., which was our student government organization, was watching the show from one of the wings on the stage. As John was running around, he ran a little too far offstage and whacked the neck of his bass guitar right between the legs of the G.O. VP. The guy doubled over in pain, but we just kept on playing.

Then came the end of the show. We played "It's All Over Now" by the Rolling Stones. This was supposed to be the cue for all the students to stand up and leave for class, but nobody moved. Instead, they all rushed the stage again and started dancing in the aisles. We were finishing our song just as the bell rang, and all the students were still in the auditorium. They were all going to be late for class. This did not go down well with the school administration, and guess who got called down to Mr. Sirota's office again? Yep, me.

When I got to the dean's office, I was asked to sit down. Mr. Sirota started by saying, "Rich, we have a problem. We need to cut your last song from the show because none of the students left the auditorium, and they were all late for class. So, for tomorrow's show, we need to cut your last song." I totally didn't see that coming. We were such a hit with the students; I was sure he was going to tell me how awesome we were.

The next day, we played our opening song and our song during the show, but we skipped our last song, just like Mr. Sirota asked. But then the students all started chanting, "We want the Puppets! We want the Puppets!" Word had obviously gotten around that we played three songs at the first show. But we weren't allowed to go back on. Still, everyone ended up late for their next class because the students refused to leave until the teachers threatened them with detention.

After the show, guess what? I was summoned to Mr. Sirota's office again. One more time, Mr. Sirota said, "Rich, we have a problem. The show is running way longer than planned because the students wouldn't sit down during your first song. They were all dancing in the aisles. It took them way too long to get to their seats. So tomorrow, we need to cut out your band's first song."

So we played just our one song during the show. And then, at the end of the show, the students started chanting again, "We want the Puppets! We want the Puppets!" And again, we weren't allowed to play at the end. And still, everyone was late for their next class.

We were a hit. The whole school was buzzing about The Tangerine Puppets. Girls who had never even looked at me before were now saying hi to me in the hallways. Girls were actually coming up to me in school to tell me their girlfriends wanted to date me. It was pretty awesome to be 16 years old and in a popular high school rock band.

John Cummings, our bass player, and Tommy Erdelyi, our guitar player, both went on to form The Ramones and became Johnny and Tommy Ramone. Randy Wolfe formed the band Spirit and was given the name Randy California by Jimi Hendrix. Freddie Lefkowitz joined the band Television and changed his name to Fred Smith.

Chapter 12

The Most Bizarre Bill in Rock History

Richard M. Adler

On July 14, 1967, at the Forest Hills Tennis Stadium, I witnessed the most unlikely rock and roll pairing in the history of concerts: The Monkees and their opening act, the Jimi Hendrix Experience. I was very excited because this was my first opportunity to see Jimi Hendrix. I was there more to see Hendrix than The Monkees, but I was curious to hear what The Monkees would sound like playing their own instruments.

Are You Experienced, Jimi's debut album, had been released in May 1967, and I had already fallen in love with it. I played that record so many times I knew every word to every song. I couldn't wait to see Jimi perform live.

Unfortunately, when Hendrix came on stage, the young Monkees fans booed him and shouted, "We want The Monkees," "We want Davy," "We want Micky." It was so bad that Jimi gave the audience the finger and threw his guitar into the crowd. After the concert, he quit the tour.

Actually, to my surprise, The Monkees were pretty good.

Mike Nesmith first heard a tape of Hendrix while at a dinner party with John Lennon, Paul McCartney, and Eric Clapton. Nesmith and his fellow Monkees, Peter Tork and Micky Dolenz, became instant Jimi Hendrix fans. After witnessing his legendary performance at the Monterey Pop Festival in June 1967, they encouraged their manager to invite the little-known but highly respected Jimi Hendrix Experience to join their upcoming U.S. tour.

"I first saw [Hendrix] when he was still Jimmy James [and the Blue Flames]," Micky Dolenz told *Forbes*. "I was in New York, and somebody said I had to come down to [Greenwich] Village to see this guy play the guitar with his teeth [laughs]."

"We were about to tour and were looking for an opening act," Dolenz added. "I said to the producers of the show that Jimi would be great because he was very theatrical, like we were. I guess my producers liked the idea, and Jimi's producers liked the idea, because sure enough, we ended up on the road together. It was wonderful."

Micky said, "I didn't even pay attention to what the audience reaction was, because I was just mesmerized by Jimi and his art. We were just blown away by him every night. I know Nez, Mike Nesmith, especially was. We would just stand in the wings in awe. I was fascinated by Jimi's showmanship, by his persona. All I knew was, I liked it. And to this day, I don't care much what people thought."

Hendrix ended up playing only seven of the tour's 29 dates, dropping out after contending nightly with thousands of nasty, impatient, jeering teenyboppers.

"Yeah, it was kind of embarrassing," Dolenz admitted to *Yahoo Entertainment*. "Jimi would go, 'Purple Haze,' and the kids would be like, 'We want Davy.' He'd go, 'Foxy Lady,' and they'd yell, 'We. Want. The. Monkees. We. Want. The. Monkees.' He was coming up against that very typical opening-act dilemma for anyone touring with a big headliner."

When Dolenz saw Hendrix at Monterey, he recalled, "All of a sudden, this act comes on, not very well known yet, but very flamboyant, the clothes, the music. And I said, 'Hey, that's the guy that plays guitar with his teeth.' I recognized him. And so, just by coincidence, we were looking for an opening act for our first tour. So, I suggested the Jimi Hendrix Experience to our producers, because obviously it was incredible music, but also very theatrical. And The Monkees were a theatrical act, if you really examine it. I guess that's why it made sense to me. I just thought it would make a great mix."

Jimi Hendrix phoned the *New Musical Express* to announce that he had quit The Monkees tour. He said, "Some parents who brought their kids to the concert complained that our show was too vulgar. We decided that this was just the wrong audience. I think they're replacing me with Mickey Mouse."

"We spent a lot of time together. We went to clubs and wandered around aimlessly, and sometimes non-aimlessly," Dolenz recalled fondly. "We got along great and had a great time. We partied, we hung around in hotel rooms jamming and just singing, having little after-show parties. I remember once we went to the Electric Circus in New York, a very famous psychedelic place back then."

"He was a lovely man, though very different from his persona onstage. He was very quiet. I don't want to say naïve, but just a real nice, quiet guy. But then, of course, he would launch into this incredible persona onstage, which was just phenomenal. We partied, and he partied just as good as anybody else, but it wasn't like he always had to be the life of the party. That's probably the reason why we got along, because I'm the same way. I get fulfillment onstage, and when I'm offstage, I want to be left alone."

Before being invited to tour with The Monkees, Hendrix had shared his opinion of the band in no uncertain terms during an interview with *Melody Maker*: "Oh God, I hate them. Dishwater. You can't knock anybody for making it, but people like the Monkees?"

"The parents were probably not too crazy about having to sit through a Monkees concert, much less see this Black guy in a psychedelic Day-Glo blouse, playing music from hell, holding his guitar like he was fucking it, then lighting it on fire. Jimi would amble out onto the stage, fire up the amps, and break into 'Purple Haze,' and the kids in the audience would instantly drown him out with, 'We want Davy.' God, it was embarrassing."

"Nobody thought, 'This is screaming, scaring-your-daddy music compared with The Monkees,'" from *I'm a Believer: My Life of Monkees, Music & Madness* by Micky Dolenz, with Mark Bego.

Actually, The Monkees were not half bad. I had expected much worse, but I was pleasantly surprised.

How was I to know that just seven years later, I would be booking concerts, first for Dolenz, Jones, Boyce and Hart, and then for The Monkees. I remember going to Michigan to cover a show, and I was sitting in the dressing room telling Davy how I met him in the elevator at Parker Towers the day he returned from auditioning for The Monkees. For some reason, he did remember meeting a band that day in his apartment building.

On July 24, 1986, The Monkees, Herman's Hermits, and Gary Puckett and The Union Gap played a show at the Orange County Fair in Middletown, NY, which was only 20 minutes from my house. This was The Monkees' 20th Anniversary Reunion Tour. I took my wife Cathy, my daughter Jennifer, who was seven years old, and my son Ryan, who was five, to see the show. After the performance, I brought my family backstage to the dressing rooms to meet both The Monkees and Herman's Hermits.

By this time, I had been out of the music business for a good seven years, but the bands still remembered me and put me on the guest list. Both groups were really nice to my kids, but unfortunately, my kids were too young to understand who they were meeting.

An interesting fact: Davy Jones, who starred as the Artful Dodger in the Broadway musical *Oliver!*, performed along with the cast on *The*

Ed Sullivan Show on February 9, 1964, the same night The Beatles made their first live U.S. television appearance.

The Monkees

The Monkees were one of the most unusual success stories in music history. Formed in 1965 for a television sitcom inspired by The Beatles' *A Hard Day's Night*, they started as a made-for-TV band with actors playing musicians. But what began as scripted entertainment quickly turned into a genuine pop phenomenon.

The four members, Micky Dolenz, Davy Jones, Michael Nesmith, and Peter Tork, won over audiences with their charm, humor, and catchy songs. Hits like "I'm a Believer," "Daydream Believer," and "Last Train to Clarksville" made them chart-toppers, and they eventually sold more than 75 million records worldwide.

At first, they weren't allowed to play their own instruments or write their own songs, which caused friction, especially for Nesmith and Tork, who were serious musicians. In time, they fought for and won creative control, proving they were more than just TV stars.

Their third album, *Headquarters*, was a turning point, showcasing their musical talent. Though their television show lasted only two seasons, their impact lasted much longer. After the show ended, they released a surreal cult film, *Head*, co-written by Jack Nicholson. The film confused fans at the time but later earned critical respect.

The group disbanded in the early 1970s, but a major revival began in 1986 when reruns of their show aired on MTV. A new generation of fans discovered their music, and reunion tours followed. Over the years, the band continued performing in various lineups, recording new material, and delighting fans old and new.

Micky Dolenz and Michael Nesmith launched a farewell tour in 2021, closing out a long and unexpected journey that began with a television casting call. The Monkees were not supposed to be a real band, but they became one anyway, and their music continues to bring joy to listeners around the world.

Richard M. Adler

Jimi Hendrix

Jimi Hendrix was one of the most influential and innovative guitarists in rock history. In just four short years, he redefined what the electric guitar could do, blending blues, rock, soul, and psychedelia into a sound that was powerful, emotional, and entirely his own.

Born in Seattle in 1942, Hendrix taught himself to play guitar as a teenager, drawing early inspiration from blues legends like B.B. King and Muddy Waters. After a brief stint in the Army, he spent years on the road playing behind artists like Little Richard and the Isley Brothers, slowly developing the stage presence and style that would later captivate the world.

In 1966, he moved to London with the help of Chas Chandler from The Animals. There, Hendrix formed The Jimi Hendrix Experience, a trio that quickly made waves with hits like "Hey Joe," "Purple Haze," and "The Wind Cries Mary." His debut album, *Are You Experienced*, released in 1967, stunned listeners with its raw power and groundbreaking use of guitar effects.

Hendrix's fame exploded after his fiery performance at the Monterey Pop Festival, where he famously set his guitar on fire. That moment, more than just a stunt, symbolized his place as a bold, visionary artist who pushed every boundary.

His second album, *Axis: Bold as Love*, and the double album *Electric Ladyland* cemented his place as a rock pioneer. Tracks like "Voodoo Child," "Crosstown Traffic," and his transformative version of Bob Dylan's "All Along the Watchtower" revealed a musician constantly evolving and never afraid to experiment.

Hendrix's performance of "The Star-Spangled Banner" at Woodstock in 1969 remains one of the most iconic moments in music history, a haunting and powerful expression of protest and artistry.

Sadly, Hendrix died in 1970 at the age of 27. Though his career was brief, his influence continues to shape music today. He changed how guitar was played, how music was recorded, and how a performer could connect with an audience.

Jimi Hendrix was more than a musician. He was a trailblazer, a cultural icon, and the gold standard for guitarists across every generation.

Richard M. Adler

Chapter 13

The Beatles at Shea Stadium

On August 15, 1965, The Beatles came back to Queens to play Shea Stadium, and of course, I had to go.

Tommy, Bob, and I got tickets on the third base line. Great seats, but we still couldn't hear The Beatles.

This time, 55,600 lucky kids got to see The Beatles.

The show at Shea Stadium was record-breaking and one of the most famous concert events of its era. It set records for both attendance and revenue. Promoter Sid Bernstein said, "Over 55,000 people saw The Beatles at Shea Stadium. We took $304,000, the greatest gross ever in the history of show business." The Beatles pocketed $160,000 of the $304,000 box office takings.

The Beatles had hoped to land on the field by helicopter, but the idea was blocked by New York City authorities. They traveled by limousine from the Warwick Hotel to a heliport, from where they were flown in a New York Airways Boeing Vertol 107-II helicopter over the city to the roof of the World's Fair Port Authority building in Queens. From there, they boarded a Wells Fargo armored van, where each member was given a Wells Fargo agent badge. They wore the badges on stage at Shea and were driven to the stadium.

The stage was located on second base, far from the audience, which was confined to the stadium's spectator areas. But from our seats behind third base, we had a great view.

Other acts on the bill were, in order of appearance, Brenda Holloway and the King Curtis Band, Cannibal & the Headhunters, and Sounds Incorporated.

The Beatles were introduced by Ed Sullivan.

"Now, ladies and gentlemen, honored by their country, decorated by their Queen, loved here in America, here are The Beatles!"

When The Beatles hit the stage, all pandemonium broke loose. The screaming was so loud, you couldn't hear yourself think. It was louder than standing next to a jet taking off at nearby LaGuardia Airport.

The Beatles had 175-watt Vox amplifiers which were not mic'd. They sang using the stadium PA system, the same one used to announce the next batter during Mets games. Hearing them was impossible. Technology wasn't ready for stadium concerts, but no one cared. The girls were there to see The Beatles, to be in the same venue, and to breathe the same air.

The Beatles performed 12 songs: "Twist and Shout," "She's a Woman," "I Feel Fine," "Dizzy Miss Lizzy," "Ticket to Ride," "Everybody's Trying to Be My Baby," "Can't Buy Me Love," "Baby's in Black," "Act Naturally," "A Hard Day's Night," "Help!" and "I'm Down."

A little over a year later, The Beatles returned to Shea Stadium for a second time.

In 1966, I attended the concert along with three members of my band, The Tangerine Puppets: John Cummings, also known as Johnny Ramone, Tommy Erdelyi, also known as Tommy Ramone, and Scott Roberts.

The concert did not sell out. 11,000 of the 55,600 tickets remained unsold. Still, The Beatles made more money than in 1965, earning $189,000, which was 65 percent of the $292,000 gross.

The support acts were The Remains, Bobby Hebb, The Cyrkle, and The Ronettes. The Beatles performed 11 songs: "Rock and Roll Music," "She's a Woman," "If I Needed Someone," "Day Tripper," "Baby's in Black," "I Feel Fine," "Yesterday," "I Wanna Be Your Man," "Nowhere Man," "Paperback Writer," and "Long Tall Sally."

Richard M. Adler

When The Beatles came on stage, Johnny, who had brought a backpack to the concert, opened it up. To our surprise, it was filled with stones.

John was a Rolling Stones fan and hated The Beatles. I actually wondered why he wanted to go to this concert. We were sitting near third base, and The Beatles were playing on a stage at second base. Johnny was a really good pitcher, and we had a lot of trouble hitting him during our stickball games. Needless to say, he had a good arm, so throwing stones from our seats to the stage was not a problem.

During The Beatles' set, John kept throwing stones at the stage. We watched them bounce off. Every time he threw one, Tommy, Scott, and I told him to stop, but Johnny would not. You couldn't make Johnny do anything he didn't want to do, and he didn't want to stop throwing stones at The Beatles.

Fortunately, none of The Beatles were injured.

Ironically, the same Johnny who once hated The Beatles became a fan sometime around the release of *Sgt. Pepper*.

Tommy and Johnny formed a new band around 1974, and John agreed to name it The Ramones, inspired by Paul Ramon, a pseudonym Paul McCartney had once used when checking into hotels during an early tour of Scotland.

Richard M. Adler

Chapter 14

Teaching Johnny to Play Guitar

John Cummings aka Johnny Ramone playing bass in the Tangerine Puppets

Richard M. Adler

In the bustling heart of 1966 New York, amidst the clamor of a city that never sleeps, our band, The Tangerine Puppets, was trying to carve out a niche in the thriving music scene. John Cummings, later famously known as Johnny Ramone, was the bassist of our band, a figure of immense potential waiting to be harnessed. As the band's dynamics evolved, I found myself in the role of a mentor, attempting to teach John the intricacies of guitar playing.

Those lessons were a blend of frustration and revelation. John, with his unorthodox approach, seemed to challenge the very conventions of guitar playing. His method of playing the A-shape barre chord was unconventional, to say the least. While most guitarists, including myself, would naturally use their pointer and ring fingers, John stubbornly used his pointer and middle fingers. No matter how much I emphasized the standard technique, he persisted with his unique style.

But it was his struggle with the upstrokes that truly tested my patience. Each attempt by John to play an upstroke ended with him missing the strings entirely. In sheer frustration, and a bit of desperation, I advised him to stick to downstrokes for the time being. Little did I know, this limitation would become the cornerstone of his iconic guitar style, revolutionizing the way punk rock was played.

Our sessions, often intense and challenging, also had their lighter moments. One day, as I was leaving John's apartment, guitar in hand and lost in the melody I was playing, an unexpected incident added a twist to our routine. Just as I stepped out of the building, I was startled by a sudden explosion of water next to me. John had launched a massive water balloon from his bedroom window. Startled, I ducked instinctively, causing my face to collide with my guitar. The impact left a cut on my chin, a scar that would remain as a memento of that day.

These experiences with John were more than just about music. They were lessons in creativity and breaking norms. His unorthodox techniques and playful antics were not just quirks but reflections of a spirit that refused to be confined by conventional standards. As I nursed my cut, I had no idea that John Cummings, the bassist struggling with guitar lessons, would soon transform into Johnny Ramone, a name that would become synonymous with punk rock's raw energy and rebellious spirit.

In those days of 1966 and 1967, The Tangerine Puppets were more than just a band. We were a crucible of creativity, each of us finding our path, sometimes in the most unexpected ways. John's journey from struggling with upstrokes to defining a new style of guitar playing is a testament to the unpredictable and transformative power of music.

Johnny Ramone. The name conjures up images of a leather-clad figure, a guitar slung low, and a wall of sound that was both simple and utterly relentless. He wasn't about flashy solos or complex chords. His was a raw, visceral approach that became the bedrock of punk rock.

Born John Cummings in 1948, Johnny's journey began with an immersion in the sounds of early rock, from The Rolling Stones and The Who to The Stooges and The Velvet Underground. He picked up his first guitar in the mid-sixties. Alongside Doug Colvin, Tommy Erdelyi, and Jeff Hyman, he formed The Ramones in 1974. This marked the beginning of a sonic revolution.

Johnny's guitar style was most defined by his strict adherence to downstrokes. Unlike most guitarists who alternate between down and upstrokes, Johnny eliminated the upstroke entirely. This created a powerful, driving rhythm, a buzz-saw sound that was both unique and instantly recognizable. The basic approach involved hitting every eighth note with a downstroke, creating a wall of sound that was both simple and intense. This technique required significant stamina and wrist strength. It took serious practice to build up the right arm.

The relentless downstrokes were not just about rhythm. They were an expression of attitude, a no-nonsense approach to guitar playing. He also reportedly used a technique similar to Jimmy Page's on "Communication Breakdown." Johnny's attack was not a constant barrage. It had accents that created a more dynamic sound. It was not just his strumming that defined his style, but also his chord choices. Johnny primarily used full barre chords rather than the simpler power chords. He transposed two barre chord positions up and down the neck of his guitar. This approach, played through a loud Marshall amplifier, created a barrage of distorted overtones that contributed to the signature fullness of The Ramones' sound.

The simplicity and sheer force of his playing became a kind of punk songwriting 101. It proved you didn't need complex techniques to create impactful music. While some might think his playing was monotonous, there were subtle shifts over time. But Johnny's downstrokes remained the foundation.

Johnny's choice of guitar was as distinctive as his playing style. He initially picked up a cheap $54 Mosrite Ventures II guitar. He later had a DiMarzio Fat Strat pickup installed, which gave his sound a chainsaw-like quality.

Beyond the technical aspects, Johnny's whole persona was an essential part of his musical impact. He adjusted his guitar strap in front of a mirror until it looked cool, and that was how it remained for his entire career. His approach to playing guitar was visceral and instinctive. He did not follow any standard practice, focusing instead on attitude, emotion, and imperfection. His black leather jacket was more than clothing; it was a way of life. He approached music with a hard-nosed, no-nonsense mindset.

Johnny Ramone's influence on punk rock is undeniable. His minimalist style showed that it wasn't about technical virtuosity but about raw energy and attitude. The first Ramones album, with its hard-panned guitar and bass tracks, became an accidental learning tool. It allowed aspiring guitarists to isolate Johnny's parts and play along.

His legacy proves that you don't need the dexterity of Jimi Hendrix to create legendary music.

Johnny Ramone wasn't just a guitar player. He was a force of nature, a sonic architect who helped shape the landscape of punk rock. He proved that sometimes, simplicity, when executed with unwavering conviction, can be the most powerful statement of all.

His downstrokes are the bedrock of punk guitar.

Johnny Ramone ranked No. 8 on *Spin*'s 2012 list of the "100 Greatest Guitarists of All Time" and No. 28 on *Rolling Stone*'s similarly titled 2015 list.

Richard M. Adler

Chapter 15

Tommy Ramone

Tommy Erdelyi 1972

Richard M. Adler

If rock and roll had a heartbeat, punk rock had a pulse, a relentless, machine-gun rhythm that never let up. At the center of that sound was Tommy Ramone, the man behind the drum kit who unknowingly set the foundation for an entire movement. While Johnny Ramone's buzzsaw guitar and Dee Dee's rapid-fire bass lines made the Ramones' sound unmistakable, it was Tommy's precise, high-energy drumming that held it all together.

But here's the twist: Tommy Ramone never planned to be a drummer.

Born Tamás Erdélyi in Budapest, Hungary, in 1949, Tommy and his family moved to New York when he was young, settling in Forest Hills, Queens. He grew up in a city teeming with rock and roll energy, watching legends like The Beatles, The Who, and The Stooges change the landscape of music. But Tommy wasn't looking to be a rock star. He was drawn to the behind-the-scenes magic of music production.

Before he ever picked up drumsticks, Tommy was a studio engineer, working at Record Plant Studios on albums like Jimi Hendrix's *Band of Gypsys*. He knew how music was constructed, how rhythm shaped a song, and how production could make or break a record. But fate had different plans.

When Tommy linked up with John Cummings (Johnny Ramone), Jeff Hyman (Joey Ramone), and Douglas Colvin (Dee Dee Ramone) in the early 1970s, they weren't a band yet, just a group of guys figuring it out. Tommy's role was supposed to be behind the scenes, managing the band and helping craft their sound.

They had the attitude. They had the vision. But they had one big problem: they couldn't find a drummer. The guys went through several candidates, but none of them fit. Tommy, who had experience playing guitar but not drums, eventually sat behind the kit out of necessity. And just like that, history was made.

What Tommy Ramone did behind the kit wasn't flashy. It wasn't technical. It wasn't rooted in jazz, blues, or progressive rock like the drummers of the time. It was something completely new.

Fast, relentless beats. The Ramones played at breakneck speed, and Tommy kept the tempo steady, never slowing down. His drumming forced the rest of the band to keep up.

No drum solos, no fills, no excess. Unlike rock drummers who filled space with elaborate rolls, Tommy kept it tight and driving, making every hit count.

The "four-on-the-floor" attack. His constant eighth-note hi-hats, simple snare patterns, and unrelenting bass drum created the punk rock template that would inspire generations of drummers.

Pure stamina. Tommy wasn't just keeping time. He was playing an entire Ramones set at lightning speed, never missing a beat. That required serious endurance.

The result was a wall of sound that was raw, fast, and stripped to its essence, the opposite of the overblown, indulgent rock of the mid-1970s.

Tommy's influence is stamped all over the first three Ramones albums:

Ramones (1976) – The birth of punk. Songs like "Blitzkrieg Bop," "Beat on the Brat," and "Now I Wanna Sniff Some Glue" feature Tommy's straight-ahead, no-nonsense drumming that became the foundation of punk rhythm.

Leave Home (1977) – Faster, tighter, and even more aggressive. Tracks like "Pinhead" and "Commando" show Tommy refining the Ramones' machine-gun approach.

Rocket to Russia (1977) – A perfect balance of speed and pop hooks, with tracks like "Sheena Is a Punk Rocker" showcasing Tommy's ability to drive a song while keeping it catchy.

Tommy wasn't just playing the drums. He was shaping punk rock as we know it.

By 1978, the Ramones were growing bigger, touring nonstop, and pushing their limits. But Tommy had had enough. The constant grind of playing at full speed, night after night, took its toll. He was never a natural drummer, and the intensity was physically exhausting.

So, he stepped away from the kit after recording *Rocket to Russia*, handing the sticks over to Marky Ramone. But Tommy wasn't done with the Ramones. He stayed on as producer, working on *Road to Ruin* and later co-producing *Too Tough to Die* in 1984.

Tommy told me that he quit the Ramones because if he stayed, he would have gone insane.

Tommy Ramone never played with wild abandon like Keith Moon, never had the technical prowess of Neil Peart, and never showed off with elaborate fills like John Bonham. And yet, his impact on rock and punk drumming is just as significant.

Why?

Because every punk drummer that came after him owes something to Tommy. Without him, there is no Paul Cook (Sex Pistols), no

Topper Headon (The Clash), no Tré Cool (Green Day), and no Travis Barker (Blink-182). His drumming was the backbone of punk, proving that you didn't need to be a virtuoso to make music that mattered. You just had to play with conviction.

Tommy passed away in 2014, the last surviving original Ramone, but his influence never faded. The moment you hear that unmistakable 1-2-3-4 count-off and the drums kick in, you know exactly where it came from.

Because punk rock starts with a beat. And that beat belonged to Tommy Ramone.

Richard M. Adler

Chapter 16

Smoking Banana Peels

It was the summer of '67, and we were, to put it mildly, easily influenced. News of a new way to get high, something cheap and readily available, had spread through our ranks like wildfire: banana peels. Yeah, you heard me right, banana peels.

It all started, as I recall, when John came running over, eyes wide, waving a tattered copy of *The Village Voice*. He claimed it had the secret to unlocking a new dimension, all through the power of the humble banana. Tommy and I were skeptical, of course, but we were teenagers with a whole lot of time on our hands and a desperate desire for a good buzz.

According to *The Village Voice*, you couldn't just chow down on a banana peel and expect to have your mind blown. No, no. This required a process, a ritual of sorts. First, we needed to gather our supplies. This meant going to the grocery store and buying about 15 pounds of bananas. We peeled them all like a bunch of chimps, eating the fruit and carefully saving the peels. Then, armed with dull butter knives, we scraped the insides of the peels like we were panning for gold, trying to extract the magical pith.

We then dumped this mess of gooey banana scrapings into a pot and boiled it for what felt like an eternity. The house smelled like overripe fruit and despair. We spread the resulting glop onto cookie sheets and baked it in the oven. Finally, after all this effort, the stuff turned into a fine black powder, which we promptly declared was bananadine. That was the name of the fictional chemical supposedly responsible for the hallucinogenic effect.

Armed with our homemade "bananadine," we rolled it up in cigarette papers. I swear, we felt like mad scientists on the verge of a major discovery. We looked at each other, grinning, and lit up. We puffed and coughed and waited... and waited...

Nothing. Absolutely nothing. We just tasted burnt banana. Maybe we just needed more. So, we smoked some more. The smoke got thicker, the coughs got louder, and the disappointment got heavier.

The high we were chasing, the mind-blowing psychedelic experience we had anticipated, never arrived. Instead, we were just a bunch of dumb kids who smelled like banana peels and had spent a whole afternoon making a mess for nothing. Later, we would learn that the FDA even set up a machine to smoke banana peels and confirmed what we had already discovered for ourselves: smoking banana peels does not get you high.

Looking back, I can't help but laugh at our naïveté. We really thought we were on to something. We thought we had discovered a secret, a shortcut to enlightenment. In reality, we had just fallen for one of the most ridiculous drug hoaxes in history. We were convinced that Donovan's song *Mellow Yellow* was about smoking banana peels, and that just made us even more committed to our quest. Now I know he wrote it about a yellow vibrator, not about smoking bananas.

That night, as we sat in a circle, still smelling like bananas, we realized that the real trip was the one we had taken together, the journey of sheer idiocy and youthful optimism. It was our own little mellow yellow moment, even if we never felt mellow or yellow.

The funny thing is, the legend of banana peels as a drug still pops up from time to time. I guess the myth is just too good to die. And honestly, I'm glad it never did. It's a story that reminds us of our younger selves and those long, strange days when we believed everything we read (especially if it involved a good high). But we should have known we were just a bunch of monkeys trying to get high on the peels instead of the banana.

Richard M. Adler

Chapter 17

The Ramp

The Thorneycroft Ramp, located at 66th Avenue between 99th and 102nd Streets in Forest Hills, led up to the top of the parking garage attached to the Thorneycroft apartment buildings. The ramp was known as a "hotspot for misbehavior."

We used that roof as our meeting place and our playground. We played football and stickball up there, as well as getting high. Some sniffed glue, others passed around a joint, and some drank Boone's Farm Apple Wine.

My friend Ira Nagel lived in the Thorneycroft apartments and became the unofficial mayor of Thorneycroft (or so he says). We hung out there with our neighborhood friends: Tommy Erdelyi, John Cummings, Jeff Hyman, Mitchell Hyman, Ira Nagel, Marc Lester, Billy Banks, John Lederer, Jeff Lane, and a host of neighborhood kids.

We were hanging out at the Thorneycroft ramp when John Lederer came over and told John Cummings that there was a portable TV on the sidewalk in front of his apartment building. Johnny and John Lederer carried the TV set to the roof of the building across the street from Thorneycroft. At this point, we were unaware of what they were going to do.

Apparently, the Johns (Lederer and Cummings) put the TV on the ledge of the building and pushed it off the roof toward the entranceway below, just as a little old lady was walking by. The TV smashed on the pavement only a few feet away from her. I thought for sure that she would have a heart attack. They were so lucky that the TV didn't hit that woman, because it would have killed her. Johnny just loved to scare and mess with old ladies.

When we would walk somewhere and an old lady was walking in front of him, Johnny would spit on his finger and then flick the spit onto the back of the coat of this unsuspecting woman. I think he used to call that a "lungy." Perhaps his name in the band should have been "Lungy Ramone."

The ramp we once gathered at, which has been dubbed the birthplace of punk, now features a mural of the band. Painted by

My Rock and Roll Fantasy
artist Ori Carino, it is based on a photograph by Bob Gruen depicting
the four original band members sitting atop the ramp.

Richard M. Adler

Chapter 18

Humping Amps & Fighting Fires: The Accidental Roadie

Richard M. Adler

September 9, 1967, was already shaping up to be an incredible night. My friend Robert Rowland and I were heading to the Village Theatre in New York City to see The Doors and The Vagrants. Not only were we going to see two great bands, but we were going with our friend Roger Mansour, the drummer of The Vagrants. That meant we had early access, backstage passes, and a front-row seat to all the behind-the-scenes action.

We arrived at the Village Theatre around 3 p.m. for the soundcheck. The theater was empty except for the crew setting up. Bob and I climbed onto the stage, sitting on the edge while The Vagrants' gear was being arranged. The stage lights were dim, and the place smelled of sawdust and cigarette smoke, just the way an old New York theater should.

Then, from the far side of the room, we saw two figures walking toward the stage. Even in the dim light, there was no mistaking them: Ray Manzarek and Jim Morrison of The Doors.

Bob and I sat frozen for a second. I mean, these guys were rock stars. They had just released their debut album earlier that year, and "Light My Fire" was all over the radio. Now, here they were, heading straight for us.

Ray, tall and wearing his signature glasses, gave us a friendly nod. "Hey, guys," he said, extending a hand. "I'm Ray, and this is Jim."

Jim Morrison barely said a word. He gave a slow, almost lazy nod and flashed a slight smirk. Even offstage, he had that mysterious aura about him, the kind that made people hang on his every word, even when he wasn't talking.

Ray, however, was full of energy. "We need a favor," he said. "Our roadies got sick and had to stay at the hotel. You guys think you can help us out? Just for today?"

Bob and I looked at each other. Did he really just ask us to be The Doors' road crew? How could we say no?

Within minutes, Bob and I were outside, unloading heavy amplifiers, keyboards, and drum cases from a truck. It was exhausting, but we didn't care. This was The Doors. Even Jim helped carry some of the gear, though, to be honest, he wasn't exactly busting his back like the rest of us.

Once we got everything onto the stage, Ray set up his new Gibson Kalamazoo G101 organ, which had just replaced his old Vox Continental. He looked excited about it, like a kid with a new toy. Meanwhile, John Densmore was adjusting his brand-new mod orange drum kit, which he had picked up that very day at Manny's Music Store.

Soundcheck was incredible. Watching The Doors perform up close, just a few feet away from me, was something I'll never forget. Jim wasn't in full rock-god mode yet. He was more relaxed, humming through the microphone as they fine-tuned everything. But there was something almost hypnotic about him, even in rehearsal.

When showtime finally arrived, Bob and I were allowed to stay backstage. The early show kicked off at 8 p.m., with The Vagrants opening the night. Bob and I were huge fans, so watching them from behind the curtain was already a thrill.

But then things got wild.

Richard M. Adler

During the set, Leslie West, The Vagrants' incredible guitarist, decided to pull off a crazy stunt. He lit his guitar on fire mid-performance.

Now, if that had been the only thing burning, it might have been fine. But Leslie was wearing a jacket made of eagle feathers. And just like that, the feathers caught fire.

The problem? Leslie had no idea he was on fire.

I didn't even think. I just reacted. I ripped off my denim jacket and ran onto the stage. Leslie was still lost in his guitar solo, completely unaware that flames were creeping up his arm. I started whacking him with my jacket, trying to put it out without making it obvious. The crowd probably thought I was some kind of crazy fan who had stormed the stage.

By some miracle, I managed to extinguish the flames without ruining the performance. Leslie barely flinched. I don't even think he realized what had happened. Once the fire was out, I casually walked off stage, trying to act like I hadn't just saved him from becoming a human torch.

After The Vagrants' fiery set, The Doors took the stage. From where I stood, I had the best seat in the house. The early show's setlist included:

"Alabama Song"

• "Back Door Man"

• "Light My Fire"

Watching Jim Morrison perform that close was like witnessing some kind of shamanic ritual. He wasn't just singing. He was channeling something bigger than himself. The way he moved, the way his voice echoed through the theater it was otherworldly.

Between shows, we hung out backstage with some music legends. Tommy James was there, along with Al Kooper and Steve Katz. They told us about a new band they were putting together, Blood, Sweat & Tears. At the time, we had no idea how big they would become.

The late show started at 10:30 p.m. and was even wilder than the first. Some of the songs The Doors played

• "When the Music's Over"

• "Horse Latitudes"

• "The End"

• "Light My Fire" (again, because, let's be honest, the crowd couldn't get enough of it)

Jim was fully in his element now. He prowled the stage like a panther, his voice rising and falling like some kind of hypnotic spell. When they launched into "The End," it felt like time had stopped. The theater was completely silent, everyone hanging onto every word.

That night was unforgettable. Bob and I had started the evening as fans in the audience, but by sheer luck (and a couple of sick roadies), we had become part of the show. We got to carry The Doors' gear, stand backstage with legends, and even save Leslie West from going up in flames.

Years later, I was sitting at Boodle's in Chester, New York, with Leslie and his brother Larry. We were reminiscing about old times, and I brought up that wild night at the Village Theatre.

Leslie looked at me, confused. "Wait... I was on fire?"

I laughed. "Yeah, man, you had no idea. Your jacket went up in flames, and I had to put it out."

Leslie shook his head, chuckling. "Well, thanks for saving me, I guess."

In a few months, the Village Theatre would be bought by Bill Graham and renamed the Fillmore East, one of the most legendary rock venues of all time. But on September 9, 1967, it was just another crazy night in rock and roll history, and I got to be a part of it.

Chapter 19

The Magical Mystery Encounter

In 1968, when I was just 18 years old, on a beautiful day in May, I decided to cut school and take the subway into Manhattan to spend the day walking around Central Park. I loved people-watching, so I was closely looking at the faces of the people in the park. As I walked close to the Bethesda Fountain, I noticed two guys sitting on the edge of the fountain who I thought I recognized, but it couldn't be. Why would they be in Central Park today? I decided to take a closer look. I stood and stared for about a minute, and I was sure I knew who they were. I wanted to go over and talk to them, but I needed something interesting to say. I thought about it and came up with a great idea. So, I got up the courage to approach them and said, "John Lennon and Paul McCartney, what are you doing here?"

John smiled and said, "We have been sitting here for a while, and you are the first person who has stopped by to say hello."

Paul also smiled and said hello, then offered to shake my hand. I shook Paul's hand, then John's.

I now had to tell them about my idea for their movie Magical Mystery Tour, which they made the year before. Magical Mystery Tour was broadcast on Boxing Day in England in 1967. It didn't get favorable reviews, and U.S. TV stations refused to show it. It was too short to be a theatrical release, so there really was no way for The Beatles to do anything else with Magical Mystery Tour. But I had an idea that would not only give them new outlets to show their film but also an opportunity to make some money as well.

I started telling them my idea for promoting the film Magical Mystery Tour on college campuses. I explained that they should find a student organization on each campus that would like to do a fundraiser. Any student organization can get a venue for free on campus for a fundraiser. Then, find a local radio station and tell them that you would like them to present the film on the nearby college campus. What rock station would turn that down? The radio station would provide free advertising and promotion. Every local radio station back then was pushing some local band, so let the local band perform before the film. All this would cost you is ten percent of the profits donated to the student organization. The Beatles would make ninety percent of the profits.

McCartney said to me, "So when can you start? Sounds like you have it well thought out. Come work for us and run your idea for real." He wrote a phone number on a piece of paper and gave it to me. It said Nat Weiss and his office phone number. I said thank you, and Paul said they had to run. I said goodbye, shook their hands again, and they were gone.

The next day, I called Nat, and when I told him who I was, he said he was expecting my call. He asked me to come to dinner at his apartment to discuss the arrangements. How cool was that?

The next day, I spent hours trying to decide what to wear to Nat's house for dinner. I finally picked out an outfit, got dressed, and took the train to my friend Joel Levy's apartment on Delancey Street on the Lower East Side of Manhattan. I told Joel my story and where I was going for dinner. Joel was so excited. Joel had played bass for the band the Strawberry Alarm Clock, but I never confirmed that, and I had my doubts.

Joel said to me, "Is that what you are wearing to dinner?" I sheepishly said, "Yes." Joel said, "No way," and proceeded to his closet and started pulling out outfits. He decided that I would wear

166

tweed pants and a light green shirt with a big collar and a leather vest. I felt ridiculous, especially because Joel was heavier than me and taller. So, the pants were a little too loose and a little too long. I tightened my belt so that the pants wouldn't fall down, but I had to live with the long pants, which touched the floor on the back of my shoes.

I left my clothes at Joel's house and took a taxi uptown to Nat's apartment.

"Nat Weiss was indisputably one of the all-time greats of the real music business, a person whom one would consider themselves very lucky to have known and very lucky to have worked with. He was the smartest person I've ever met and certainly one of the strongest.", Steve Forbert

Nat was Brian Epstein's business partner and was The Beatles' American representative. Brian and Nat had formed Nemperor Artists to represent Brian's acts in America, and I was having dinner with him. Wow!

I had just turned 18 and was getting ready to go off to college in the fall.

I got out of the taxi on East 73rd Street and headed up to Nat's apartment. The doorman stopped me and asked who I was there to see. I told him Nat Weiss, and he called upstairs to find out if he was expecting me. The doorman said that Nat was expecting me and told me the apartment number.

I took the elevator up to Nat's floor and rang his bell. I was so nervous. Nat's houseboy opened the door and asked me to sit in the living room, and Nat would be with me in a few minutes. I spent that time looking around. Nat had a beautiful apartment. He had paintings by some well-known artists and gold records on his wall. I noticed that he had no family photos displayed. His apartment was very nicely furnished. It was the nicest New York City apartment that I had ever been in during the first 18 years of my life.

After a few minutes, Nat came out of his bedroom. As we shook hands, he apologized because he had been on a business call. Nat offered me a drink, which I accepted, and we sat and chatted for about an hour about music. He told me that John Lennon and Paul McCartney stayed in his apartment while they were in New York City and that he moved out to the St. Regis Hotel to give them some privacy. Nat hired a pretty girl to act as a maid for the time John and Paul stayed there, and this made John happy. He frequently took her to bed. Linda Eastman was a friend of Nat's and begged him to allow her to visit Paul while he stayed at his apartment. Nat asked Paul if he was okay with it, and Paul agreed. So, Linda and the maid were the only two females permitted in Nat's apartment while John and Paul stayed there.

Nat had the houseboy pour me another drink as we sat down for dinner. During dinner, Nat wanted to hear about the idea that I had for Magical Mystery Tour. I laid out the plan to Nat, and he was delighted. Nat said, "If we charge five dollars a ticket in a one-thousand-seat hall and do two shows, the gross would be ten thousand dollars. Now you are telling me that my entire cost would be one thousand dollars for the student organization plus your travel expenses and salary?"

"Yes, that is correct," I answered him. Nat was intrigued. There was a lot of work to do before we got started. First, Nat would need to have a couple of 16mm prints made. Then we would need to begin booking colleges. This most likely could not begin until 1969 since most colleges were booked for the 1968–69 season. Nat asked the houseboy for more drinks, and we continued talking.

It was now time for dessert, and I figured after dessert we would wrap things up for the night and I would leave. But no.

Nat started a new conversation.

"Richie, Paul was very impressed with you. He asked me if you would consider being on the next Beatles album cover."

What?

Nat continued, "The Beatles' next album will have a western theme, and they are looking for a young, good-looking man such as yourself to play an American Indian on the album cover."

I said, "I am not a model, and I don't really want to be on the next Beatles album cover. I prefer to work for them doing this Magical Mystery Tour project."

Nat then said, "Paul was very specific. He asked for you, and he usually gets what he wants. I happen to have an Indian headdress in my bedroom. Please go in there, take off all of your clothes, and put on the headdress, and I will come in and take some Polaroids to send to Paul."

Now I was suddenly very uncomfortable. I said to Nat, "I think you need to get someone else. This is one time Paul isn't going to get what he wants."

At this point, I was unaware that Nat was gay, but I did suspect that this had nothing to do with Paul or The Beatles.

Nat was very disappointed. He too seemed to usually get what he wanted. Nat then said,

"Look, I can help you with your Magical Mystery Tour project, but I need you to help me give Paul what he wants."

How do I answer him? I just said,

"Sorry, no. This is a deal that is mutually beneficial to you, The Beatles, and me. Let's not let this get in the way of that."

With that said, Nat decided it was time to call it a night. We agreed to keep talking about working on Magical Mystery Tour after Nat did a few things to solidify his deal with The Beatles on this project.

Less than a year later, I did my first Magical Mystery Tour presentation at the University of Oklahoma. Two shows in a 1,500-seat auditorium. The requests for tickets were overwhelming.

We sold out both shows. The next night, I did a second show at Texas Christian University in Fort Worth, Texas. We sold out two shows there as well. My proof of concept was a success. The big problem that I did not think about was the amount of cash I had to carry. Almost twenty thousand dollars in small bills, and no banks were open on the weekend. Since the student organizations handled the ticket sales, there was no provision to pay us by check. The night of the performance, I had to sit and count ten thousand dollars out in small bills, twenties, tens, fives, and ones.

Hello? Yeah, right!

When I was promoting the movie Magical Mystery Tour on college campuses, Paul McCartney called my house. My sister Mindy, who was eleven years old at the time, answered the phone. The voice on the other end of the phone asked if I was home. She asked who was calling, and in his best English accent, he said it was Paul McCartney.

My sister said, "No really, who is this?" and once again he said, "Paul McCartney."

I was not home, but my sister didn't know what to do, so she asked Paul to hold on and she ran out of the apartment, down the stairs, and was running all over the neighborhood looking for me. She couldn't find me, and after fifteen minutes of searching, she went back upstairs and guess what, Paul had hung up.

When I got home, she told me Paul called. I asked, "Did you take a number?"

She said, "No, I went looking for you instead."

Kids!

Richard M. Adler
Dueling Ukuleles

One day, Nat called me up and invited me to his apartment for dinner. This time, I wore sneakers just in case he tried to chase me around the apartment. He did, but he didn't catch me.

When I got there, I found George Harrison. Wow, I did not expect that. A few of Nat's friends were there as well.

Nat whispered in my ear that a special guest was coming that night, but George did not know he was coming. Nat said that when he gave us a signal, we should all get up and walk to one of the bedrooms and leave George to answer the door.

When the doorman rang up to tell Nat that the special guest had arrived, Nat gave the signal, and we all got up and left the room. When the doorbell rang, George, sitting all alone in the living room, got up to answer it. I heard George yell, "Tiny Tim, what are you doing here? Please come in."

Tiny Tim screamed, "Oh, Mr. Harrison, I had no idea you were going to be here."

George loved the ukulele, and he and Tiny Tim played the ukulele together in Nat's living room. Tiny Tim played his version of "Nowhere Man," and I could see that George was beaming. This session was recorded, and it was released one month later on The Beatles' 1968 Christmas Album.

During the party, I sat on the couch with George, talking about his guitar playing, and I complimented him on his playing on "And Your Bird Can Sing." George looked at me and said, "That wasn't me. Paul played both guitar parts."

To this day, I don't know if George was telling me the truth or just wanted to get a rise out of me. Now only Paul knows the truth, but he is not saying.

Photography

By 1972, I was getting into every rock concert in NYC through the stage door. I would hang backstage and in the dressing rooms with the bands. One day, I decided to bring my Nikon camera and start taking photos of the bands. I sold many of my photos to Rock Magazine, Crawdaddy Magazine, and Circus Magazine.

Nat invited me to his apartment to take photos of John McLaughlin and the Mahavishnu Orchestra. The next day, he asked me to photograph the Mahavishnu Orchestra performing live at Carnegie Hall. Nat had signed the Mahavishnu Orchestra to a management deal with his company, Nemperor Artists. He bought all my photos of the Mahavishnu Orchestra for a very nice sum of money.

Nat also represented James Taylor. James was playing at Carnegie Hall, and once again, Nat asked me to take the photos. I went to Carnegie Hall, shot the photos, stayed up all night processing the film, and brought the photos to Nat's office the next morning. I was showing the photos to Nat when James Taylor walked in. He saw the photos laid out on the table and said that he wanted all of them. He told me to send an invoice to Peter Asher, his manager and producer, and said Peter would pay me for the photos. I sent the invoice but never heard back and never received a check.

In 2020, Peter Asher called me because he wanted to use my photo of Nat Weiss standing in front of his closet door for a book he was writing about The Beatles. Unfortunately, I had to turn him down, telling him I was writing a book and the photo would appear in my book. Peter was very persistent. He told me how close he was to Nat and how much he would love to have that photo for his book. He asked what it would take to get my permission. I told him, half-jokingly, that he still owed me money for the James Taylor photos from 1972. Peter started making excuses, saying things like, "I never saw the invoice or I would have paid it." I stopped him and said it was water under the bridge. I told Peter I had many other photos of Nat he could use, and I sent them to him. Peter chose one, and I was happy to give him permission to use it. He sent me a copy of his book, so we can now call it even.

Nat invited me to another dinner party at his apartment. This time, his guest was Ahmet Ertegun, the President of Atlantic Records. Ahmet brought a date, whom he introduced as a journalist. I felt uncomfortable because it appeared that I was Nat's date. I had never been pursued like that before and didn't know how to handle the situation. On one hand, it was good for business. On the other hand, I was not gay and had tried to tell Nat this many times. He didn't care. He just kept trying. I took photos that night of Nat standing by his open closet door, alone and with Ahmet's journalist.

This was the last time I saw Nat Weiss. I think I made it clear that I was only interested in a friendship and business relationship and that nothing romantic was going to happen. After being chased by Nat Weiss for over four years, it was finally over. I think Nat got the message.

I didn't tell many people about my association with Nat Weiss back in the day. One day, I was talking with my friend and former bandmate Robert Rowland, and he told me a story about Nat.

Robert's parents owned a small hotel in Atlantic City. In the summer of 1965, Robert took a bus to Atlantic City to visit them. He struck up a conversation with the man sitting next to him, who introduced himself as Nat Weiss. Nat told Robert he was going to Atlantic City to scout some bands. He said he was a business partner of Brian Epstein and that they were looking for new talent. Robert told him to go see The Rhondells at the Alibi Bar in Atlantic City. Nat was pleased to get the tip and actually went to the Alibi Bar. He was impressed with The Rhondells and recommended to Brian Epstein that they sign the band to a management contract. They renamed the band The Cyrkle, and John Lennon provided the spelling for their name. The Cyrkle had my dear friend Robert to thank for their success. The band had a couple of big hits, including "Red Rubber Ball" and "Turn-Down Day."

Richard M. Adler

The Beatles Secret NYC Hideaway

The following is an article written by Woody Lifton. It was published on his Beatles website, www.BestBeatlesHistory.com, on June 14, 2009.

When you operate a fairly popular Beatles website that has a "Share Your Beatles Story" section, you are likely to get all kinds of stories. These range from the usual "The Beatles are the greatest thing since sliced bread" to unusual tales about women having John's baby, with a conspiracy theory thrown in for good measure.

Finding a story about moments in the Beatles' career that I don't already know is incredibly rare. So when my Facebook friend Richard Adler (who was in a high school band with two members of the Ramones) sent me the story of Nat Weiss' closet door (Nat was Brian Epstein's partner), along with two pictures of the closet door signed by John Lennon, George Harrison, and Paul McCartney, I was thrilled. Richard told me these pictures had never been posted on any website.

While lengthy, this story is actually a combination of three different sources talking about the same time frame in Beatles history:

- Richard Adler's story, with actual pictures of the infamous "closet door"

- An excerpt from Danny Field's book *Linda McCartney – A Portrait*

- 60s musician Hash Howard's story

Note: After I listed this story on my website, the one and only "Hash Howard" read it and added a comment, which I have included at the end of the story.

First, here is Richard's story in his words, along with the two pictures of the door and Nat Weiss:

"It was the spring of 1968 when John Lennon and Paul McCartney came to New York City to promote Apple Corp. They stayed at the apartment of their American manager Nat Weiss, who was a business partner and close friend of Brian Epstein. Nat packed a suitcase and stayed at the St. Regis Hotel, giving John and Paul their privacy. When Nat returned to the apartment a week later, John and Paul were gone. Opening his closet door, he found a surprise. A huge autograph was written on the inside of his closet door. It read:

'Nathaniel certainly is. Love Paul McCartney and John Lennon. Much love.'

This is the largest known autograph of John Lennon.

George Harrison also stayed at Nat's apartment when he was in New York City. Not to be outdone, he autographed Nat's closet door. George wrote:

'To Nat, the king and queen of FUH. Love from George Harrison 30/11/68.'

Does anyone get George's reference to FUH? Most people don't. That doesn't surprise me. Most people had never heard of the song or the artist behind it. But I knew exactly what George was talking about.

My photo of Nat Weiss and his famous closet door

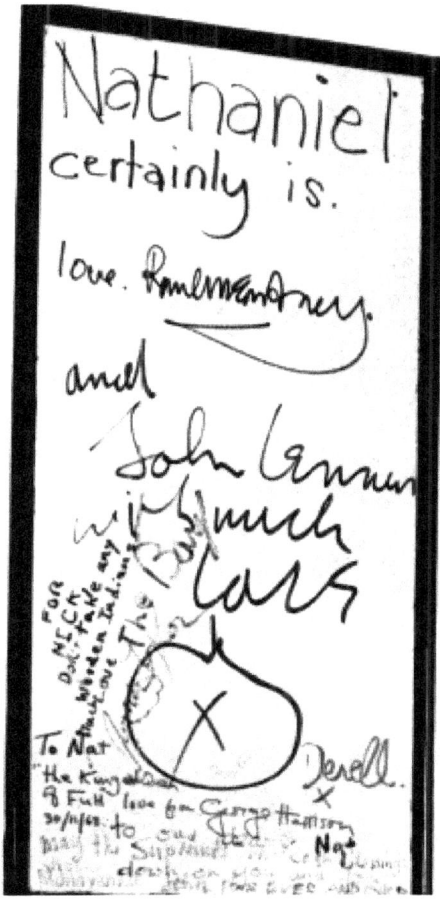

Close up of closet door autographs

FUH wasn't just a random word. It came from a song by Stephen Friedland, also known as Brute Force. Brute Force was an Apple Records artist who never quite became famous under that name, but his music certainly made an impression, especially on George Harrison and John Lennon. Before adopting the Brute Force persona, Stephen Friedland joined The Tokens in the mid-1960s as a singer, songwriter, and pianist. Brute Force may not have been a household name, but he did something that no one else had ever dared to do. He wrote and recorded a song so cheeky and rebellious that it nearly never saw the light of day. The song was called "The King of Fuh," and if you say it out loud, you might catch on to why it was so controversial.

Nat and Me by the Closet Door

The lyrics told the story of a king who ruled over the imaginary land of Fuh, and naturally, he was called the "Fuh King." You can probably guess why that caused a problem.

The song was originally produced by The Tokens, the same band that sang "The Lion Sleeps Tonight," and when George Harrison heard it, he loved it. He even arranged the record himself. John Lennon liked it too. They both thought it was clever, funny, and exactly the kind of rebellious spirit they admired in music.

But there was one big problem: Apple Records' distributor, EMI, was never going to let this song get released. There was no way they would print and sell a record that could so easily be misunderstood, or worse, banned.

Of course, George and John weren't the kind of guys to back down easily. So instead of giving up, Apple Records decided to take matters into their own hands. They pressed 2,000 copies of the record themselves and distributed them independently in 1969. It was released under catalog number Apple 8, but good luck finding one today. It's a rare collector's item, almost impossible to track down.

There was even a special American version of the record. It didn't have a catalog number at all because it wasn't meant for the public. It was made as a personal copy for an Apple Records employee in the United States. That version is even rarer than the original.

The first line of the song was legendary:

"There once was a King of the land of FUH, and everyone called him the FUH King."

It was bold, it was funny, and it was exactly the kind of thing that made the music industry exciting back then.

Nat's door was also autographed by Ahmet Ertegun, who was the President of Atlantic Records.

Ahmet wrote: "To My Dear NOT, He is not only Love, he is also your date. Amet."

In addition, James Taylor, Carly Simon, Cat Stevens, and I believe John McLaughlin also autographed the door. There are a few other autographs, but I am not sure whose they are. I took this picture in 1969, and it is difficult to read.

Nat's closet door sold at auction for approximately $52,000. These pictures of Nat Weiss and his closet door have never been published.

Richard M. Adler

Magical Mystery Tour

In 1967, The Beatles decided to try something new by making a movie without a script. *Magical Mystery Tour* was a wild and colorful film where a group of people took a bus trip filled with strange and unexpected events, all guided by mysterious magicians (played by The Beatles themselves). Inspired by fun coach trips in England and the free-spirited adventures of American writer Ken Kesey and his Merry Pranksters, the idea came mostly from Paul McCartney, though even he was not sure if it was a good one.

The band filmed much of the movie at an old military airfield, improvising as they went. With no real script, they simply made things up as they filmed, filling the movie with weird and wacky moments like a race where everyone used different kinds of transportation, a crazy restaurant scene where a waiter dumped piles of spaghetti on a table, and even a strip show.

The movie also included some fantastic Beatles music, featuring performances of "I Am the Walrus," "Blue Jay Way," and "Your Mother Should Know." There was even a guest performance by The Bonzo Dog Doo-Dah Band, singing "Death Cab for Cutie."

The Beatles were excited to share *Magical Mystery Tour* with the world, but when it premiered on BBC1 on December 26, 1967, something went very wrong. It was shown in black and white instead of color. Because of this, the trippy visuals looked dull and boring, and the press and public hated it. Even when it was later broadcast in color, most people still did not get it. The film never aired in the U.S. and was not widely seen until years later, although it was shown on college campuses across the country.

Many people, including the band's assistant Peter Brown, blamed Paul for the failure. He had believed in the project, but when the first audience reaction was terrible, The Beatles had to defend their work. Paul even went on television to explain, saying, "If we goofed, we goofed."

Despite the bad reviews, the *Magical Mystery Tour* soundtrack was a huge success, featuring some of The Beatles' most creative songs. Over time, the movie gained a cult following, especially as people began to appreciate its experimental style. In fact, Monty Python, the British comedy group famous for *Holy Grail*, even considered re-releasing it in the 1970s because they saw its comedic potential.

Looking back, even George Harrison admitted it was more like a homemade movie than a professional film. But years later, fans and critics began to see *Magical Mystery Tour* as a unique, if unusual, piece of Beatles history, an ambitious, colorful, and sometimes confusing trip into their creative minds.

Richard M. Adler

Chapter 20

My Woodstock Experience

On the morning of August 15, 1969, I called my good friend Kenny at work with an exciting idea.

"Do you want to go to Woodstock this weekend?" I asked.

Kenny sounded confused. "Why would I want to go to Woodstock, New York, today?"

I explained that there was a rock festival happening, not in Woodstock, but in Bethel, New York. I told him it was shaping up to be the biggest music event of the decade. I had recently become a huge fan of Crosby, Stills, and Nash, and this would be my first chance to see them perform live.

Kenny agreed to go and picked me up right after he got out of work. He told me that our friends Michael, Steve, Simon, and Jack were camping just down the road from Bethel at Ten Mile River Scout Camp. He was sure we could find an empty tent to sleep in for the two nights we would be there.

We had already heard the horror stories. Traffic was backed up for miles, and part of the New York State Thruway had even been shut down. But that did not worry us. Kenny and I knew the area well. I had spent summers at Ten Mile River Scout Camp, and one year I even worked as an Assistant Quartermaster at Camp Kernochan at TMR.

We decided to avoid the gridlocked highways altogether. Instead, we took Route 84 to Port Jervis, then followed the Delaware River up to Route 55, which led us straight to Bethel. It was our secret shortcut.

As we drove, it started to rain. The downpour was so heavy that Kenny could not see the road, so we pulled over under a bridge to wait it out. When the rain finally eased up, we continued on our way.

We got within two miles of the festival before we hit complete chaos. Cars were parked everywhere, on the side of the road, in ditches, even on front lawns. Some were just abandoned. Thousands of people were walking, some hitching rides on slow-moving vehicles. You could feel the excitement in the air. Kenny pulled onto a patch of grass and asked a cop where we could park. The cop grinned and said, "You're parked. Just leave it there."

That was Woodstock.

As we walked toward the festival grounds, I kept looking for a ticket booth. I had my money ready to buy our three-day passes. But we never found one.

Then we crested a hill.

What I saw below took my breath away. A massive sea of people stretched out toward a giant wooden stage. I turned to Kenny in shock.

"How did we get in without tickets?"

It turned out that the fences meant to secure the festival had been knocked down almost immediately. The festival had become a free concert, not on purpose, but in true Woodstock spirit.

The moment we stepped into the crowd, I realized just how unprepared the organizers were for this kind of turnout. The event was originally designed for 50,000 people, but over 400,000 had shown up.

Food ran out quickly. Vendors had only stocked up for a much smaller crowd and were completely wiped out within hours. The ones who still had food started charging ridiculous prices, one dollar for a hot dog, five dollars for a sandwich. That might not sound like much today, but back then it was highway robbery.

Luckily, a hippie commune called the Hog Farm had set up a free food station. They gave out rice and vegetables to make sure people did not go hungry. If you were not picky, you could eat. If you were, you were out of luck.

Then came the rain.

One minute we were lying in the grass, listening to Santana play an incredible set. The next minute the sky opened up. Within hours, Yasgur's farm had turned into a giant mud pit. Sleeping bags were soaked, blankets were ruined, and there was no way to escape it. People tried using plastic sheets, ponchos, even garbage bags, but in the end, most of us just gave up and accepted the mud as part of the experience.

But the smell was something I will never forget. Wet cow manure mixed with the rain and mud made an awful stench that stuck with us for the rest of the festival.

The bathrooms were even worse. They had not been built to handle half a million people. By the second day, the porta-potties were practically overflowing. The smell was unbearable. You learned to hold your breath and move fast.

Drugs were everywhere. Weed, acid, and pills were being passed around. Some were given out for free, others sold cheap. I stuck to a few joints, just enough to enhance the music but not enough to lose control. Others were not so lucky. I saw people freaking out on bad trips, wandering aimlessly, talking to people who were not there. The medical tents were overwhelmed, with volunteers and medics working nonstop to help people who had taken too much acid or had simply collapsed from exhaustion.

The military even had to fly in doctors and field hospital equipment. When I saw military helicopters flying over the festival, I felt paranoid. Here we were, all in one place, most of us against the

Vietnam War and the government. I feared they might open fire on us all. Fortunately, someone on stage announced that the helicopters were here to help and only bringing in medical personnel and supplies. That calmed me down, and I went back to enjoying the music.

But in the end, it was the music that made it all worth it.

I was there when Richie Havens opened the festival. He strummed his guitar so hard it felt like his soul was bursting through his fingertips.

I watched Janis Joplin give everything she had in her performance. Her voice was raw, untamed, and electric. The Who played a set so powerful it felt like the ground was shaking beneath us.

Then came the moment I had been waiting for.

Late Sunday night, Crosby, Stills, and Nash took the stage. This was only their second time performing live as a trio. I stood there, soaked from the rain, exhausted but completely mesmerized. When they sang "Suite: Judy Blue Eyes," their harmonies soared over the crowd like magic.

Finally, as if to end Woodstock on a legendary note, Jimi Hendrix took the stage on Monday morning. His version of "The Star-Spangled Banner" was unlike anything I had ever heard. It was haunting, chaotic, and powerful. His guitar made the sounds of bombs, sirens, and screams. It was not just a song. It was a statement.

Despite the hunger, exhaustion, rain, mud, and madness, we stayed. There was no violence. No riots. Just people coming together for music, peace, and something bigger than all of us. Looking back, I do not know how we made it through, but I would not trade it for anything.

Woodstock was not just a concert. It was a moment in history. It was larger than some cities in the US but with almost no crime. Only one person died when he was accidentally run over by a tractor while he was asleep in a field.

And I was there with my friend Kenny. Even over fifty years later, Kenny and I are still good friends and still talk about that unforgettable weekend.

The first performer we saw was Richie Havens. He was not supposed to go first at Woodstock, but when traffic jams stopped many of the scheduled acts from arriving on time, the festival organizers asked him to open the show. With only his acoustic guitar, a strong voice, and steady strumming, Havens stepped onto the stage on August 15, 1969, and set the tone for the historic festival.

Havens was only supposed to play a short set, but as the organizers struggled to get other bands ready, he kept performing. He sang songs like "High Flying Bird" and "I Can't Make It Anymore," pulling the crowd in with his powerful energy and deep emotions. The more he played, the more the audience cheered, and their excitement pushed him to keep going far longer than planned.

Eventually, he ran out of songs. But instead of stopping, he created one on the spot. That song, "Freedom," became one of the most famous moments of Woodstock. He took inspiration from the old spiritual "Sometimes I Feel Like a Motherless Child" and turned it into a bold and passionate anthem. It was completely improvised, but it captured the feeling of the festival and the hopes of a generation.

His performance was the perfect way to start the weekend. It was a call for peace, togetherness, and freedom. His unforgettable opening set not only launched Woodstock but also secured his place in history as the man who set the festival in motion.

Next up was Bert Sommer, who had written songs for The Vagrants, Leslie West's former band. Leslie West, a Forest Hills boy like me, was now with Mountain, scheduled to perform the next day. Kenny and I carefully made our way through the crowd, politely weaving our way closer to the stage. We settled onto a patch of grass and stayed there until Joan Baez finished her set around 4 a.m.

That night, we listened to Ravi Shankar, Tim Hardin, Melanie, Arlo Guthrie, and Joan Baez, who closed her set with a haunting rendition of "We Shall Overcome." The energy of so many people gathered for peace, love, and music was overwhelming.

When the music ended, I turned to Kenny. "Where are we sleeping?" Fortunately, Boy Scout Troop 56 and 280 were camping at Ten Mile River, just a few miles away. We hiked back to Kenny's car and drove to TMR where our friends had a tent and two cots waiting for us.

The next afternoon, we returned to Woodstock, joined by some of our Boy Scout friends. Michael, one of the scout leaders and a friend of ours, actually Michael and I were blood brothers. In sixth grade, we cut our hands and mixed our blood together like Native Americans. Michael knew a shortcut on a dirt trail through Ten Mile River Scout Camp, though I think his car's muffler might still be somewhere along that bumpy dirt road.

We parked near the same spot as before, hopped onto passing cars for a ride, and arrived just in time to catch Quill's opening set.

Up next was Country Joe McDonald, the lead singer of Country Joe and the Fish. As the festival faced delays, producer John Morris noticed McDonald near the stage. He asked if McDonald could perform a solo acoustic set to fill time while Santana's equipment was being set up. Although unplanned, McDonald agreed. A guitar was found for him, and a rope was fashioned into a strap. Dressed in a green Army shirt with sergeant stripes and a name tag reading "EVERETT," along with scarves on his head and arm, McDonald took the stage. Emcee Chip Monck introduced him as his "very fond friend, Mr. Joe McDonald."

Greeting the massive crowd, McDonald asked, "Are you having a good time?" He began his set with "Janis," a song he wrote two years earlier for his former girlfriend, Janis Joplin. The song, featured on the album *I Feel Like I'm Fixin' to Die*, had a slow tempo and complex melody, receiving polite applause from the audience. He continued with "Donovan's Reef" from the album *Here We Are Again*, followed by three country classics: "Heartaches by the Number," "Ring of Fire," and "Tennessee Stud." These songs would later appear on his solo album *Tonight I'm Singing Just for You*.

Despite his efforts, the audience's response remained subdued. McDonald then played "Rockin' Round the World" from the upcoming album *CJ Fish* and "Flying High" from their debut album. He concluded with "I Seen a Rocket," which would later be released as a single. Feeling disheartened by the lackluster reaction, McDonald consulted his tour manager about performing "The 'Fish' Cheer/I-Feel-Like-I'm-Fixin'-to-Die Rag" as an encore, even though it was planned for the band's set the next day. His manager replied, "Nobody's listening to you, so what difference does it make?" Determined, McDonald returned to the microphone and initiated the now-famous cheer: "Gimme an F! Gimme a U! Gimme a C! Gimme a K! What's that spell?" The crowd erupted, enthusiastically shouting back the letters. This bold call-and-response electrified the atmosphere, transforming the audience's energy. He then launched into the satirical anti-war anthem, "I-Feel-Like-I'm-Fixin'-to-Die Rag," with the crowd singing and clapping along. This spontaneous performance not only revitalized the audience but also solidified the song as a defining protest anthem of the era.

Reflecting on the impact of this moment, McDonald later acknowledged that his solo performance at Woodstock was a pivotal point in his career, stating, "It launched me as a solo performer."

The unexpected encore, coupled with its inclusion in the *Woodstock* film and soundtrack, propelled both McDonald and his signature song into the cultural zeitgeist, resonating with audiences worldwide and providing a unifying anthem for those opposing the Vietnam War.

The next band was a then-unknown band from San Francisco called Santana, led by the talented guitarist Carlos Santana. Their journey to the Woodstock stage was unique. Promoter Bill Graham, who managed Jefferson Airplane and the Grateful Dead, insisted that if the Woodstock promoters wanted to book the Airplane and the Dead, Santana must also be included in the festival lineup. This was despite Santana not yet having released an album. Graham's influence ensured that Santana had a spot at Woodstock.

As the festival progressed, unexpected schedule changes occurred. Santana was called to perform earlier than planned. Some band members had taken psychedelic substances, anticipating a later performance. This sudden change meant they had to take the stage while still feeling the effects. Carlos Santana later recalled that during the performance, his guitar felt like a "snake," making it challenging to play. Despite this, the band delivered an unforgettable set.

Santana's performance began with the instrumental "Waiting," showcasing Gregg Rolie's keyboard skills and Carlos's mesmerizing guitar solos. They continued with "Evil Ways," a track that would later become one of their signature songs. The band's fusion of rock, Latin, and African rhythms captivated the audience, many of whom were hearing this unique sound for the first time.

One of the standout moments was the song "Soul Sacrifice." This intense instrumental featured a legendary drum solo by 20-year-old Michael Shrieve, one of the youngest performers at Woodstock. His energetic performance, combined with the band's tight musicianship, electrified the massive crowd. The audience responded with enthusiastic applause, clearly moved by the raw energy and passion of the music. If you look closely at the director's cut of the Woodstock movie, you will see me up and dancing to Santana.

Reflecting on their Woodstock experience, Carlos Santana acknowledged the profound impact it had on their career. The festival not only introduced their music to a vast audience but also solidified their place in rock history. Santana's Woodstock performance remains a testament to the power of live music and the enduring spirit of artistic expression.

I will never forget the moment John Sebastian walked onto the Woodstock stage. It was not planned, and that made it even better.

It was Saturday afternoon, and the rain had just stopped. Everyone was still wet and covered in mud, but the music kept us going. Suddenly, a skinny guy in tie-dye and jeans strolled onto the stage, holding an acoustic guitar. It was John Sebastian, the lead singer of The Lovin' Spoonful, who I used to see at the Nite Owl in Greenwich Village.

He was not even supposed to perform. He was just visiting the festival like the rest of us. But with the rain delay and the crowd needing a lift, someone handed him a guitar and said, "Go play." And he did.

The moment he started singing, it felt like the whole crowd took a deep breath. His voice was soft, warm, and full of emotion. He played songs like "Rainbows All Over Your Blues" and "How Have You Been," songs that felt perfect for that moment.

Then he sang "Younger Generation." Before he started, he told us he had written it for a friend who had just become a father. It was about growing up, change, and hope for the future. As he played, I looked around and saw people swaying, hugging, and wiping their eyes. It was a real, honest moment, something that made Woodstock more than just a concert.

John Sebastian did not have a band, flashing lights, or a big show. He just had his guitar, his voice, and a little bit of magic. And that was more than enough.

The Keef Hartley Band and The Incredible String Band were next, though they did not hold my attention as much.

It was Saturday evening, 8:00 PM, and the crowd was buzzing. The sun was going down, but the energy was just getting started. Then out came Bob "The Bear" Hite and the rest of Canned Heat, ready to take us on a wild ride.

From the first note, it was clear we were about to boogie. They kicked things off with "I'm Her Man," and the crowd started moving. Their bluesy, electric sound filled the air, and suddenly, the mud, the hunger, and the exhaustion did not matter.

Richard M. Adler

Then they launched into "Going Up the Country." That song felt like the anthem of Woodstock, a song about freedom, escape, and starting something new. It was the perfect soundtrack for the festival's free-spirited vibe.

When Bob Hite belted out the lyrics, we all sang along. But the real magic happened when they played "On the Road Again." That steady, hypnotic beat, Alan "Blind Owl" Wilson's high, eerie voice, it was impossible to stand still. People were dancing, spinning, clapping, totally lost in the music.

Canned Heat did not just play songs; they created a feeling. A wild, free, unstoppable boogie that pulsed through the crowd like electricity. And even after they left the stage, that energy stayed with us.

It was Saturday night, around 9:15 PM, and we were ready for something loud. Mountain was a new band back then, but the second they started playing, it felt like they had been stars forever. Leslie West, the lead guitarist, was a big guy with a bigger sound. His guitar roared through the speakers, shaking the ground beneath us.

They kicked off their set with "Blood of the Sun," and the whole place erupted. The music was heavy, bluesy, and full of power. It was not folk, it was not psychedelic, it was pure, raw rock.

Then came "Theme for an Imaginary Western," a slower song but just as powerful. The melody felt like a journey, and for a moment, we all got lost in it.

By the time they played "Long Red," the crowd was hooked. The drumming, the guitar solos, the deep, rumbling bass, it was like a wall of sound crashing over us.

Mountain played loud, hard, and with everything they had. And even though they were not as famous as some of the other bands at Woodstock, they played like they belonged there. That night, I walked away knowing one thing: Mountain was not just another band. They were a force of nature. And oh, Leslie West's guitar tone was incredible. Just think, Leslie West, another Forest Hills boy makes good.

Next up was the Grateful Dead. I was excited to see The Dead at Woodstock. They were already legends, and I knew their set would be something special. But what happened that night was something none of us expected.

It was late Saturday night, around 11:00 PM, and by the time the Dead took the stage, the rain had turned the festival grounds into a muddy mess. The air was damp, the stage was soaked, and the band was facing a nightmare. Their equipment kept shorting out from all the moisture.

Still, they powered through. They started their set with "St. Stephen," and for a moment, it felt like they might pull it off. The crowd swayed to the music, and the band jammed the way only the Dead could.

But then things got worse. The sound system kept failing, and every time a cable sparked or a mic cut out, the band had to adjust. Jerry Garcia and the guys did their best, but they looked frustrated.

They went into "Mama Tried" and "Dark Star," but something felt off. The band, known for their long, trippy jams, seemed stuck in slow motion. The rain, the sound issues, and maybe even the heavy doses of LSD they had taken all seemed to weigh them down.

Then came "Turn On Your Lovelight." This should have been the big finish, a wild, free-flowing jam. Instead, it dragged on, with Pigpen trying to keep the energy up while the rest of the band struggled to keep it together.

By the time their set ended, I could tell they were not happy. Jerry Garcia later called it one of their worst performances. But to me, it was still something to remember. Even on a bad night, the Grateful Dead gave us something real, a moment of chaos, music, and a band pushing through the storm. Woodstock was not their best show, but it was a night I would never forget.

At midnight, Creedence Clearwater Revival kicked off their hour-long set with "Born on the Bayou," followed by hits like "Green River," "Bad Moon Rising," and "Proud Mary." Their extended jams on "I Put a Spell on You," "Keep On Chooglin'," and "Suzie Q" showcased their incredible musicianship.

I was beyond excited to see Creedence Clearwater Revival at Woodstock. Having seen CCR twice before, I knew they would not disappoint, and they lived up to every expectation. But by the time they got on stage, things did not go quite as planned.

It was after midnight on Sunday, and most of the crowd was exhausted. The Grateful Dead had played before them, and their set had gone on way too long. A lot of people had fallen asleep in the mud, while others were too out of it to pay attention. But when John Fogerty and the band started playing, they woke up whoever was still listening.

CCR did not waste time. They blasted right into "Born on the Bayou," and suddenly, the night felt alive again. That deep, swampy guitar riff cut through the night, and even though it was late, I could feel the energy pick up.

Then came "Green River," "Bad Moon Rising," and "Proud Mary." Song after song, they delivered pure rock and roll, with John Fogerty's voice cutting through the cool night air like a howl from the bayou.

At one point, Fogerty looked out at the sleepy, half-conscious crowd and realized a lot of them were not even paying attention. He later said it felt like he was playing to a bunch of "drunk and stoned people lying in the mud," which, honestly, was not far from the truth.

But that did not stop them. They tore through their set, giving it everything they had. The people who were awake were dancing, shouting, and loving every second. They finished with "Keep on Chooglin'," stretching it into a long, bluesy jam that left the stage smoking.

Creedence never made it into the official Woodstock movie or soundtrack, which was a shame, because their performance was one of the best of the weekend. Even though it was late, and even though half the crowd was asleep, I will never forget the night CCR rocked Woodstock.

I had been waiting all weekend to see Janis Joplin perform at Woodstock. I knew she was going to be amazing, but nothing could have prepared me for the raw power of her voice that night.

It was late Saturday night, actually early Sunday morning around 2:00 a.m., by the time she took the stage. The festival was running way behind schedule, and the crowd was tired. But the moment Janis stepped up to the microphone, everything changed.

She looked a little different from her usual wild, carefree self. She had been drinking backstage, and you could tell she was feeling it. But when she started singing, none of that mattered.

She opened with "Raise Your Hand," and instantly, that scratchy, bluesy voice cut through the night air. The crowd woke up fast. It was like pure fire coming from deep inside her soul.

Then she went into "Try (Just a Little Bit Harder)," and her voice just kept getting stronger. Every note was filled with emotion, pain, joy, heartbreak, and power all at once. One of the best moments was when she sang "Piece of My Heart." The way she belted out those lyrics, "Take another little piece of my heart now, baby!", it felt like she was giving every single one of us a piece of herself.

She closed with "Ball and Chain," and by the end, she looked exhausted, but the crowd was on fire. People were screaming, cheering, and completely blown away.

Janis did not just perform; she lived her music. Her voice was not perfect that night, and she was a little rough around the edges, but that made it even more real.

Woodstock had a lot of legendary performances, but for me, Janis Joplin was one of the best.

I had seen a lot of great performances at Woodstock, but Sly and the Family Stone brought something completely different. Their music was not just rock or blues, it was funk, soul, and pure energy. And when they hit the stage in the middle of the night, they turned Woodstock into the biggest dance party I had ever seen.

It was 3:30 in the morning on Sunday, and most people were half-asleep in the mud. But the second Sly and the band started playing "Stand!", it was like a jolt of electricity ran through the crowd. Suddenly, everyone was up, moving, clapping, and singing along.

Sly Stone was a wild frontman. He knew exactly how to get the crowd going. Every time he yelled, "I want to take you higher!", we all screamed it right back. The horns blasted, the bass thumped, and the backup singers kept the groove going. It felt like the music was controlling our bodies. We could not stop dancing even if we wanted to.

Then came "Dance to the Music," and the whole field turned into one big, grooving, sweaty mess. It did not matter if you were covered in mud or had not slept in two days, everybody was feeling it.

By the time they finished with "I Want to Take You Higher," I was out of breath, but I did not care. Sly and the Family Stone had just put on one of the most exciting, high-energy performances of the whole festival.

The Who finally took the stage at 5:00 a.m. on Sunday morning and played a scorching hour-long set that included almost all of their rock opera, *Tommy*. Their performance was indeed intense, and that intensity was matched by the chaotic goings-on in and around the concert area.

This show included what is known as the "Abbie Hoffman Incident." Following the band's smash hit "Pinball Wizard," the radical political activist Abbie Hoffman jumped onto the stage shouting in typical Abbie fashion, "I think this is a pile of shit!" He continued, "While John Sinclair [sentenced to nine years for smoking marijuana] rots in prison..." He was quickly interrupted by Pete Townshend, who took over the mic screaming, "Fuck off! Fuck off my fucking stage!" and then hit Abbie Hoffman in the head with his guitar.

Shortly afterwards, the evidently temperamental Townshend added, "The next fucking person that walks across this stage is gonna get fucking killed!" as the crowd roared with frenzied delight.

The famed performance ended just after 6:00 a.m. as Townshend thrilled the captivated audience with his trademark smashing of the electric guitar.

Besides *Tommy*, The Who also played "Heaven and Hell," "I Can't Explain," "Summertime Blues," "Shakin' All Over," "My Generation," and "Naked Eye."

The Who are still one of my favorite bands, and they did not disappoint at Woodstock.

Jefferson Airplane, a prominent band from San Francisco, was originally slated to headline the Saturday night lineup at the Woodstock Festival. However, due to numerous delays, their performance was postponed, and they eventually took the stage at 8:00 a.m. on Sunday, August 17. This unexpected schedule change led them to perform for a weary audience that had been up all night, creating a unique atmosphere for their set.

As morning broke over the vast sea of festival-goers, Grace Slick, the band's dynamic vocalist, took to the microphone. Dressed in a fringed white doeskin vest and matching bell-bottoms, she exuded an aura of effortless cool. With a sly smile, she addressed the crowd:

"Alright friends, you have seen the heavy groups. Now you will see morning maniac music. Believe me, yeah. It's a new dawn!"

Her words resonated with the audience, signaling the start of a performance that would become legendary.

The band was joined by the esteemed session pianist Nicky Hopkins, whose keyboard skills added depth to their sound.

They opened their set with a rendition of Fred Neil's "The Other Side of This Life," a staple in their performances during that era. The familiar tune served to captivate the audience, setting the tone for what was to come.

Without missing a beat, Jefferson Airplane launched into "Somebody to Love," one of their most recognized hits from the 1967 album *Surrealistic Pillow*. Grace Slick's powerful vocals soared over the instrumental backdrop, energizing the crowd despite the early hour. However, the performance was not without its challenges. Grace experienced electric shocks from her microphone each time she touched it, likely due to grounding issues, but she powered through, demonstrating her professionalism and dedication.

The set continued with "3/5 of a Mile in 10 Seconds," showcasing Marty Balin's distinctive voice. The song's upbeat tempo and engaging lyrics transported the audience back to the Summer of Love in San Francisco. Following this, the band eased into a medley of "Saturday Afternoon" and "Won't You Try" from their 1968 album *After Bathing at Baxter's*. The gentle melodies provided a soothing contrast, allowing the crowd to relax and absorb the music's nuances.

Introducing new material, Jefferson Airplane performed "Eskimo Blue Day," an environmentally conscious track from their then-upcoming album *Volunteers*. Grace Slick's compelling lead vocals highlighted the song's message, emphasizing the band's evolving musical direction. They then revisited "Plastic Fantastic Lover," a critique of television culture penned by Marty Balin, maintaining the momentum of their performance.

A notable highlight was "Wooden Ships," a collaborative piece co-written with David Crosby and Stephen Stills. The song's narrative of a post-apocalyptic journey resonated deeply, and the band's extended jam session allowed each member to showcase their instrumental prowess. Guitarist Jorma Kaukonen then took center stage with "Uncle Sam Blues," an unrecorded anti-war song that reflected the era's sentiments. The title track "Volunteers" followed, its rousing chorus inspiring a sense of unity and purpose among the attendees.

The main set culminated with "The Ballad of You and Me and Pooneil," during which bassist Jack Casady delivered an impressive solo, stretching the song beyond its usual length and demonstrating the band's improvisational skills. The audience, though fatigued, clamored for more, leading to an encore.

Returning to the stage, Jorma Kaukonen led a soulful rendition of "Come Back Baby," a classic blues number. The performance built up to "White Rabbit," where Grace Slick's dramatic delivery captivated the crowd, her voice weaving a tapestry of psychedelic imagery. To conclude, they revisited "The House at Pooneil Corners" from their 1968 album *Crown of Creation*, leaving the audience in awe. As the final notes echoed, the time was 9:40 a.m., marking the end of a historic set that left an indelible mark on the Woodstock legacy.

This performance not only solidified Jefferson Airplane's status as pioneers of psychedelic rock but also encapsulated the spirit of an era defined by musical innovation and cultural revolution.

Kenny and I were exhausted and in dire need of sleep. We headed back to TMR for some well-deserved rest, then breakfast and a much-needed shower.

It was now time to return to Woodstock for Day 3 of this incredible festival.

Today, I was determined to get a good seat. I had been eyeing the light tower as the best way to view the concert. I saw other people already climbing up the tower, and I decided to join them. Kenny thought I was crazy. There were thunderstorms in the area, and lightning could have hit the tower and killed us all. But it was too good to pass up. I climbed the tower like a kid on the monkey bars in a playground and found a good place to perch and watch the rest of the concert.

At 2:00 p.m., Joe Cocker kicked off Day 3 and performed an incredible set. Joe Cocker did not just perform at Woodstock; he possessed it. On that rain-soaked Sunday afternoon, August 17, 1969, the relatively unknown British singer unleashed a performance that would cement his place in rock history, transforming the chaotic mud pit into a soulful revival meeting.

Before Cocker took the stage, the festival had already been a whirlwind of music, mud, and mayhem. Delays, overcrowding, and equipment malfunctions plagued the event. The crowd was weary, wet, and perhaps even a little skeptical. But the moment Cocker and his Grease Band launched into their opening number, "Dear Landlord," all that seemed to melt away.

Cocker's unique style was a revelation. He was not just singing; he was channeling the music through every fiber of his being. His body contorted, his arms flailed, and his face twisted in a symphony of expressions, mirroring the raw emotion he poured into each song. He resembled a marionette controlled by the strings of his own soul, a stark contrast to the polished and often restrained performances of other artists.

The setlist was a masterclass in blues-rock interpretation. Cocker took familiar songs like "Feelin' Alright" and transformed them into intensely personal anthems. His gritty vocals, dripping with soul and punctuated by his signature guttural cries, captivated the audience. The Grease Band, a tight and energetic ensemble, provided the perfect backing, laying down a groove that was both raw and undeniably funky.

But it was Cocker's rendition of the Beatles' "With a Little Help from My Friends" that truly set the Woodstock crowd ablaze. He transformed the song from a whimsical pop tune into a desperate plea for connection and support. The music swelled, building to a fever pitch as Cocker roared the chorus, his voice cracking with emotion. The audience responded in kind, singing along at the top of their lungs, united in that shared moment of catharsis.

Legend has it that the performance was so intense that it short-circuited the sound system, momentarily silencing the stage. But even the technical difficulties could not dampen the energy. The crowd continued to sing, fueled by the fire Cocker had ignited within them.

He was like a man possessed. He poured his heart and soul into every note. It was impossible not to be moved by it. Joe Cocker's Woodstock performance was more than just a concert. It was a visceral experience, a moment of raw emotion, unbridled energy, and undeniable artistry that transcended the mud and the chaos. It was a performance that not only launched his career but also cemented his place as one of the most electrifying performers of his generation. He brought a soulful inferno to Yasgur's Farm, leaving the crowd forever warmed by the afterglow. His Woodstock set remains a testament to the power of music to connect, to heal, and to ignite the human spirit.

At around 4:30 PM, a heavy storm and rain raged over Woodstock. The concert was put on hold until the storm passed. The stage was covered by plastic rolled out by the stage crew to protect the equipment. By this point in the festival, the crowd had endured rain, mud, and logistical nightmares. The rain had halted the concert, and everyone tried to find shelter from the storm.

When the storm ended, Country Joe and the Fish took the stage. Their set didn't start until 6:30 PM due to the storm. While their set wasn't quite as legendary as some other Woodstock performances, Country Joe and the Fish carved out a memorable niche with their quirky mix of psychedelic rock and anti-war sentiment, along with a dose of politically charged levity for the mud-soaked masses.

While their equipment had suffered from the rain and delays, they managed to deliver a set that showcased their signature blend of psychedelic rock and folk sensibilities. Tracks like "Rock and Soul Music" and "Not So Sweet Martha Lorraine" offered moments of trippy musical exploration, providing a welcome change of pace from some of the heavier acts.

While their performance might not have been the most technically polished of the festival, Country Joe and the Fish captured the spirit of Woodstock perfectly. They were authentic, politically engaged, and willing to connect with the audience on a deeply personal level. They weren't just playing music; they were making a statement, and the Woodstock crowd was listening.

Next up was Ten Years After. They didn't just play at Woodstock; they conquered it with a blistering performance that remains a defining moment in the festival's history. Their set, arriving late Sunday at 8:30 PM, provided a jolt of high-octane energy that reignited the crowd after days of mud, rain, and intermittent performances.

Richard M. Adler

Led by guitar virtuoso Alvin Lee, Ten Years After unleashed a torrent of blues-infused rock that showcased their instrumental prowess and Lee's unparalleled speed. While the band had already built a solid following in Europe, Woodstock provided the platform for them to explode onto the American scene.

The setlist included a selection of their best-known tracks, but it was their electrifying rendition of "I'm Going Home" that stole the show. Lee's extended guitar solo in "I'm Going Home" became legendary. His fingers flew across the fretboard with astonishing speed and precision, unleashing a barrage of notes that left the audience in awe. It was a display of technical brilliance combined with raw emotion, a sonic explosion that perfectly captured the spirit of the era.

The visuals of Lee shredding his guitar, his face contorted in concentration, became iconic images of the festival. He looked every bit the rock god, and the audience responded with wild enthusiasm.

Ten Years After's performance at Woodstock was more than just a great set; it was a showcase of their musical talent and a defining moment for the band. Alvin Lee's guitar solo in "I'm Going Home" became synonymous with the energy and excitement of the festival, cementing their legacy as one of the most memorable acts to grace the stage at Yasgur's Farm. They came, they saw, they conquered, leaving an indelible mark on Woodstock and rock history itself.

Next up was The Band. Amidst the chaos and spectacle of Woodstock, The Band offered a moment of grounded authenticity with their performance, which started around 10:00 PM. Already respected musicians, though perhaps not yet the household names they would become, The Band delivered a set that highlighted their unique blend of rock, folk, country, and blues, showcasing their exceptional musicianship and songwriting.

Unlike many of the acts who aimed for sonic explosions and crowd-rousing theatrics, The Band approached their Woodstock set with a quiet dignity. They were there to play their music, and they did so with a level of professionalism that was both refreshing and captivating.

Their setlist was a journey through their Americana-infused songbook. "Chest Fever," with its iconic Garth Hudson organ introduction, got the crowd moving. Tracks like "Tears of Rage" and "The Weight" showcased their lyrical depth and their ability to blend various musical influences seamlessly. They were storytelling through song, painting vivid pictures of American life and history.

While the rain and the delays had taken their toll on the crowd, The Band's performance offered a moment of respite. Their music was familiar and comforting, yet also challenging and thought-provoking. They weren't trying to change the world with their music; they were simply trying to tell stories, and they did so with remarkable skill.

Although plagued with technical difficulties and some of their performance being cut from the film, the band's set was solid. They delivered a thoughtful and skillfully rendered performance of their trademark sound.

The Band's performance at Woodstock may not have been the most visually arresting or the most talked about, but it was a testament to their musical integrity and their ability to connect with an audience on a deeper level. They brought a touch of Americana to the festival, reminding everyone that even amidst the chaos and spectacle, there was still beauty and meaning to be found in the simple things.

Next up was Johnny Winter, who took the stage at around midnight. The festival's crowd was already buzzing from days of groundbreaking performances. Yet, the Texas-born blues rock guitarist and singer still managed to carve his own place in the annals of music history with a blistering set that showcased his exceptional talent, raw energy, and deep connection to the blues tradition.

By the time of Woodstock, Johnny Winter had already earned a reputation as one of the finest blues guitarists of his generation. With his fiery guitar playing, soulful voice, and striking albino appearance, he was impossible to ignore. His self-titled album, released earlier that year, had introduced him to a national audience, and anticipation for his Woodstock performance was high.

Winter performed in the early hours of Sunday morning, a slot that could have challenged any artist given the long, rain-soaked days the crowd had endured. But Winter's presence and musicianship quickly captured the audience's attention.

Backed by his band, which included Tommy Shannon on bass (later known for playing with Stevie Ray Vaughan), Uncle John Turner on drums, and his brother Edgar Winter on keyboards, Johnny delivered a set steeped in blues roots but electrified with rock intensity.

Winter's Woodstock setlist was a potent mix of blues classics and his own material. His rendition of "Mean Town Blues" is often cited as one of the festival's standout moments, with his rapid-fire slide guitar work and gritty vocals epitomizing the power of electric blues. Winter also paid tribute to one of his musical heroes, Chuck Berry, with a high-octane cover of "Johnny B. Goode" that had the crowd dancing despite their exhaustion. Adding a unique family dynamic to the performance, Edgar Winter joined his brother onstage for several songs, contributing his multi-instrumental talents on keyboards and saxophone. Their synergy brought an added layer of depth and spontaneity to the set.

While Johnny Winter's Woodstock performance did not receive as much immediate media attention as those of Jimi Hendrix, Janis Joplin, or Santana, it has since become recognized as a crucial moment in his career and a testament to his virtuosity. The performance helped solidify his reputation as a blues rock powerhouse and paved the way for his subsequent success, including collaborations with blues legends like Muddy Waters. Winter's appearance at Woodstock also underscored the festival's eclectic spirit, blending rock, blues, folk, and psychedelia into a cultural phenomenon that defined a generation. His music bridged the gap between the traditional blues of the Mississippi Delta and the electrified rock scene of the late 1960s, leaving an indelible mark on both genres.

Johnny Winter's performance at Woodstock remains a testament to the power of blues rock and the enduring appeal of a musician who stayed true to his roots while pushing the boundaries of the genre. His fiery guitar work, soulful vocals, and passionate stage presence not only captivated the Woodstock audience but also cemented his place as one of the greatest blues guitarists of all time. Today, his Woodstock set is remembered as a defining moment in the career of a true blues rock legend.

Next up was Blood, Sweat and Tears, who hit the stage around 1:30 AM, delivering a performance that blended rock, jazz, and blues in a way few other bands could match. Known for their sophisticated horn arrangements and fusion of musical styles, the band's appearance at the legendary festival added a unique dimension to the weekend's lineup.

By the time of Woodstock, Blood, Sweat and Tears had already achieved commercial success with their self-titled album, which featured hits like "You've Made Me So Very Happy," "Spinning Wheel," and "And When I Die." Their blend of brass-heavy arrangements and rock rhythms made them stand out in the late 1960s music scene, and their performance at Woodstock was an opportunity to showcase this innovative sound to a massive audience.

Taking the stage after days of performances that leaned heavily into rock, folk, and psychedelia, Blood, Sweat and Tears brought a polished, jazz-infused energy that contrasted with the rawer sounds of many other acts. Their setlist included their signature hits as well as deeper cuts, with the band's tight musicianship and dynamic horn section captivating the crowd:

"Spinning Wheel" – one of their biggest hits, known for its catchy melody and jazz-rock fusion.

"You've Made Me So Very Happy" – a soulful, horn-driven track that had become a radio staple.

"And When I Die" – a folk-influenced song with themes of mortality, written by Laura Nyro.

David Clayton-Thomas's powerful vocals, combined with the band's sophisticated arrangements, highlighted their ability to fuse jazz and rock into something fresh and compelling.

While their performance was musically impressive, Blood, Sweat and Tears' appearance at Woodstock has often been viewed through a different lens compared to other bands. Unlike many of their festival peers, who were closely associated with the counterculture movement, Blood, Sweat and Tears had a more mainstream image, which some critics and fans saw as a departure from Woodstock's rebellious spirit.

Despite these perceptions, their Woodstock performance remains a testament to their musical talent and the diverse range of sounds that defined the festival. The band's tight, horn-driven sound brought a level of sophistication that broadened the scope of what was heard at Woodstock, reinforcing the festival's reputation as a melting pot of genres and styles.

Although their set was not included in the original Woodstock film or soundtrack, which may have limited its historical visibility, Blood, Sweat and Tears' performance remains a key part of the festival's legacy. Their appearance at Woodstock showcased a band at the height of its powers, delivering a blend of jazz, rock, and blues that resonated with the festival's diverse audience and added yet another layer to the rich musical tapestry of Woodstock.

Next up was Crosby, Stills and Nash, who walked out on stage at 3:00 in the morning. After days of music, rain, and mud, I was tired but excited. You see, Crosby, Stills and Nash were the main reason I had come to Woodstock. Their music had touched something deep inside me, and I knew I had to see them live. What made the night even more special was that this was only the second time they had ever played in front of an audience. I felt like I was witnessing history.

They took the stage late at night, sometime after midnight. The air was cool, and the sky above was dark and endless. When the first notes of their music floated through the air, the crowd fell silent. It was as if everyone knew something magical was happening. Their harmonies were perfect, soft and sweet but powerful enough to reach the hearts of thousands. I could feel the music in my chest, like it was a part of me.

They started with "Suite: Judy Blue Eyes," a song that had already become a favorite for many of us. The mix of Stephen Stills' guitar, David Crosby's rich voice, and Graham Nash's high harmonies created a sound like no other. The crowd swayed and sang along, caught up in the beauty of the moment. After that, they played "Guinnevere" and "Marrakesh Express," two more songs that showed off their unique blend of folk and rock.

Then came a moment that made the night even more special. Neil Young stepped onto the stage, joining the trio to become Crosby, Stills, Nash & Young. I remember the cheers from the crowd as he picked up his guitar. With Young on stage, the music took on a new energy, grittier, louder, and full of raw passion. Together, they played "Helplessly Hoping" and "Wooden Ships," songs that seemed to echo the spirit of the festival itself: freedom, hope, and the power of coming together.

One of the highlights of the night was their performance of "Long Time Gone." The lyrics felt like a message to all of us, urging us to stand up and make a difference in the world. The music was loud and strong, and I could feel the ground vibrating beneath my feet. When they played "49 Bye-Byes," I knew the night was nearing its end, but I didn't want it to stop.

Looking around, I saw faces lit up with joy, wonder, and sometimes tears. The music had brought us all together, people from different places with different stories, standing side by side, united by the sound of guitars and voices.

After their set ended, the cheers and applause seemed to go on forever. As I stood there, surrounded by thousands of people, I knew I had witnessed something I would never forget. Crosby, Stills & Nash, and Neil Young had created a moment that would live in my heart forever.

To this day, I still hear those harmonies when I think of Woodstock. And whenever I listen to their music, I remember that night: the night that music, hope, and togetherness filled the air, and I was lucky enough to be there.

I was tired, but I wanted to see Jimi Hendrix, who still had not performed. Crosby, Stills & Nash's set ended around 3:45 a.m., and I was in need of sleep. I fell asleep on the ground right where I had been sitting all day, but I told Kenny to wake me up once the music started again. Kenny and I both slept through the Paul Butterfield Blues Band and Sha Na Na. When I woke up, it was about 8:45 a.m. Jimi Hendrix was getting ready to take the stage. I looked around, and wow, most of the crowd had left. There were only about 30,000 people remaining to see Jimi play.

I'll never forget the day I saw Jimi Hendrix play at Woodstock. It was August 18, 1969, the last day of the festival. A three-day festival had now become a four-day festival, and there was no way to let my boss know that I was not coming into the office that day. People had been listening to music for days, but everyone who stayed was waiting for Jimi. Even though it was early in the morning, no one wanted to miss his performance.

When Jimi finally took the stage at 9:00 a.m., the crowd went quiet. Then he started playing his guitar, and the music filled the air. His fingers moved so fast across the strings that it looked like magic. Jimi and his band, Gypsy Sun and Rainbows, began with a song called "Message to Love." It had a strong beat that made everyone

215

want to move. After that, they played "Hear My Train A Comin'," a blues song that showed off Jimi's incredible guitar skills. I loved "Foxy Lady," and Jimi did not disappoint.

As the sun rose higher, Jimi played some of his most famous songs. "Fire" had the crowd dancing and cheering. Then came "Izabella," a song with powerful guitar riffs. But the moment that everyone remembers most was when Jimi played "The Star-Spangled Banner," the national anthem.

Jimi's version of "The Star-Spangled Banner" wasn't like anything I had ever heard. He made his guitar sound like bombs, sirens, and airplanes, capturing the feeling of the world at that time. It was loud, emotional, and unforgettable. When he finished, the crowd erupted into applause.

After that, Jimi played "Purple Haze," one of his biggest hits. The wild guitar sounds and powerful lyrics had everyone hooked. He ended the performance with "Hey Joe," a song about a man on the run. As the final notes rang out, the crowd knew they had witnessed something special.

Jimi Hendrix's performance at Woodstock wasn't just a concert. It was a moment in history. His music brought people together and made them feel things they couldn't put into words. Even now, I can still hear the sound of his guitar echoing in my mind. That day, Jimi Hendrix showed the world why he was one of the greatest guitar players of all time.

I left Woodstock with memories that would last a lifetime. The sense of unity, the incredible music, and the once-in-a-lifetime atmosphere made those three days truly unforgettable. Woodstock wasn't just a concert. It was a moment in history, and I was lucky enough to be part of it.

That's me at Woodstock circled at the bottom right. *"Best seat at the festival"*

Richard M. Adler

Chapter 21

The Beach Boys

In May of 1969, I promoted my first Beach Boys concert in the Field House at the University of Oklahoma, where I was attending college at the time.

I met the Beach Boys when they arrived a day before the show at their hotel. I introduced my girlfriend at the time, Joanne Leff, to Bruce Johnston. When Bruce heard her last name, he asked if she happened to know someone named Ricky Leff. Joanne said, "Yes, he's my brother." Bruce replied, "Ricky is my new roommate." What are the chances of that happening?

Ticket sales were going well, and I was looking forward to a sold-out show and a nice profit. I was lucky to book the Beach Boys for a $5,000 guarantee against 50 percent of the profits. I couldn't believe I got them so cheap. It turned out that two nights before the show, they were in Chicago, and the night after, they were in Dallas, Texas, so it made sense for them to take the gig at a reduced rate.

The Beach Boys' agent insisted that I do this show with an experienced promoter since I had never promoted a Beach Boys concert before. I agreed. I never saw the promoter until the day of the show.

The Beach Boys were great that night. I made friends with Dennis Wilson and Billy Hinsche, who was a member of the Beach Boys' touring band and a former member of Dino, Desi & Billy. Billy was also Carl Wilson's brother-in-law.

While the concert was going on, I went into the office with the promoter the Beach Boys' agent insisted I use. I brought all the

219

money to the office, and we began counting it. After we finished, I gave the promoter all the receipts for the expenses that needed to be deducted from the gross before we paid the Beach Boys their 50 percent share of the profits. This left 25 percent for the promoter, 15 percent for me, and 10 percent for the student organization that helped secure the Field House for free, created and posted all the banners and posters on campus, and sold tickets.

After paying the Beach Boys and their road manager, I asked the promoter for our 25 percent split for Student Action and me. The promoter pulled out a gun and placed it on the table.

He said, "Thank you for a good show, but you're not getting any money."

With that, he closed his briefcase and left the building.

I realized I had made a mistake. I never signed contracts with the promoter. He signed the contracts with the Beach Boys, and I had no legal right to the money. That experience taught me a lesson that served me well throughout my business life: everything must be in writing and checked by a lawyer.

I was depressed. I was leaving school for home the next day and had to pack because I had an early flight the next morning. I told Billy Hinsche I was heading back to the dorm. Billy said he'd come with me. We packed up my room and then met up with the Beach Boys at their hotel. Dennis, Billy, and I remained friends for many years. I would be backstage at every show they did in the New York area between 1969 and 1976.

Whenever the Beach Boys came to New York, I was backstage hanging out with the band. When they played Nassau Coliseum, they arrived a day early. I met up with Dennis Wilson, Billy Hinsche,

Blondie Chaplin, and Ricky Fataar. Somehow, we all ended up back at my apartment in Queens. I guess they'd had enough of hotels and were happy for the distraction.

They had to be at the Coliseum by 4 p.m. for soundcheck, and I told them I'd drive them to the gig. What I didn't tell them was that I had only had my driver's license for about a week. I'd been to the Coliseum many times, but only as a passenger. I thought I knew the way.

Well, I made a wrong turn, and they all started panicking, everyone except Dennis, because they would get fined if they were late. Eventually, I found the way, and they arrived with five minutes to spare.

The Beach Boys hit the stage, and the concert was going great. During one song, Dennis came off stage. He said he didn't have anything to do on that number and asked me to join him in the dressing room, which meant smoking a joint and having a beer.

After a few minutes, it was time for Dennis to go back. The odd thing about the Coliseum setup was that you needed a stage pass to get from the dressing rooms to the stage. Dennis had left his pass on his jacket, on stage. He knocked on the stage door, and a security guard opened it. Dennis tried to walk in like he belonged, but the guard stopped him and asked for his pass.

Dennis said, "I'm Dennis Wilson of the Beach Boys. I need to get on stage."

The security guard replied, "Yeah, and I'm Goldilocks. If you were Dennis Wilson, you'd be on the stage. Where's your pass?"

Dennis couldn't reason with him, so he tried to push his way in. Six more security guards came over. Dennis fought back. It was like running the gauntlet. He got beat up pretty badly but made it to the stage.

He was bleeding badly from his nose, and his T-shirt was soaked with blood and sweat. He grabbed the mic from Mike Love and shouted, "Seven against one, seven against one, and I won!"

It was a bizarre scene, but I was used to seeing Dennis with an assortment of cuts and bruises over the years.

Once, I saw his eye completely red, with no white visible. I asked him what happened. He said he was surfing and a board from the guy next to him popped up and hit him. I asked what the other guy looked like. He just smiled.

Sometime in the early '70s, Dennis called and asked if I was coming to that night's gig. I said yes. He asked, "Can you bring some coke tonight?" I paused and said I'd try.

I didn't want to let Dennis down. I always had weed for us, but I had never gotten coke before. I needed rolling papers, so I stopped by a head shop. I told my friend behind the counter what I needed. He said, "Don't worry. I've got just the thing."

He showed me a little bottle filled with white powder. I asked him what it was. I knew he didn't sell coke. He said it was Cocoa Leaf Incense and that it was legal. "Dennis will never know the difference," he said.

I was concerned. I didn't want to mess Dennis up, so I tried it first. My friend was right. It passed. And it only cost $3.50 a bottle.

When I got to the gig, Dennis asked if I got the coke. I said I did, and we did a few lines. I was so nervous he'd know it wasn't real coke. At the end of the night, Dennis asked if I had more. I said we finished it.

He told me it was the best coke he ever had. I never told him the truth. Does that make me a bad person?

One day backstage at a Beach Boys concert, Dennis told me an incredible story.

In 1968, Dennis was driving through Malibu when he picked up two female hitchhikers. Later, he saw them again and this time took them to his house at 14400 Sunset Boulevard, near Will Rogers Park.

Dennis told me, "I told them [the girls] about our involvement with the Maharishi, and they told me they had a guru too, Charlie, who just got out of jail after 12 years. He drifted into crime, but when I met him, I found he had great musical ideas. We're writing together now. He's dumb in some ways, but I accept his approach and have learned from him."

Dennis left for a recording session. When he came home at 3 a.m., he was met in the driveway by "Charlie," aka Charles Manson.

When Dennis walked in, about a dozen people, mostly women, were already living there. Dennis became fascinated by Manson and his "family," who stayed at his house at Dennis's expense.

Initially impressed, Dennis introduced Manson to people in the music industry, including Terry Melcher (Doris Day's son). Dennis asked Melcher to sign Manson to a deal. Melcher invited Manson to audition. After hearing his songs, Melcher said he was busy but might set up a recording session when he had time.

Nothing ever happened. The Beach Boys released a Manson song, originally called *Cease to Exist*, as *Never Learn Not to Love* on the *20/20* album.

Manson later showed up at Melcher's house looking for a session. Melcher wasn't home. His guests were rude to Manson. He didn't take it well.

According to Beach Boys collaborator Van Dyke Parks, "One day, Charles Manson brought out a bullet and showed it to Dennis. Dennis asked, 'What's this?' Manson replied, 'It's a bullet. Every time you look at it, I want you to think how nice it is your kids are still safe.' Dennis grabbed Manson by the throat and pummeled him until Charlie said, 'Ouch!' Dennis beat the shit out of him. Charlie was weeping in front of a lot of hip people. The point is, Dennis Wilson wasn't afraid of anybody!"

Eventually, Dennis realized how dangerous Manson was and simply moved out, leaving Manson behind. When Manson tried to get more money, he left a bullet with Dennis's housekeeper. Dennis took it as a threat.

In August 1969, Manson sent his followers to Melcher's former house, now occupied by Roman Polanski and Sharon Tate. The Manson Family committed the Tate murders there. Dennis rarely spoke of his connection to them.

The Beach Boys were in town for a Carnegie Hall concert. Billy called and asked if I wanted to go shopping for clothes. I told him we should go to Granny Takes a Trip, where all the rock stars shopped.

Billy tried on a lot of things but only bought a silk scarf. We went back to the Warwick Hotel, where the band was staying. Carl Wilson wasn't feeling well, so we went to check on him. He answered the door in sweats, with a towel around his head, soaking his feet in a bowl of hot water. He was shivering. I called the front desk and asked for a doctor.

The doctor gave him a prescription, which I filled. Carl looked so sick I thought he'd miss the show, but he made a speedy recovery and performed beautifully. Backstage, he wanted to rehearse *Marcella* before the show. I got a private a cappella performance. I've always loved that song.

When the Beach Boys played Queens College, I took my sister Mindy to meet them. Dennis asked me to meet him at a coffee shop because he was hungry.

Mindy and I got there first. I went to the restroom while she waited at the counter. Dennis came in and started hitting on her. Billy, who was with him, said, "That is Richie Adler's sister," just as I came out of the bathroom. Dennis was embarrassed. We all laughed. My sister never forgot it. We still talk about it to this day.

I met a lot of people through the Beach Boys. On one tour, Toni Tennille and Daryl Dragon, the Captain and Tennille, played keyboards in the band. Toni always sat on the floor backstage. I'd sit next to her and ask, "So what are you knitting?"

She'd give me a look and say, "I'm not knitting, I'm crocheting."

It became a running joke. Fifty years later, I was chatting with Toni online and said, "I remember you always knitting backstage." Without missing a beat, she replied, "I was not knitting, I was crocheting."

She remembered.

Richard M. Adler

Chapter 22

A Trip to Highland Park

It was 1968, and I was a student at the University of Oklahoma. The Beatles were the biggest thing in the world, almost like superheroes with guitars.

My good friend Rick Vittenson invited a bunch of us to spend the weekend at his parents' house in Highland Park, a nice neighborhood just outside of Chicago. The lawns were perfect, and the cars were nicer than anything we had.

Richard M. Adler

One of our friends had a Volkswagen Beetle, you know, one of those tiny little cars that somehow keeps going. Well, this one barely kept going. Still, six of us squeezed into that tiny car. It was like stuffing six raccoons into a shoebox. We were practically sitting on each other's laps, but we were young and didn't care.

We drove 750 miles to Chicago, which took 12 hours. No air conditioning, no GPS, just a map and a lot of bad jokes. The weekend was fun, but the big deal was what was happening Sunday night:

The Beatles were going to be on TV!

They were performing *Hey Jude* and *Revolution* on *The Smothers Brothers Comedy Hour* at 8 p.m. We had to get back to campus in time.

The Beatles on TV in the '60s was a major event. This was a time before videotape or DVRs, a time when you had to wait for The Beatles to appear on TV or in the movies because they had stopped touring in 1966.

So, needless to say, if you missed the show on TV, you missed it. And chances are, they would never show it again. It was an amazing time, and you had to be there, because there was no tomorrow. This was before the internet, where you can watch your favorite band anytime you want. There was no outlet except live shows, TV, or movies. So, when The Beatles were going to perform on TV, it was a major event.

We piled back into the Beetle and headed out Sunday morning, full of snacks and excitement. But less than an hour outside of Chicago, the Beetle made some strange noises, like a robot coughing, and then just stopped. The engine was dead.

We were stuck on the side of the road, six sweaty college kids with no car and no plan.

There were no cell phones back then, so we did what people did. We stuck out our thumbs and hoped for a ride. Amazingly, a guy in a beat-up car stopped and asked where we were going.

"Norman, Oklahoma," we said, kind of joking.

"Hop in," he said. "I'll take you."

We couldn't believe it. This guy was going to drive us all the way back to school, just like that. Along the way, he told us he used to be in a group called the Hollywood Argyles and sang on the record *Alley Oop*. Rick and I were skeptical, but he seemed nice, and more importantly, he had a running car.

He promised to get us back in time for The Beatles, and he meant it. We were cruising down the highway like it was a race. But just five miles from campus, his car got a flat tire.

Now, most people would pull over. Not this guy.

He wanted to keep his word and see The Beatles too.

So he drove the last five miles on the rim, sparks flying everywhere. It sounded like someone banging pots and pans down a staircase. But he got us there.

We ran into the girls' apartment, turned on the TV, and made it just in time to see The Beatles Walk on stage. *Hey Jude* started, and for a few minutes, nothing else mattered. The car, the flat tire, the stress, all forgotten. It was magical.

Now, here's where things got weird.

The girls were so thankful that they let the guy stay the night.

Then he stayed the next night.

And the next week.

And then... another week.

By week three, they were over it. They asked me to kindly tell him it was time to go. He agreed, but he also took one of the girls' checkbooks and started writing checks. She had to cancel her account.

Even with all that, the broken-down car, the mystery musician, the checkbook situation, we all agreed on one thing:

We got to see The Beatles live on TV. And back then, that meant everything.

We might've lost a car and a little trust in strangers,
but we got a great story. One that, just like *Hey Jude*,
keeps going and going.

Chapter 23

Hanging with Napolean XIV

Jerry Samuels aka Napolean XIV

In the grand tapestry of my life, there are certain threads that shimmer with a unique kind of magic, a rock and roll fantasy come to life. One of those threads is woven with the eccentric brilliance of

Richard M. Adler

Jerry Samuels, better known as Napoleon XIV, the man behind the novelty hit *They're Coming to Take Me Away, Ha-Haaa!*

But my story with Jerry is more than just about a catchy tune. It's a tale of late-night parties, bizarre recording sessions, and the kind of uninhibited creativity that only comes from someone truly marching to the beat of their own drum.

It all started in the early '70s in Forest Hills, where I was just 20 years old and hanging out with my friends Bob Berman and Alan Lakin. Bob's next-door neighbor was none other than Jerry Samuels. Jerry's apartment was like a magnet for all the cool kids in the neighborhood, including some of The Ramones.

Every night, his place was a party scene. Jerry, who was about twelve years older than me, was this fascinating, eccentric guy. I mean, it was June, and he still had his Christmas tree up. A real tree, mind you, which looked pretty rough. When I asked him if he was ever going to take it down, he simply said "no," and it stayed up indefinitely.

Jerry was generous. Since I still lived with my parents, he would let my girlfriend and me use his apartment so we could have some alone time. Nice guy, right? But Jerry was not just some party host. He was a songwriter, a recording engineer, and the mind behind that crazy hit record *They're Coming to Take Me Away*. It was surreal to be hanging out with the guy who created that song. During this time, he was also working on a new album titled *For God Sake Stop the Feces*.

I remember one day Jerry invited me to the studio to watch him record the track "Rape." It was intense. Watching Jerry work was like watching a mad scientist. He was disheveled and manic, turning knobs, pushing faders, setting up mics in his mad lab.

While recording "Rape," instead of a typical musical break, he recorded himself and his girlfriend making love in the middle of the song while the studio lights were turned off but the monitors were still on. It was definitely a bit strange to be sitting there, listening to all that. Jerry had this ponytail in front of his head that reminded me of a unicorn. He was a true original, and a lot of my friends from Forest Hills loved to hang out at his place.

Jerry would often put on little impromptu concerts in his apartment, playing the piano and singing for us. He was always creating and sharing his music. One day, he invited me, my girlfriend Rochelle, and his girlfriend to take a trip to Croton Dam. On the way, Jerry passed out Orange Sunshine (LSD). We all spent the day tripping at Croton Dam. It was a wild, strange trip, and the first and last time I ever dropped LSD.

Looking back, I realize that Jerry Samuels, this eccentric neighbor, was more than just a party host. He was a musical force who made a lasting impact. Born in 1938, he started his career in 1954. He recorded his first song in 1956, called "Puppy Love." He co-wrote "As If I Didn't Know" for Adam Wade in 1961. He also wrote "The Shelter of Your Arms" for Sammy Davis Jr. in 1964.

But it was in 1966, under the name Napoleon XIV, that he created his most iconic work, *They're Coming to Take Me Away, Ha-Haaa!* He conceived of it while stoned and sitting in a vibrating chair. The song, a rant from a mental patient with a simple drum loop and a siren, was incredibly unique for the time. It became a massive hit, reaching number three on the Billboard chart. The B-side was the song played in reverse, with a mirror image label.

The success of the single led to an album of the same name, which continued the mental illness theme. The album featured tracks like "Bats in My Belfry," "Split Level Head," and "I'm in Love with My Little Red Tricycle." There was even a woman's perspective of the hit single called "I'm Happy They Took You Away, Ha-Haaa!" Despite the song's popularity, radio stations banned it after complaints that it hurt the image of doctors and institutions. Jerry only performed the song once, feeling that the audience was laughing at him.

Even though *They're Coming to Take Me Away, Ha-Haaa!* is his most well-known work, Jerry's career was diverse. He later became a booking agent and an entertainer, playing the retirement home circuit. He released a compilation album called *The Second Coming* in 1996, which included new recordings, unreleased tracks, and classic songs from his 1966 album.

My time hanging out with Jerry was a wild ride through the heart of rock and roll. He was the embodiment of the idea that music can be both genius and strange, and that sometimes, the most memorable people are the ones who don't quite fit the mold. Jerry Samuels, also known as Napoleon XIV, was a rock and roll fantasy I was lucky enough to live.

Chapter 24

Granny Takes a Trip

The early '70s in New York City were a total rush of music, clothes, and nights that stretched on forever. One adventure that sticks out is when my buddies, Tommy Erdelyi (who you might remember as Tommy Ramone), Jeff Salen (later the guitarist for Tuff Darts), and

Richard M. Adler

I went on a mission to Granny Takes a Trip, the legendary New York clothing boutique. This store, originally founded in London in 1966, was known for its unique blend of traditional English styles with flamboyant and psychedelic fashion. The boutique was a popular destination for rock stars and aspiring musicians seeking fashionable clothing.

It wasn't just a store. It was a place where rock stars and anyone who was anyone in the music scene went to get their hands on the coolest, most English-style clothes.

Granny Takes a Trip was a huge deal, a total game-changer in fashion in the '60s and '70s. It started in 1966 in London, on King's Road, by John Pearse, Nigel Waymouth, and Sheila Cohen. It became known for its psychedelic and cutting-edge look, with a crazy storefront that even had a Jean Harlow art face. It drew in everyone from famous rock stars to fashion lovers, and they were all about mixing traditional English looks with wild, colorful, and psychedelic designs. It was a cultural landmark for modern fashion. They opened a shop in NYC on 62nd Street in 1970.

Our trip started with the subway, buzzing with the anticipation of what cool things we'd find. The shop was something else, a total sensory experience. That's where I made a fashion choice that, looking back, wasn't the smartest. I spotted these burgundy boots that just called out to me. They weren't basic boots. They laced up almost to my calves, with a two-inch heel that looked great but was secretly a torture device. They were super narrow, a tight fit that seemed like a challenge. I also grabbed these slick black velvet pants to go with them, the perfect match.

Dressed to kill, we started hitting up Max's Kansas City, where all the night owls hung out. Each night, my feet would be in agony, but it was worth it. Then, one night at the Roundtable, another one of the city's hotspots, things got really interesting. We were there to see the New York Dolls. I was just leaning against the bar, and this stunning woman came up and asked me to dance. We hit the dance floor just as this slow, sensual song came on, and there was this instant connection. It ended with a passionate kiss, the kind that makes you forget about everything else.

After the dance, I went back to Tommy and Jeff, who were still standing at the bar where they had seen it all unfold on the dance floor. Jeff, with a total smirk, said, "Dude, you know that was a drag queen you were dancing with!" I just brushed it off, saying she was an amazing kisser and definitely not a drag queen. We kept the banter going all the way home, with Tommy and Jeff giving me endless grief. The next day, Tommy came over with a knowing look and admitted that he and Jeff had totally made up the drag queen story out of pure jealousy. They couldn't believe how easily I'd won over such an incredible girl on the dance floor. Although, Tommy was still jealous that I got her phone number.

Those times in NYC, whether it was the laughs with friends, the fashionable shoes that hurt like hell, or that unexpected romance, had a special, '70s-style kind of magic to them.

Here's a cool story about Tommy Ramone from 1972. At the time, I was a photographer working for a number of magazines on a freelance basis. I was fortunate to have photographed many music and movie stars, from John Lennon to Sissy Spacek.

While at a party in Brooklyn, I was talking to Linda, another guest at the party who found out I was a photographer. She told me that she was looking to break into the porn industry and asked if I would photograph her in the nude and create a portfolio for her. We set up a date for the shoot, and one of the other guests said we could use her house for it.

I went home and met Tommy coming out of our apartment building. I mentioned the photo shoot to him. Tommy loved to make art films and asked if he could tag along. I told him he could be my assistant. Tommy brought along a Super 8 movie camera and proceeded to shoot some footage with Linda's permission. Tommy was shooting from all angles, and he kept filming throughout the entire photo shoot.

The shoot lasted about an hour. As we were packing up to leave, I asked Tommy how many rolls of film he had shot. He told me he brought one roll of film, and it ran out about five minutes after he started filming. I asked him why he kept shooting without film. He said he wasn't shooting; he was just using the zoom lens to get a better look.

That was my friend Tommy!

Chapter 25

Photography

It all began around 1972, a time when the world was awash in experimentation and reinvention, when I first discovered my passion for photography. Eager to learn, I enrolled at the School of Visual Arts, where I was fortunate to study under the talented and renowned photographer Cora Kennedy. Her keen eye and unwavering dedication to the craft inspired me to see the world through a lens in ways I had never imagined.

Determined to master the business of photography, I decided that the best way to learn was by immersing myself in its professional side. After a series of interviews, I was hired as an assistant by Larry Silver, a brilliant commercial photographer whose work graced the pages of the era's most popular magazines. Larry shared his busy studio with two other accomplished photographers, and from day one, I found myself swept up in a whirlwind of creative energy and technical challenges. The constant buzz of the studio, with cameras clicking and lights flickering, offered endless opportunities to absorb practical knowledge. I was fortunate enough to work with all three photographers, each imparting unique lessons that would shape my future.

Even amid the bustle of commercial shoots, my heart harbored a secret ambition: I yearned to become a rock music photographer, capturing the raw energy of legendary rock stars and seeing my work celebrated in the glossy spreads of music magazines. I imagined the thrill of freezing electrifying moments in time, immortalizing the pulse of a generation.

One ordinary day in the studio, while preparing for an advertisement shoot, I was busy rolling out a pristine white background paper and setting up the intricate lighting arrangements. That's when she walked in, a would-be model named Sissy. With a confident yet curious air, she asked if I needed a model for any test shots. I agreed, and she proposed that in exchange for posing, she'd receive copies of the photos for her portfolio.

The testing session quickly took an unexpected turn when Sissy shyly requested to be photographed nude, as she needed some tasteful nudes for her portfolio. Although it was an unconventional request, I sensed her earnest desire to build her portfolio, so I agreed. The session unfolded with a creative intensity, the soft studio light accentuating her features and the vulnerability of the moment. It was a lesson in both technical precision and the art of capturing genuine emotion.

After the session, as I began tidying up, I noticed a guitar propped in the corner. Curiosity got the better of me, and I asked if she played. Sissy casually mentioned that she was a decent guitarist and could accompany her singing. Before I knew it, she began strumming a familiar tune, "In My Life" by The Beatles. Her voice was unexpectedly soulful, a tender yet powerful rendition that resonated deeply. In the midst of our conversation, she inquired if I played an instrument. I confessed that I did, though my guitar was tucked away back in my apartment. With an impish grin, she suggested we head over there to "jam" together. I couldn't resist the opportunity for a spontaneous musical interlude, so we hailed a cab and set off for my apartment in Forest Hills.

Inside my cozy bedroom, the walls adorned with my own photographic prints and scattered musical memorabilia, we began our impromptu session. The air was filled with creativity and the sweet strains of melody when an unexpected interruption occurred. My 14-year-old sister, curious and a little mischievous, wandered in. Sissy, ever candid, asked why she was there, to which I replied that it was my home. Confused by the presence of a teenager, she inquired whether I lived with my parents. The situation, though awkward, added a layer of humor to the otherwise enchanting afternoon. With a polite nod, Sissy gathered her things, her guitar in hand, and quietly departed. I guess Sissy was hoping to crash at my house and realized that it was not going to happen with my parents and my sister there.

That chance encounter with Sissy left an indelible mark on me, a memory interwoven with the themes of art, music, and spontaneity. Years passed, and the vibrant tapestry of my early career continued to unfold. Then, in an unexpected twist of fate, I found myself in a movie theater one night to see the film *Carrie*. As the lights dimmed and the screen flickered to life, I was startled by a familiar face. There, illuminating the screen, was Sissy Spacek. It was a surreal moment of recognition, a flashback to that singular afternoon in my apartment, when art and life danced together in perfect harmony.

Before she became a celebrated actress, Sissy had even ventured into the music scene. Under the stage name Rainbo, she released a novelty record titled "John, This Time You Went Too Far," a playful, cheeky scolding directed at a certain Beatle for "showing off his Norwegian Wood." This quirky piece, full of humor and irreverence, encapsulated the spirit of the times and added yet another fascinating chapter to the story of that remarkable day in the studio.

Reflecting on those days, I realize how each moment, the lessons at the School of Visual Arts, the vibrant chaos of Larry Silver's studio, the daring photo session, and that unexpected musical jam, contributed to a journey of discovery that blended the worlds of photography and rock music. It was a time when every encounter, no matter how fleeting, left a trace, a reminder that life's most memorable stories often begin with a single, unanticipated moment.

Chapter 26

Concert for Bangladesh

George Harrison (photo by Richard Adler)

One of the first concerts I photographed was George Harrison's Concert for Bangladesh.

In the summer of 1971, the rock world witnessed an extraordinary convergence of music, activism, and sheer willpower. No one could have predicted that a single evening at Madison Square Garden would change the way the world viewed charity concerts, and it all started with George Harrison's dream.

Long before Live Aid became a household term, George Harrison was quietly plotting a musical rescue mission for a people in

243

desperate need. Moved by the harrowing plight of refugees fleeing the Bangladesh Liberation War, Harrison transformed his sorrow into action, determined to harness the unifying power of music. It was an idea so radical that many in the industry doubted its feasibility. How could rock and roll, the pulsing heartbeat of youth culture, be marshaled to confront a global humanitarian disaster?

Harrison's answer was as simple as it was profound: rally the biggest names in music for a live event that would serve as both a beacon of hope and a call to action. His vision, fueled by compassion and the defiant spirit of rock, eventually coalesced into what is now immortalized as the Concert for Bangladesh.

Imagine a night when the usual boundaries between rock royalty and world-saving activism evaporated into the night air. Harrison's guest list read like a who's who of musical legends. Ravi Shankar, whose sitar had already enchanted global audiences, lent a transcendent Eastern mysticism to the proceedings. Ringo Starr, Harrison's loyal bandmate from The Beatles, added his signature warmth and rhythm, while Bob Dylan's raw poetic intensity echoed the deep undercurrents of social change. Billy Preston, often hailed as the "Fifth Beatle," and Leon Russell, whose soulful energy could ignite any stage, further underscored the event's brilliance.

Each artist brought their unique voice, uniting the realms of rock, folk, and world music into one extraordinary tapestry. The concert wasn't just a series of performances; it was a bold experiment in cross-cultural collaboration and humanitarian outreach.

Yet behind the scenes of this historic event lay a saga of challenges that tested even Harrison's steady resolve. The logistics of orchestrating a benefit concert of such scale were enormous. Harrison faced skepticism from industry insiders, government officials, and fellow musicians. Critics questioned whether the rock community could rise above its reputation for excess and embrace a cause of global urgency.

Among the legends on Harrison's list, Bob Dylan's participation was perhaps the most hotly discussed. Known as much for his genius as for his unpredictability, Dylan's involvement was far from guaranteed. In the weeks leading up to the event, rumors swirled about his hesitations. Since his 1966 motorcycle accident, Dylan had withdrawn from the public eye and limited his performances. Even on the day of the show, his commitment remained uncertain.

For Dylan, the stakes were high. The event wasn't just another concert; it was a public stance on a humanitarian crisis. As George Harrison later recalled, "He never committed himself, right up until the moment he came onstage. On the night before Bangladesh, we sat in Madison Square Garden as the people were setting up the bandstand. He looked around the place and said to me, 'Hey, man, you know, this isn't my scene.'"

Despite these doubts, Dylan showed up the next morning. Harrison explained, "I had a list, a sort of running order, that I had glued on my guitar. When I got to the point where Bob was going to come on, I had Bob with a question mark. I looked over my shoulder to see if he was around, because if he wasn't, I would have to go on to do the next bit. And I looked around, and he was so nervous. He had his guitar and his shades, he was sort of coming on, coming. So I just said, 'My old friend, Bob Dylan!' It was only at that moment that I knew for sure he was going to do it."

After the second show, Dylan even admitted, "God! If only we'd done three shows." His decision to perform, despite personal uncertainty, added an emotional depth and vulnerability to the concert. It was a reminder that even the most guarded artists can be moved to action, and that music still holds the power to unite.

Among the anticipated performers was John Lennon, long a vocal advocate for peace. Initially, Lennon accepted the invitation with enthusiasm. However, Harrison told Lennon that Yoko Ono would not be permitted on stage. For Lennon, whose personal and artistic partnership with Yoko was inseparable, this condition was unacceptable. A heated argument erupted between John and Yoko, ending with Lennon storming off to the airport and flying to France. His sudden departure left the concert without one of its biggest expected stars. Harrison also invited Paul McCartney, but Paul, then suing The Beatles, felt it would be inappropriate to appear alongside his former bandmates.

Financial hurdles and bureaucratic red tape added to the strain. Organizing a multi-artist benefit in the heart of New York City meant navigating city permits, coordinating security, and managing a constellation of high-profile performers, each with their own expectations and demands.

Still, Harrison's determination never wavered. His clarity of purpose and personal appeal brought together this diverse and often difficult group of artists for a single, noble goal. Every challenge was met with a belief that rock and roll was not just about entertainment. It was about empathy, action, and the willingness to take risks for a greater cause.

When the lights dimmed and the first notes rang out on that August night, the air crackled with energy. The Concert for Bangladesh became a defining moment, proving that music could be more than a soundtrack, it could be a lifeline. Every performance carried a sense of urgency, a shared purpose. Behind each chord and lyric was a message of compassion for a people halfway across the world.

Harrison's groundbreaking initiative not only raised critical funds for Bangladeshi refugees but also set a precedent for future charity concerts. It redefined the role of the rock musician in society, establishing that rock could be both a form of artistic expression and a powerful vehicle for social justice.

In the annals of rock history, the Concert for Bangladesh stands as a testament to the transformative power of music. It demonstrated that when icons of rock unite for a cause, they can shatter barriers and mobilize global communities. George Harrison's indomitable spirit and willingness to risk everything for humanitarian ideals paved the way for generations of artists to follow.

Even decades later, the echoes of that night continue to resonate, reminding us that in the realm of rock, the power of a well-struck chord can do far more than entertain, it can change the world.

From the chaotic backstage negotiations to the soaring melodies that filled the air, the Concert for Bangladesh remains one of the most compelling chapters in rock history, a night when music transcended boundaries, bridged cultures, and proved that compassion is the ultimate rock and roll anthem.

I was new to concert photography. I loaded up my two Nikon cameras with Kodak Tri-X film. My photos came out either overexposed or underexposed. I was so depressed. My first opportunity to photograph a rock concert turned out to be a historic event, and I was not up to the task. I managed to get a few photos that were okay, but not good enough for publication. Still, the events of the day were burned into my brain forever.

Richard M. Adler

Chapter 27

One to One Concert

John Lennon (photo by Richard Adler)

About a year later, I received a call from John Lennon asking me to photograph his One to One concert at Madison Square Garden on August 30, 1972. He told me he was only granting all-access passes to three photographers, and I couldn't believe he had chosen me. He explained that he had heard from Nat Weiss that I was photographing concerts, and since I had been associated with The Beatles and Nat, he wanted to give me a shot. From that call until the concert, I was on a high. This was huge.

249

Richard M. Adler

I contacted the editor of *Rock Magazine* and asked if he would be interested in using my photos. His response was an enthusiastic, "Hell yes!" With that, my press pass was arranged and personally delivered to my office by May Pang, who was working for Allen Klein at the time. Klein was still managing John Lennon.

There I was, a rock music fan and a John Lennon fan, standing in the pit at MSG, photographing one of my heroes. It was surreal. I had the best seat in the house, and I was loving every moment of it.

I captured some incredible photos of John and Yoko, and I was immensely proud that I had done better for John than I had for George.

After the concert, I was invited to the after-party at Tavern on the Green in Central Park. John and Yoko sat at a table by themselves, and I took plenty of photos of them dressed in white. They wore white berets. Eventually, John asked me to take pictures of other people besides just him and Yoko. To be honest, I didn't care much about anyone else who was there, and I barely remember them. I was laser-focused on John and Yoko. I eventually decided to give them a break so they could eat.

When I got home, I spent the rest of the night in my darkroom. I processed all my film, printed contact sheets, and then printed a few of my favorite shots. By 7:30 a.m., I was on my way to the city to present my photos to *Rock Magazine* before anyone else could submit theirs. In this case, the early bird truly got the worm. *Rock Magazine* purchased eight of my photos, images of John, John and Yoko, Yoko alone, as well as shots of Stevie Wonder, Roberta Flack, and Sha Na Na.

John Lennon's One to One concert remains one of rock's most enigmatic and defining live moments, a once-in-a-lifetime event that still reverberates through music history. On August 30, 1972, the former Beatle, long ensconced in the studio since The Beatles' farewell, stepped onto the stage of Madison Square Garden with a raw, urgent energy that defied his years away from full-length live performances. The event, organized as a benefit for the Willowbrook State School for children with special needs, was more than just a concert, it was a bold statement of artistic reinvention and political commitment.

For Lennon, who had grown accustomed to the controlled confines of studio work, the One to One shows marked an almost painful reawakening to the immediacy of live performance. In the weeks leading up to the concert, whispers of nervous energy and uncertainty filled the backstage corridors. Yet when the lights hit the stage, Lennon transformed that anxiety into a searing, passionate performance. Accompanied by Yoko Ono and his Plastic Ono Elephant's Memory Band, his setlist was a carefully curated journey through his evolving solo repertoire. Classics like "Instant Karma!" and "Mother" were interwoven with just one Beatles song, "Come Together," which he reimagined in a new key. The night culminated in a unifying singalong of "Give Peace a Chance," a moment that truly captured the spirit of the era.

The concert was more than just a musical performance; it was an embodiment of Lennon's growing role as a political and social activist. At a time when America was deeply divided over the Vietnam War and social upheavals were reshaping the cultural landscape, Lennon used his platform to support those who could not speak for themselves. The benefit, arranged at the urging of Geraldo Rivera, was a rallying cry for compassion, a call to arms for the disenfranchised, and a reminder that rock and roll could be a vehicle for radical hope.

As Lennon launched into "New York City," his impromptu revised lyrics underscored his commitment to turning personal artistry into a force for collective change.

Despite the immense pressure and weight of expectations, Lennon's performance radiated a rare blend of vulnerability and defiance. His delivery was starkly honest, each note and lyric imbued with the weight of his personal and political struggles, transforming Madison Square Garden into a crucible of emotional and cultural expression. It was a night where the boundaries between artist and activist blurred, and the raw immediacy of live sound cut through the noise of a turbulent world. Decades later, the performance still feels timeless, a snapshot of an artist at the pinnacle of his creative and ideological power.

For rock music fans of the era, the One to One concert offers an intimate glimpse into an artist who was both larger than life and deeply human. It stands as a testament to John Lennon's enduring influence, an echo of his belief that music, when driven by passion and purpose, can change the world. As we revisit that historic night, we are reminded that even in the face of personal doubt and a shifting cultural landscape, Lennon's revolutionary spirit shone brighter than ever. His performance wasn't just a comeback, it was a declaration that in rock and roll, authenticity and activism will always go hand in hand.

Chapter 28

Traffic at the Academy of Music

Steve Winwood (photo by Richard Adler)

I was a huge Traffic fan in 1972 and managed to get on the guest list for their show at the Academy of Music. As usual, I entered through the stage door and headed straight to the dressing room. When I walked in, I asked Steve Winwood if I could take some photos before the show. Not only did he agree, but he also invited me to sit with them for a bit.

So, there I was, sitting on the floor with Steve Winwood and Jim Capaldi, when Steve started rolling the biggest joint I had ever seen, made of tobacco and hashish. It must have been a foot long and as thick as a cigar. He lit it up and passed it to me. Suddenly, I found myself getting high with Steve Winwood and Jim Capaldi, an almost surreal moment.

As they started posing for pictures, I realized just how high I was and worried I wouldn't be able to focus the camera properly. Fortunately, I still managed to get some great shots. When it was time for Traffic to take the stage, Steve brought me along, telling me to stay in the wings and photograph the show from there.

Once again, I went home, processed the film, made contact sheets and prints, and ended up selling my photos to *Circus Magazine*.

It was a time when every encounter, no matter how fleeting, left a trace, a reminder that life's most memorable stories often begin with a single, unanticipated moment.

Chapter 29

The Woodburne Lunatic Fringe

In the summer of 1973, I produced concerts in the Catskill Mountains at the Woodburne Theater in Woodburne, New York.

I rented a house in Monticello for the summer and made it a working vacation. I booked a number of shows that season, ranging from Commander Cody and His Lost Planet Airmen and Climax Blues Band to comedians Lenny Schultz and Robert Klein.

Lenny Schultz

Before observational humor became the dominant force in stand-up, before meticulously crafted narratives ruled the stage, there was Lenny Schultz. He wasn't known for biting social commentary or introspective anecdotes. Instead, Lenny Schultz was a whirlwind of manic energy, a human sound machine, and a master of physical comedy, carving out a unique and memorable career in the world of laughter.

For those of us growing up in Forest Hills, Lenny was more than just a name on TV. He was a local legend, a neighbor who lived just a few blocks away.

Lenny Schultz was not just a comedian. He was also a dedicated gym teacher and the energetic gym director at the Rego Park Jewish Center. Even before his national breakthrough, he was honing his craft, often asking local musicians and concert promoters like me to book him as an opening act. He had played the circuit in the Catskills, the legendary Borscht Belt, where his high-energy, prop-filled comedy was already winning over audiences, especially the hotel staff who lived and worked there.

Schultz burst onto the national scene in the late 1960s and early 1970s, a time when variety shows and late-night television were king. He wasn't just telling jokes, he was the joke. His act was a frantic, breathless performance, a symphony of bizarre noises and exaggerated movements. Imagine a comedian who could seamlessly transition from the sound of a revving motorcycle to a creaking door to a flock of seagulls, all using only his voice and body. That was Lenny Schultz.

His big break came with appearances on *The Merv Griffin Show*, which led to further success on *The Tonight Show Starring Johnny Carson*, *The Ed Sullivan Show*, and countless others. He became a fixture on shows like *The Mike Douglas Show*, captivating audiences with his sheer absurdity and infectious enthusiasm. He didn't rely on punchlines so much as pure, unadulterated silliness. He would contort his face, flail his arms, and unleash a torrent of sound effects, often leaving audiences in stitches without uttering a single traditional setup.

I enjoyed watching him on Jim Bouton's *Ball Four* as Lenny "Birdman" Siegel.

His catchphrase, "Go crazy, Lenny!" became a rallying cry for his fans, urging him on to even more outrageous antics. And crazy he certainly could be.

I booked Lenny at the Woodburne Theater. He assured me he would draw a crowd, boasting about his popularity with the Catskills hotel staff. He was right. As soon as Lenny hit the stage that Wednesday night, the audience erupted, shouting, "Go crazy, Lenny!" And he delivered in spectacular, messy fashion.

He brought out a watermelon, sliced it open, and proceeded to smash pieces all over himself, the stage, and even the front rows of the audience. Not stopping there, he then produced a jar of peanut butter and slathered handfuls of it across his body. It was pure Lenny Schultz, visual, visceral, and undeniably unique.

While some critics might have dismissed his style as simply silly, it was undeniably effective. He tapped into a primal sense of humor, a childlike delight in mimicry and physical comedy that transcended language barriers and intellectual pretenses.

Often assisted by his wife Helen with props, Lenny's live stand-up act, unlike his more sanitized television appearances, could even delve into lewd or adult humor, showcasing his versatility.

Despite his growing fame, Lenny remained grounded. He continued working as a high school gym teacher throughout his comedy career. He was known to leave clubs early on school nights, balancing the glitz of the stage with the responsibilities of his day job. He even recounted how principals and fellow teachers would ask for autographs after seeing him on TV the night before. That was a testament to his widespread appeal.

Within the comedy community, Lenny was respected as a hard act to follow. His unique and energetic performances left lasting impressions.

While he might not have achieved the household-name recognition of some of his contemporaries, Lenny Schultz enjoyed a long and successful career. He toured extensively and performed in clubs and casinos for decades. His influence is undeniable. Comedians like Gallagher, Carrot Top, and Angel Salazar often cite his kinetic style as an inspiration. He garnered praise from across generations, from Brett Butler and David Letterman to Jon Stewart and Billy Crystal. The latter two attested to his consistent ability to kill and earn standing ovations.

Lenny Schultz might not be the first name that comes to mind when discussing comedy legends, but his contribution to the art form is undeniable. He proved that laughter could be generated not just through words, but through movement, sound, and sheer unbridled energy. He was a one-of-a-kind comedic force, a human sound machine who left audiences breathless with laughter. He reminded us of the joy of pure silliness.

His legacy lives on in comedians who embrace physical comedy and in the enduring appreciation for a performer who dared to be utterly, wonderfully, and hilariously bizarre.

And for some of us, he was also just a neighbor from Rego Park, and my friend.

Robert Klein

Robert Klein was a famous comedian in the 1970s. He was known for his smart jokes and funny songs. He appeared on *The Tonight Show* with Johnny Carson and had his own comedy specials on HBO. Many comedians today say he inspired them.

One day, I booked Robert Klein to perform at the Woodburne Theater. It was a big deal. People loved his comedy, and we sold out every seat in the theater. The show was going to be great, or so I thought.

Robert Klein showed up around 3:00 p.m. that afternoon. He walked in, looked around, then turned to me with a strange request.

"Got any coke?" he asked.

I was surprised. "No, sorry," I told him.

His face got serious. "I won't go on unless you get me some coke."

I wasn't sure if he was joking.

"Show me where in your contract it says I have to get you coke," I said.

He didn't answer that. He just repeated, "I need it."

"Well, I'll try," I told him. But I didn't.

A few hours passed, and it was almost showtime. The theater was packed. People were excited to see him. But just before the lights went down, I couldn't believe my ears.

"Did you get me some coke?" Klein asked again.

I looked him right in the eye and said, "No."

He shook his head. "I can't go on without it."

I pointed toward the audience. "Look out there," I said. "Do you want me to go onstage and tell them that Robert Klein isn't performing tonight because I didn't get him cocaine?"

He was silent for a moment. Then he took a deep breath.

The lights dimmed. The crowd cheered. And Robert Klein went onstage. He did his act, and the audience loved it.

In the end, the show was a success. But I never forgot that strange request. I had worked with many performers before, but this was one of the oddest moments of my career.

And Robert Klein? He kept making people laugh for years. But I always wondered, did he ever ask anyone else for coke before a show?

New Riders of the Purple Sage

Based on our success in Woodburne, we booked the New Riders of the Purple Sage at the Palace Theater in Albany, New York.

The New Riders of the Purple Sage were a country-rock band that formed in 1969. They started out as an offshoot of the Grateful Dead, with Jerry Garcia playing pedal steel guitar. Their music blended country, folk, and rock, and they became famous for songs like "Panama Red" and "Henry." Fans loved their laid-back sound, and they toured with big names like the Grateful Dead and the Allman Brothers.

By the mid-1970s, the New Riders had built a strong fan base, especially among people who loved country rock. That's why we thought they would be the perfect band to book for a concert in Albany.

We set our sights on the Palace Theater, a grand old venue with a lot of history. To make it happen, we needed money.

We approached a man who owned a movie theater in Monticello, New York, and asked if he would back us financially. He agreed, but for some reason, he always called us the Woodburne Lunatic Fringe, or WLF for short. We never quite understood why, but he seemed to enjoy saying it.

At first, everything seemed to be going well. We booked the New Riders, secured the Palace Theater, and started selling tickets. But as the concert date got closer, ticket sales were not looking good. We were worried.

I decided to take a trip up to Albany to see if I could figure out what was going wrong. I managed to get an interview on a local TV station. It was my chance to tell people that the New Riders of the Purple Sage were coming to town.

But while I was on the air, I learned something that made my stomach drop. Emerson, Lake & Palmer were playing in Albany on the same night.

ELP was one of the biggest rock bands in the world at the time. They played huge arenas, and their fans were some of the same people who might have come to see the New Riders. There was no way we could compete with that.

I went back to our financial backer and told him the bad news.

"I think we should cancel the show," I said.

He was furious. He had already paid a 50 percent deposit to the band's agent and had spent money on advertising. Now all of that money was gone.

"You're telling me I just threw my money away?" he yelled.

I felt terrible. I tried to explain that when we booked the show, ELP had not announced the Albany concert yet. There was no way we could have known.

Richard M. Adler

In the end, there was nothing we could do. We canceled the show and took the loss. Our backer was not happy, but at least we didn't end up playing to an empty theater and paying all the additional expenses. That's show biz.

Summer was ending, and it was time to head back to Queens. The Catskills were quieting down, and so were our concert plans, for now.

Even though we never got to see the New Riders of the Purple Sage take the stage that night, we learned a tough lesson about the music business.

Timing is everything.

Chapter 30

Fairport Convention

In the grand tapestry of rock and roll history, certain bands redefine an entire genre, leaving an indelible mark on the musical landscape. Fairport Convention is one such band. Emerging in the late 1960s from the folk clubs of London, they pioneered British folk rock, blending traditional English ballads with electrified instrumentation in a way that had never been done before. While their influence might not be as mainstream as The Beatles or The Rolling Stones, their impact on the folk-rock movement is undeniable, making them one of the most important and enduring bands in rock history.

Richard M. Adler

Fairport Convention was formed in 1967 in North London by guitarist Simon Nicol and bassist Ashley Hutchings. They were soon joined by guitarist Richard Thompson, drummer Martin Lamble, and vocalist Judy Dyble. Their early sound reflected the American folk-rock scene, drawing inspiration from The Byrds, Bob Dylan, and Jefferson Airplane. Their self-titled debut album, *Fairport Convention* (1968), showcased this transatlantic influence with a mix of originals and covers.

However, the band's trajectory shifted dramatically when Dyble was replaced by the unmistakable voice of Sandy Denny, a singer whose ethereal yet powerful vocals would become one of Fairport's defining characteristics. With Denny at the helm, the band began to explore British traditional folk music with a rock twist, forging a sound that was entirely their own.

By 1969, Fairport Convention had undergone significant changes, both musically and personally. After the tragic death of drummer Martin Lamble in a road accident, the band regrouped with drummer Dave Mattacks and violinist Dave Swarbrick, doubling down on their folk roots. The result was *Liege & Lief*, a landmark album that would set the template for electric folk music.

Liege & Lief was a revelation, blending traditional English ballads like "Matty Groves" and "Tam Lin" with rock energy and instrumental prowess. The album also featured original compositions like "Come All Ye," which felt just as ancient and timeless as the centuries-old songs they reinterpreted. This fusion of the old and the new would go on to define Fairport Convention's legacy and influence generations of folk and rock musicians alike.

Like many legendary rock bands, Fairport Convention's history is marked by a revolving door of talented musicians. After *Liege & Lief*,

Sandy Denny left to form Fotheringay and later embarked on a solo career before her untimely passing in 1978. Richard Thompson, whose virtuoso guitar playing had become a band trademark, also departed to pursue a solo career, ultimately becoming one of the most revered songwriters and guitarists in British music. Dave Pegg joined Fairport Convention in 1969, replacing Ashley Hutchings as the band's bassist.

Despite these losses, Fairport Convention pressed on, adapting their sound while staying true to their folk-rock roots. Albums like *Full House* (1970) and *Babbacombe Lee* (1971) showcased their ability to evolve while maintaining their identity. The latter was a bold concept album about a 19th-century English convict, further cementing their reputation as musical storytellers.

While many of their contemporaries faded away, Fairport Convention endured. In the late 1970s, they established the Cropredy Festival, an annual gathering in Oxfordshire that became a celebration of folk-rock music. What began as a small reunion event turned into one of the most beloved festivals in the UK, drawing fans from around the world and keeping Fairport's music alive for new generations.

Their influence extends far beyond their own discography. Acts like Steeleye Span, Pentangle, and even Led Zeppelin, who dabbled in English folk elements, owe a debt to Fairport Convention. Their pioneering blend of electric rock and traditional folk music paved the way for countless artists who sought to bridge past and present in their music.

In an era when rock was all about excess and rebellion, Fairport Convention took a different path, honoring tradition while fearlessly experimenting with it. Their ability to weave ancient ballads into modern rock arrangements set them apart, ensuring their music remains timeless.

Fairport Convention's story is one of resilience, reinvention, and reverence for the past. Whether through their classic albums or their legendary Cropredy Festival, they continue to shape the world of folk rock, proving that some sounds are truly timeless.

For anyone who loves rock and roll, folk music, or the blending of the two, Fairport Convention stands as a beacon of authenticity and innovation, a band that may not have chased fame but instead built a legacy.

In 1972, my good friend Shawn Becker asked me if I was interested in going on the road with Fairport Convention. She told me they needed an American roadie and that she had some pull with the band since her fiancé was Dave Swarbrick, the fiddle player and lead singer. I was busy with my photography at the time, but I thought a change of scenery might do me some good, so I accepted Shawn's offer.

I would be traveling with Andy, their English roadie, in the band's rented van. This was my first tour as a roadie, and I didn't really know what to expect, but I was game. The tour was set to last about six weeks, mostly covering the East Coast, with two dates on the West Coast, San Francisco and Los Angeles. The band was booked at some interesting venues, including Alice Tully Hall at Lincoln Center, an armory in Tampa, Florida, where we played with The Kinks and Lindisfarne, and several college shows, including one with Billy Joel.

On our way to the show with Billy Joel, we got caught in a snowstorm. As luck would have it, we ended up stuck in a snowbank, and the van refused to move. Andy and I tried everything to get it out, but nothing worked. One of us driving while the other pushed wasn't cutting it. Frustrated and on the verge of exhaustion, we decided to give it one last try before hiking to the nearest town for a tow truck. This time, we managed to literally rock the van out of the snowbank and continue on our way. We arrived at the college just in time to set up for soundcheck.

At soundcheck, I got to hang out with Billy Joel. I had known him from the Action House when he was with The Hassles. This was my first time seeing him perform as a solo act, and he absolutely blew me away. His performance was electrifying, and I was mesmerized.

One of our shows was on Long Island, which was familiar territory for me. I had lived in Bethpage from 1958 to 1961 before my family moved to Forest Hills. After the show, we returned to the hotel, where I spotted a young woman who looked like a groupie. There was something incredibly familiar about her. I found myself staring at her, trying to place her face, until it suddenly hit me. She was my former next-door neighbor from Bethpage. We had been friends as kids, but after moving away, I hadn't seen her in over a decade. Now, here she was, trying to hook up with one of the band members. When she noticed me staring, recognition flashed across her face. She turned bright red, clearly embarrassed, and without saying a word, she bolted out of the hotel lobby. I never saw her again.

For our San Francisco gig, we flew out of JFK. Traveling with a band and all their gear was no easy task. Dragging equipment through the airport was exhausting, and by the time everything was finally loaded onto the plane, it was already time to board.

At the time, I wasn't a great flyer. I was incredibly nervous, and Dave Pegg, who we all called Peggy, tried to calm me down, assuring me that everything would be fine.

Richard M. Adler

The flight was uneventful until we reached San Francisco and had to circle the airport. It felt like an eternity, and my nerves were on edge. At one point, Peggy got up to use the restroom and stopped to chat with a flight attendant. When he returned to his seat, I could tell something was wrong. I asked him what was up, and he hesitated before telling me the bad news.

He said the flight attendant had told him that the front landing gear was stuck and wouldn't deploy. The pilot had tried to release it manually, but it wouldn't budge. Meanwhile, the airport was laying down foam on the runway, preparing for an emergency landing. I went white as a ghost. My biggest fear was coming true.

Then, the descent began. I assumed the crash position, you know, bend over and kiss your ass goodbye. As we approached the runway, I braced myself for impact. The back wheels touched down. The nose of the plane started to drop. I held my breath, waiting for the inevitable crash. But instead, the plane rolled to a smooth stop. At that moment, the entire band erupted into laughter.

Turns out, they had been playing a cruel prank on me. There had never been a problem with the landing gear. We had simply been in a holding pattern due to heavy air traffic. They knew how much I hated flying and decided to have a little fun at my expense. I was so relieved to be alive that I couldn't even be mad. Once we were inside the terminal, they all came up to apologize, and I let it go. I guess I'm a good sport.

In San Francisco, we stayed at the Miyako Hotel, a beautifully designed Japanese hotel that reflected traditional Japanese architecture. The hotel featured Zen gardens, a koi pond, and a stunning six-million-dollar Japanese art collection. The blend of

Japanese and Californian styles created a unique and serene atmosphere.

Shawn Becker was on tour with us, as she was about to marry Dave Swarbrick. One night, after a heated argument, things took a dramatic turn. Shawn was furious about something and, in a fit of rage, grabbed Dave's Martin guitar, which was safely stored in its anvil case, and hurled it off the sixth-floor balcony.

The guitar smashed through the windshield of a car parked in front of the hotel. Shortly after, the hotel manager called my room and asked to see me. He asked if we had lost a guitar. Unaware of what had just transpired, I told him I would need to see it to confirm. He then informed me that I would have to retrieve it from the car's windshield.

Sure enough, when I went outside, I saw the familiar anvil case lodged in the shattered glass. Miraculously, despite the dramatic fall, the guitar itself was unharmed. I retrieved it and returned it to its rightful owner.

Life on the road was never dull, and this tour was proving to be one for the books.

Fairport played three nights at Winterland in San Francisco with King Crimson.

The day after the last San Francisco gig, we drove down to Los Angeles to do a show at the Santa Monica Civic Auditorium. We stayed at the Tropicana Motel, which had become the place to stay for rock bands in LA.

The Tropicana Motel was a hotspot for rock bands in the 1970s for several key reasons. Located at 8585 Santa Monica Boulevard in West Hollywood, it was close to legendary music venues like the

Whisky a Go Go, The Roxy, and the Rainbow Bar & Grill, all central to the rock scene. Unlike upscale hotels such as the Chateau Marmont or the Beverly Hills Hotel, the Tropicana offered a laid-back, affordable alternative that catered to musicians' lifestyles. It became famous for its rock star–friendly policies, allowing for wild parties, loud music, and eccentric behavior. The management was accustomed to dealing with late-night antics, trashed rooms, and impromptu jam sessions, making it an ideal retreat for musicians who wanted to let loose without consequences.

The motel's guest list included some of the most legendary rock stars of the era. Tom Waits lived there for years, often writing songs in his room, while The Ramones were regular guests whenever they were in LA. Other notable names who stayed there included Elvis Costello, Blondie, Iggy Pop, Led Zeppelin, Van Halen, and The Runaways, all of whom used it as a crash pad. Adding to its appeal was Duke's Coffee Shop, an attached diner that became a hangout for musicians, groupies, and industry insiders. Known for its cheap food, it was the perfect spot to nurse hangovers and network with fellow rockers.

The Tropicana cultivated an "outlaw" reputation, gaining a cult status as a place where bands could be themselves without judgment. It was immortalized in rock documentaries and song lyrics, further cementing its mystique. However, by the late 1980s, as the rock scene evolved and shifted, the Tropicana lost its relevance. In 1987, it was demolished to make way for office buildings. Despite its demise, the Tropicana remains legendary, often regarded as the West Coast's answer to the Chelsea Hotel in New York City, a gritty, no-frills haven where rock musicians could live by their own rules.

I have a lot of family in Los Angeles, and I invited my cousin Carol to the show. I put her name on the guest list and made sure there were tickets left at the box office for her. Carol and her children still talk about that night. I was happy to include them.

Touring with Fairport Convention and playing a show with The Kinks and Lindisfarne was the kind of experience that blurred the lines between dream and reality. Each band carried its own energy, its own chaos, and its own legends in the making. The Kinks were the quintessential British rock rebels, Ray and Dave Davies constantly at odds but creating music that would outlive them. Fairport Convention, with their folk-rock mastery, gave every show a sense of timelessness, especially when Dave Pegg and Dave Swarbrick let loose with their intricate melodies. And Lindisfarne? They were the Geordie folk-rock powerhouse, their harmonies as tight as their camaraderie. Together, we were a traveling circus of music, alcohol, and misadventure.

It was a humid Florida night, the kind where the air sticks to your skin and the whiskey flows just as easily as the conversation. We had a night off in Tampa, so naturally, we found ourselves in a club, looking for trouble, or at least for a decent band and a few drinks. Along for the ride were Ray and Dave Davies, Dave Pegg and Dave Swarbrick from Fairport, and a couple of other bandmates, including the phenomenal guitarist Roger Hill and drummer Tom Farnell. It didn't take long before the drinks started working their magic, and we got loud enough to draw attention.

The house band, a solid barroom rock-and-roll outfit, recognized us (well, Ray and Dave) and asked if we wanted to jump onstage for a jam. These kinds of spontaneous gigs could go either way. You either embarrass yourself beyond redemption, or you make the night unforgettable.

Richard M. Adler

We chose the latter.

Ray counted us in, and we launched into Chuck Berry's "Sweet Little Sixteen," a song we all knew like the back of our hands. The crowd, mostly local rock fans and bar regulars, ate it up. Ray and Dave Davies were in rare form, trading off vocals, while Pegg and Swarbrick held down the groove like they'd been born to it.

Then, it happened.

During a musical break, Ray pointed at me for a solo. Now, I'd had just enough to drink that my brain thought, why not have a little fun? Instead of keeping it straight Chuck Berry, I ripped into the guitar solo from "Surfin' USA" by The Beach Boys. Same chords, different vibe.

The band cracked up. Peggy was practically crying from laughter, and Ray nearly dropped his mic. It was one of those musical inside jokes that only made sense in the moment, but damn, it landed. We rolled through a few more tunes, the kind of loose, raw rock and roll that felt alive in a way no carefully structured concert ever could.

Somewhere around the third or fourth song, I noticed the club owner standing at the edge of the stage, motioning me over. At first, I figured he wanted to thank us or maybe even offer us another round. Instead, he leaned in close and said in a loud, urgent voice:

"You have to stop playing. Now!"

I turned to the band. "I think we need to wrap it up."

Dave Davies grinned. "Just one more."

So we kept going.

Ten minutes later, the owner was back. Only this time, he wasn't alone. In his hands was a shotgun, and he wasn't just holding it for show.

Everything stopped. The band. The music. The laughter. The booze-fueled bravado.

He pointed the gun at my head and glared at me. "We have a 1:00 AM curfew. If I don't shut this place down, I lose my liquor license."

In that moment, I was completely sober.

We put down our instruments faster than a band getting stiffed on a paycheck. The owner, satisfied that the message had been received, lowered the shotgun and muttered something about loving the music but needing to keep his business intact.

We slipped out of the club, still buzzing with adrenaline, and found ourselves back on the streets of Tampa, laughing in that way you do when you just narrowly avoided disaster. Dave Davies, years later, would bring up that night when I visited him backstage at one of his solo gigs in Suffern, New York, and we cracked up all over again.

"Remember the guy with the shotgun?" he'd say.

"Oh yeah. And you wanted to play just one more song."

And that, in a nutshell, was rock and roll.

The Fairport Convention tour had finally come to an end. It had been a long run, filled with the usual chaos, stunning performances, and the occasional near-disaster. But as the last gig wrapped up and the crew packed up their gear, the band's fiddler, Dave Swarbrick, had his mind on something else, his upcoming wedding to Shawn Becker.

It was an unexpected pairing, but Swarb had always been full of surprises. Shawn, a sharp and witty woman with a deep love for music, had captured his heart somewhere between the green rooms and the soundchecks. And so, not long after the tour bus was parked for good, the invitations went out.

The wedding was a proper Jewish affair, and seeing the members of Fairport Convention decked out in yarmulkes was a sight I'll never forget. Roger Hill adjusted his nervously every few minutes, as if it might fly off at any moment. Tom Farnell, ever the stoic one, wore his with a quiet dignity, while Dave Pegg spent half the night making jokes about how it made him look like a rabbi.

And then there was Swarb, beaming, laughing, and completely in his element. The ceremony itself was beautiful, full of tradition and warmth. And the reception? Absolute mayhem in the best way.

I was snapping photos the whole time, knowing full well that *Circus* magazine would eat them up. The sight of Fairport Convention celebrating in such an unexpected setting was too good to pass up. And sure enough, the shots of Swarb hoisting a glass of wine under the chuppah and the band linking arms in a raucous hora ended up in print, immortalizing the night in all its chaotic glory.

But of course, we all knew it wouldn't last. There were signs, little cracks in the fairytale. The infamous guitar incident said it all: Shawn, in a fit of rage, hurling one of Swarb's prized instruments off a balcony. It was dramatic, ridiculous, and completely unsurprising to anyone who had been around them long enough.

Not long after, the marriage unraveled. It didn't take a psychic to predict that it would end in divorce. When the dust settled, Fairport moved on. The tour cycle began again, and the yarmulkes were packed away in dresser drawers as odd souvenirs of a night that felt, in hindsight, like a dream.

Still, for that one night, it was magic, a wild, unexpected chapter in the never-ending, often chaotic story of Fairport Convention.

Dave Swarbrick (photo by Richard Adler)

I interviewed Dave Swarbrick about Fairport Convention's album *Babbacombe Lee* for *Circus Magazine.*

Fairport Convention and "The Man They Could Not Hang" was the title of the article.

"Miss Keyse was found lying on her dining room floor with her throat horribly cut. The murderer had obviously attempted to burn the body."

David Swarbrick's story of what could be the year's most unusual LP by Richard Adler

It is the morning of Monday, February 23, 1885. In a shed behind Exeter Prison, England, a chaplain opens his Bible and nervously begins to read aloud. The hangman leads a tall, clean-shaven young man to a trapdoor set into the floorboards, straps his ankles together, places a black bag over his head, slips the noose around his neck, and steps to the side.

John Lee stands alone, his throat dry, his teeth clenched, waiting for his death. The bell clangs, the bolt is pulled, the trap door falls two inches and stops. John Lee's heart beats frantically, but he is alive, standing on his toes, the rope still loose around his neck.

Fifteen minutes later, they try to hang him again.

Bizarre headline: Fairport Convention, the peculiarly unstable group that spearheaded Britain's electric-folk revival, has just unleashed what could be one of the strangest albums of 1972, the musical tale of John Babbacombe Lee.

Dave Swarbrick, Fairport Convention's short, elf-like fiddler, had been browsing in a cluttered antique shop when he spotted a bundle of newspapers whose yellowing pages sported a bizarre headline:

"John Lee of Babbacombe: THE MAN THEY COULD NOT HANG."

Swarbrick bought the bundle and took it home, determined to use it as the basis for a new song. But as he became more absorbed in the distressing details of John Lee's life, what had begun as a single song soon grew to three, then six, and finally nine.

The result was a milestone in Fairport Convention's tumultuous career, *John Babbacombe Lee* (on A&M Records), an album of hypnotic melodies and brooding themes, the last LP the group was to record with its only remaining original member, Simon Nicol.

Ever since 1966, Fairport Convention has pioneered the electric exploration of folk music in England. That was the year in which Simon Nicol, Richard Thompson, Ashley Hutchings, Judy Dyble, and the late Martin Lamble got together in Simon's house, adopted the title of the Ethnic Shuffle Orchestra, and began to wed folk music's soft sounds and social themes with rock's crisp rhythms.

Disastrous itch: Since then, the organization has garnered the kind of historical respect reserved for the Byrds in America, but it has also been plagued by a nearly disastrous itch for change. Fairport has shuffled members as regularly as James Bond trades in mistresses, leaving in its wake many a distinguished alumnus. Ian Matthews entered the group, then dropped out to form Matthews' Southern Comfort. Ashley Hutchings left to organize Steeleye Span. Judy Dyble was replaced by Sandy Denny, who split to go solo and eventually captured the title of England's Best Female Vocalist. Drummer Martin Lamble was killed when Fairport's van crashed. And the story goes on and on. Dave Swarbrick finally fell in with the group two and a half years ago and injected the jig-like rhythms of his violin into the total sound.

Swarbrick flew to New York not long ago to round out arrangements for his wedding to American Shawn Becker and spent several hours outlining the story of John Babbacombe Lee to photographer Richard Adler.

Adler reports:

I picked Swarb up at the airport, and we spent the weekend together. Two hours before he took off for England again, we set up the tape recorder in my girlfriend's bedroom, a converted dinette done up completely in white except for the red rug on the floor. The four of us, Swarb, his fiancée, my girlfriend Bernice, and I, were sitting together on the bed.

Swarb, who's an energetic little guy, 5'3", with a mustache and an earring, rested up against the white wicker headboard until I started to ask him questions. Then he got excited and leaned forward to illustrate his points with his hands, while his intense facial expressions drove home the seriousness of what he had to say.

What inspired the *John Babbacombe Lee* album?

I was knocking around junk shops and came across a bunch of old newspapers collected together and placed in a folder that had been autographed by this cat John Lee. The file turned out to be his life's story, so I bought them, took them home, and read them up.

What's the story about?

Babbacombe Lee is a story about a bloke who was convicted of murder. They put him on the gallows, but they couldn't hang him.

They tried three times and failed. English law prohibits attempting to hang a man more than three times, so they gave him 22 years in prison instead.

The album goes into the chapters of his life which I felt were the highlights. John Lee was in the Navy for 18 months and was discharged with pneumonia, which seemed to him at that time to be the worst thing that could ever happen to him. He couldn't have known what fate had in store for him later.

What actually happened to him?

They put him on the gallows three times, and it failed to work. Actually, since the album came out in England, I've had a talk with a guy whose relative was one of the carpenters who built the gallows for John Lee. It was sort of a working man's organization that this bloke belonged to, and they were very much on the side of John Lee. They thought he'd been framed.

The story I get is that they rigged the gallows so that it wouldn't open. They did it by putting a plank of wood on the platform that was warped. It was warped at the exact spot where the priest would stand (the place where the priest stood was regulated by law at this time and was marked off by a painted white square), so that when the priest's weight rested on the plank of wood, it would unwarp, straighten out, come against the flange of the trap door, and stop it from opening. So, every time they put the priest on the gallows with John Lee, it wouldn't work. When they took John Lee off to test the gallows, obviously the priest wasn't going to be standing in the same spot. Then they would try it with a man holding onto the rope, and of course it would work. It only wouldn't work when the priest was standing on that spot. But that story isn't the gospel.

Richard M. Adler

Could you go through the record and Lee's story track by track?

Yeah. It opens with the death sentence being read, which leads into a cut called "Little Did I Think."

This is a song in which John Lee states that he never thought he would be set free. I wrote that one, it was one of the first. The song is based on broadside ballads. When people were hanged in public, professional songwriters would follow the cart, get the story from the condemned man, and then write a song as if it came from the mouth of the condemned person. It gave the story in his words, right up to the point where he'd say something like, "The rope was around my neck, and it hurt." So the first song is based on that form. It has the same format and the same kind of stanzas.

The instrumentation is very simple. We used mandolin, guitar, bass, and drums, and it's written in fifths.

Then comes a song called "When I Was 16," which is a flashback showing that John Lee is fed up with being working class. It's like him saying, "What is expected of me? I don't want to be a servant. I want to see the world." But everything's against him: his background and his station in life. What's he supposed to do? What his parents think, what everyone thinks.

Is this the old case of running away to sea to escape a depressing life?

If you like, yeah, except that he's got his parents' permission to get away.

The song also deals with him working for the woman who was murdered, Miss Keyse, as sort of a downstairs boy. Then he convinces his parents to let him join the Navy.

280

"When I Was 16" was written by Peggy and Simon. In the middle of that composition, there's another song which gives Lee's parents' point of view. The parents say that the sea is fickle and land isn't, with words like: "John, my son, don't join the Navy. There's no good in it, I know. Plant your seeds on solid ground and watch your harvest grow."

After "When I Was 16," we do an instrumental which is sort of nameless, with a couple of hornpipes. They won't mean much in America because they're actually signature tunes used on British naval radio shows. They're a little camp, but they don't really get it in England either.

The last verse of "When I Was 16" leads you right into the Navy.

His father gives him permission to join and signs the papers. Then John Lee goes down to get the papers signed by the Admiral. The instrumental and the "Sailor's Alphabet" were designed as a light spot because being in the Navy was really the only bright spot in his life. The "Sailor's Alphabet" serves as an interlude. If you want to get clever about it, you can say it symbolized an interlude in his life. Being a sailor was his ambition, and it was the only thing he really enjoyed doing. Apart from that, everything was heavy.

After the "Sailor's Alphabet," there's a long track. Then comes a song called "John Lee," which is the first intimation on the record that everything is not quite right. See, up until that point, everything has been hunky-dory and the music has been a bit pretty. But "John Lee" is a heavy song that bangs straight in. When it ends, there's a reading of a newspaper item that states a woman has been found murdered. She's Miss Keyse, the woman John Lee worked for when he was fifteen. You see, he goes back to work for her after he's discharged from the Navy.

Lee had been forced to leave the service after a bout with pneumonia. When he was discharged, he tried his hand at various trades but was unhappy with all of them. He was overjoyed when Miss Keyse asked him to return to her household, "The Glen," as a servant.

The newspaper article states that Miss Keyse was found lying on her dining room floor with her throat horribly cut, and that the murderer had obviously attempted to burn her body. It doesn't say anyone has been charged.

The next song dates the incident and shows it through the eyes of a middle-aged couple living in a fashionable area, where problems like those John Lee faced were unheard of.

They're discussing the incident over breakfast. It's the usual case of people reacting callously to someone they don't know. The husband reads the article aloud to his wife, but neither of them is truly interested. To them, it's just conversation. The song ends with her saying, "So put that paper down before your breakfast goes quite rotten."

A short time before the murder, Miss Keyse, knowing John Lee was anxious to find a better position in life, he had intentions of marrying, suggested that he join the Army and said she would get her friends to promote him. She was always fond of Lee and very kind to him, so John regarded Miss Keyse as his best friend.

After discovering her murder, John said, "I have lost my best friend," and he meant it. But he was immediately arrested on suspicion of her murder.

The next piece is "The Trial Song," and again it's given from John Lee's point of view, in the first person. In this song, the words are the most horrifying because there's such a typically English attitude toward the court. John Lee's mindset is, "I'm right, but I must be wrong if they're trying me, because they're better than me." One line in the song is: "The judge sits high and mighty, and he asks me who I am." Which is pretty bizarre, because of course the judge knows who he is.

Then the song continues: "The robes he wears impress me, but he looks a kindly man," which is really quite horrible, because he isn't kindly at all, but it's the image of justice.

We come out of that into "The Condemned Song." This is probably the best song on the record for me. It's ultra-simple because it's a subject most people can relate to in some way or another. Not many of us have been accused of a serious crime or been in the Navy, but all of us are waiting to die. What I tried to do was describe everyday events inside John Lee's cell, like a bird sitting on the window sill. If I say, "I'm sitting here waiting to die and watching a bird on the sill," everybody can picture what it's like.

What people have missed in this track is that it's a parody of a Victorian song. Instrumentally, it's flowery. You know, Victorians were the only ones who could sing about the most terrible subjects so flippantly and sentimentally. They'd tell you the worst aspects of sad and terrible things and turn them into something glorious, very sentimental, hand-over-the-heart and all that.

After the condemned song, things get really heavy. You're getting very near the time it's going to happen. You're also dealing with a magical incident: a dream John Lee had the night before they were supposed to execute him. When he gets up in the morning, he tells his guards about the dream. He dreamt he was on the gallows and heard the bolt being drawn to open the trapdoor below him, but the scaffold wouldn't work. He sees this happening three times in his dream. Each time they try to hang him, they fail.

It is now eight o'clock in the morning, and the door of John Lee's cell is opened. The governor, the executioner, and the priest enter. After all is made ready (a belt is placed around John Lee's waist and the executioner straps Lee's arms to it, then straps his wrists together near the buckle), the procession starts on its way to the gallows. This path leads through a part of the prison John Lee has never seen before, but he recognizes it anyway.

He tries to remember where he's seen it and suddenly realizes it is the same place that appeared in the dream. He is then led into the garden, and this too is the same as in his dream. He's going over the same path, the same ground. John Lee thinks, "Good heavens, this part of the dream has come true. Suppose the other part comes true as well. Suppose I am not executed at all."

The album comes straight out of the "Dream Song" and right into a factual account of what happened when they attempted to hang John Lee, a very understated, factual song.

Public opinion at that time held that John Lee's mother was a witch and that a coven gathered on the moors the night before the scheduled execution to try to save him.

Was public opinion on his side?

I think that the working man's opinion was very much on his side. He was sort of a hero.

Do you feel that John Lee really committed the murder?

Well, I don't think so, and he says no.

Was it a frame-up?

This is where it gets into some sort of social commentary. Lee worked from 1840 to 1860 in England, which at that time was almost feudal. John Lee was as working-class as you could get, and Miss Keyse was as aristocratic as you could get. All the courts and the government were aristocrats, so naturally they weren't going to give John Lee a fair trial.

Would you say this album was musically different from your other albums?

Well, yes and no. A lot of people think so, but I don't.

What I wanted to do was have eight or nine incidents that were related and led up to the attempted hanging, so that every incident told its own story and didn't have to be directly related to the next one, although they were all parts of John Lee's life.

It wasn't designed as an opera. I didn't sit down and say, "This is where it's going to start, and this is where it's going to finish." In fact, the LP finishes at the point where they're hanging him three times, but John Lee doesn't finish there. He did 22 years in prison, but the album doesn't go into that.

You know, all I was thinking of at that point was being hanged three times and getting away with it. It's incredible. How could it have happened to him? What was he thinking?

One of the tracks sounds like a group of men singing in an English pub. What track was that?

It's the "Sailors' Alphabet." What we tried to do with this song was make it as rough and as much like an 1800s Navy song as we could. We wanted it to sound as if it was really being sung by sailors, and you didn't get professional singers on board Her Majesty's warships. The song actually comes from the 1860s. It's the only composition on the album not by Fairport Convention.

I can tell that you were trying to get that old English folk sound.

Well, it's deliberately under-arranged. The group is involved in the folk scene, and that's just naturally the way you do it if you're doing a traditional song. In fact, we never actually arranged it.

One of the criticisms of this record in England is that it doesn't finish dramatically or on a high note. You see, John Lee's story doesn't finish there. He went on to serve 22 years in prison (which Lee said were the most harrowing years of his life). Other critics have said that the words in this album overshadow the music, and if that's so, then I am pleased. I feel that the chords and the music have equal importance, but what the critics say is really garbage. I don't think anyone will understand "Babbacombe Lee" for another five years.

Chapter 31

Buzzy Linhart

Buzzy Linhart (photo by Richard Adler)

Buzzy Linhart's name might not immediately ring bells like those of Hendrix or Joplin, but his influence in the 60s music scene was as pervasive as it was profound. Here, we delve deeper into examples of his impact and why he remains an essential figure in music history.

In the vibrant year of 1963, the streets of New York City became the new home for a young, ambitious Buzzy Linhart. It was here that his journey took a pivotal turn. Buzzy forged a close friendship and shared living quarters with John Sebastian, another burgeoning talent of the time. In this bustling artistic hub, Linhart found himself under the tutelage of renowned guitarist and folk singer Fred Neil, whose influence would play a significant role in shaping his musical direction.

One of Linhart's earliest forays into the music scene was with his band, Seventh Sons. Alongside fellow musicians Steve De Naut, Serge Katzen, and Max Ochs, Seventh Sons carved a niche in the evolving genre of raga-rock. Their groundbreaking LP, released under ESP Records, was a testament to their innovative sound that blended traditional rock elements with the mystical rhythms of Indian raga.

The late 1960s to the mid-1970s marked a prolific period for Linhart, as he embarked on a solo career that would solidify his place in the music world. His debut album, fittingly titled "buzzy" (with an intentionally lowercase "b"), released in 1969 under Philips Records, was just the beginning. This period saw Linhart unleashing his creative prowess, exploring a range of musical styles that reflected his eclectic taste and versatility.

1971 was another landmark year for Linhart, as he signed with Eleuthera Records. Though he was deeply entrenched in the Greenwich Village folk-rock scene, his first full-fledged solo album was recorded across the Atlantic in London and Wales. For this venture, he teamed up with the Welsh progressive rock band Eyes of

Blue, who lent their unique sound as his backing band. This collaboration underscored Linhart's ability to blend diverse musical worlds seamlessly.

Linhart's mastery of the vibraphone, an instrument not typically associated with rock music, made him a sought-after session musician. His distinctive touch on the vibraphone can be heard in recordings by a spectrum of artists, from Buffy Sainte-Marie's haunting melodies to Richie Havens' soulful folk tunes, Carly Simon's evocative songs, and the innovative sounds of Cat Mother & the All Night Newsboys. Notably, Linhart's collaboration with Jimi Hendrix stands out, contributing to the song "Drifting" on the legendary Cry of Love album and receiving credits on Electric Ladyland. Buzzy played vibraphone on the Hendrix track "Drifting" and drums on a live jam session with Hendrix, Noel Redding, and Al Kooper, which included "Like a Rolling Stone" at an uptown club called The Scene in 1969, showcasing Linhart's versatility and ability to blend with various music styles.

Fast forward to 2005, Linhart continued to make waves in the music scene. He recorded "Mr. Cool" for the CD Life Goes On, collaborating with artists Monica Dupont and Gary Novak. This track reflected his enduring talent and adaptability, showcasing his ability to remain relevant and impactful in a constantly evolving musical landscape.

Buzzy was responsible for Jesse Colin Young's big hit "Get Together." Jesse had heard Buzzy play the song at Café Au Go Go one afternoon during an open mic jam. After Buzzy's set, Jesse asked him to show him how to play it. Buzzy not only taught him the chords and arrangement but also wrote out the lyrics and chords so Jesse wouldn't forget them. The song would eventually become an anthem for the 1960s peace culture.

Richard M. Adler

"I will never forget the first time I heard it, when I just dropped by the Café Au Go Go where the Youngbloods were playing regularly, and heard Buzzy Linhart on stage with his bass player and drummer singing 'Get Together.' Those words just went through me like a spear. It was like one of those movies about the Bible where the clouds open up and the light comes in. That's what happened to me. I ran backstage and asked him to write down the lyrics because I had to   sing   it."
– Jesse Colin Young

Linhart's songwriting talents shone brightly with his work for other artists. The most notable is "Friends," co-written with Mark "Moogy" Klingman, which Bette Midler turned into an anthem of love and unity. This song alone showcases Linhart's knack for creating timeless tunes that resonate across generations.

Linhart was a pioneering figure in popularizing the vibraphone in rock music. His use of the instrument added a unique layer to the 60s sound palette, influencing bands to experiment with less conventional sounds in their compositions.

Buzzy was also an early adopter of Eastern musical influences. His incorporation of these sounds predated the more celebrated forays of The Beatles and other contemporaries into Eastern music. This aspect of his work highlights his role as a precursor to trends that would later dominate the music world.

Beyond his tangible musical contributions, Linhart's role as a mentor and inspiration to other musicians cements his importance. Stories from peers illustrate how he generously shared his knowledge and enthusiasm, impacting numerous artists' careers and creative directions.

Buzzy Linhart's significance in the 60s music landscape extends beyond mere song credits or collaborations. He was a forerunner, a mentor, and an innovator whose influence rippled through the music of the era and beyond. While he may not have sought the spotlight, his legacy in shaping the sound and spirit of a pivotal musical decade is undeniable. As we celebrate the icons of the 60s, let us also remember the instrumental figures like Linhart, who helped orchestrate the era's unforgettable soundtrack.

In 1974, I was the road manager for Buzzy Linhart. Buzzy had also just hired a new band, which he named Shoo-Fly after his song "Shoo That Fly" from his album Pussycats Can Go Far. The band consisted of some awesome musicians from Long Island, led by Jim Roberge on keyboards, Chris Carberry on guitar, Carl Mignano on drums, and Terry Woodward on bass.

We had a gig lined up in Cleveland at the Agora, and after a long day of travel, Buzzy, the band, and I found ourselves unwinding over dinner at the Holiday Inn in downtown Cleveland. The hotel restaurant was relatively quiet, the low hum of conversation mixing with the clinking of silverware against plates. As we ate, I noticed a man approach our table from the corner of my eye. Figuring he was just another fan looking for an autograph or a quick conversation with Buzzy, I didn't even bother looking up. But then, a familiar voice rang out with unmistakable enthusiasm:

"Richard Adler! What are you doing in Cleveland?"

I looked up from my plate, and there, standing in front of me, was Walter Becker from Steely Dan. Walter and I had played together back in high school, part of the vibrant and unpredictable music scene of the 1960s. Walter, Randy California, and I had a band called Newport News that played a few clubs in Greenwich Village.

Seeing him there, years later, both of us now firmly entrenched in the business, was a surreal moment. We caught up briefly, reminiscing about old times, our days in bands together, and our journeys since. I introduced him to Buzzy and the band, and after a bit of conversation, Walter grinned and said,

"Listen, we're playing tonight. You guys should come to the show."

It was an incredible offer. Steely Dan was one of the most respected acts of the time, and getting a personal invite from Walter himself was an opportunity I couldn't pass up.

Fortunately, Buzzy didn't go on until 10:30 p.m., so we had enough time to make it work. After dinner, as we stepped out of the hotel to get some air, a large tour bus pulled up to the entrance. The doors swung open, and out stepped a familiar face, Jock, an old friend of mine who had been in the touring business for years.

"Jock! What are you doing in Cleveland?" I called out, genuinely surprised to see him.

Jock and I had worked together when I promoted Magical Mystery Tour.

With a grin, Jock walked over and said, "I'm James Taylor and Carly Simon's road manager. We've got a show tonight. You should come."

It was a small world, indeed. As much as I wanted to check out their concert, I explained that we had already accepted Walter's invitation to Steely Dan's show. But then I had an idea.

"Why don't James and Carly come to Buzzy's show later tonight?" I suggested.

Jock considered it, then said he'd run it by James and Carly. After a quick discussion, he returned with the answer: they were in.

Now, there was an interesting wrinkle here. Carly Simon and Buzzy had once been an item. In fact, he had written "Love Still Growing" about her. I had no idea how that reunion would play out, but I figured the music would carry the night and any potential awkwardness would be overshadowed by the incredible talent that would soon converge in one place. I also decided to keep it a surprise for Buzzy. After all, what's rock and roll without a little drama?

That night, we made our way to the Steely Dan concert, where Walter greeted us warmly and insisted, we watch the show from the wings of the stage. Seeing them perform live for the first time was an experience like no other. The musicianship, the precision, the sheer artistry that defined Steely Dan was on full display. The band was tight, the crowd electric, and even though we couldn't stay for the entire set, we were absolutely blown away. At one point, I caught Walter's attention from the side of the stage and gestured that we had to head out. He gave a nod and a thumbs-up, understanding that duty called.

That was the first time I ever saw Steely Dan live. The last would be decades later, in 2016, but that night in Cleveland would always stand out.

We rushed back to the Agora, arriving just in time for Buzzy to take the stage around 10:30 p.m.

The set was in full swing, the crowd grooving along, when, around midnight, James Taylor and Carly Simon quietly entered through the backstage area. I greeted them and gave them a quick rundown of what was happening on stage. Buzzy had just begun playing "Love

Still Growing," the song he had written for Carly. I turned to her with an idea and handed her a live microphone.

"You know the song," I said with a grin.

From the darkness of backstage, Carly started singing backup to Buzzy's lead vocals. The moment her voice floated into the microphone, Buzzy visibly reacted, his face scrunched in confusion as he heard a female voice harmonizing with him. He looked around, trying to locate the source. Then, as if perfectly timed for maximum impact, Carly stepped onto the stage.

The crowd erupted. Buzzy, still mid-song, was stunned, but he kept playing. Carly continued singing, their voices blending in a way that was both nostalgic and magical. It was an incredible moment, charged with history and raw emotion.

And just when it seemed like the night couldn't get any more surreal, James Taylor walked onto the stage. The audience went absolutely wild. Without hesitation, James and Carly launched into "Mockingbird," and the energy in the room skyrocketed.

Then, as if fate had arranged it, James's band, David Spinozza, Hugh McCracken, and Rick Marotta, joined in, seamlessly merging with Buzzy's band, Shoo-Fly. What followed was an impromptu jam session that felt like something out of a dream. James, caught up in the moment, grabbed one of Buzzy's Stratocasters to join the jam. But as soon as he started playing, he paused, a puzzled expression crossing his face.

"What the hell," he muttered, looking down at the guitar.

Buzzy burst out laughing. The Strat was tuned to open E, something James hadn't expected. He fumbled for a moment, then adjusted and rolled with it, diving into the groove like the pro he was.

The music continued late into the night, a once-in-a-lifetime jam session featuring some of the greatest musicians of the era, all sharing a stage in Cleveland. The audience was in awe, witnessing something truly special, something that wasn't planned, couldn't be rehearsed, and would never happen the same way again.

That night in Cleveland was more than just another gig. It was a perfect storm of music, fate, and old friendships reconnecting in the most unexpected way. It was proof that in rock and roll, the best moments are the ones you never see coming.

We were on the road, staying in a Holiday Inn. It was late, about 3:00 a.m. I was fast asleep until I heard someone banging on my door and calling my name. I rushed to the door and opened it. It was Buzzy, jumping up and down and stark naked in the hallway of the Holiday Inn.

I asked Buzzy what was wrong, and he said that he figured it out.

I asked, "What did you figure out?"

He said, as he was jumping naked at my door, "I figured out how to make it ten inches long."

I said, "How?"

And Buzzy said, "Fold it in half," as he started running back to his room.

It was never dull on the road with Buzzy.

Tommy Ramone

I may have been indirectly responsible for Tommy Erdelyi joining the Ramones.

The summer of 1974 was a whirlwind. I was the road manager for Buzzy Linhart, a wild, unpredictable ride filled with late nights, long drives, and the kind of music that made your bones vibrate. It was my job to keep things moving. Schedules, equipment, people, everything had to be in sync. One of the people I brought on board was my old friend Tommy Erdelyi.

Tommy worked as an assistant engineer at the Record Plant. He was sharp, talented, and had a good ear for sound. I figured he'd be perfect as our soundman and roadie. Turns out, I may have been wrong.

Tommy and I had known each other for years. We'd played music together back in Forest Hills in the Tiger 5 and The Tangerine Puppets. He was the kind of guy you could count on. I trusted him, which was why I offered him the gig. He jumped at the opportunity. After all, who wouldn't want to be on the road with a musician like Buzzy? But life on the road wasn't glamorous. It was brutal. The hours were long, the work was grueling, and sometimes, you had to do things you didn't want to do.

The day everything fell apart, we had just arrived at a venue, one of those nondescript spots you'd never find again if you weren't looking for it. We had a Hammond B-3 organ with us, a beast of an instrument, heavy as hell and not exactly easy to move. Normally, we'd use the hydraulic tailgate on the truck to lower it down. That day, though, the tailgate was shot. Dead. We had to do it the old-fashioned way: pure muscle and sweat.

I turned to Tommy and told him he needed to help us unload it. It wasn't a request. It was part of the job. But Tommy wasn't having it.

"I didn't sign up to schlep heavy equipment," he snapped.

"I am not taking a chance on hurting my fingers," he said. At the time, Tommy was a guitar player and was very protective of his hands.

I was stunned. We were all in this together, and everyone pulled their weight.

"Tommy, we don't have a choice. It's got to come off the truck."

He shook his head. "No way. That's not my job."

I told Tommy that he was hired as a soundman and roadie, so yes, it was his job.

I could feel the heat rising in my face.

"You think you're too good for this? We all have to do things we don't like."

The argument escalated fast. Voices got louder, tempers flared. Neither of us wanted to back down. I told Tommy either he helped or we would have to replace him on the crew.

Tommy didn't like that.

In the end, Tommy made the call. He quit, right then and there. Grabbed his stuff and walked away. I watched him go, fuming.

If I had given in, if I had let him slide, maybe he would've stayed. Maybe he would have spent years on the road with us. Maybe he never would have joined The Ramones.

The fight had left a crack in our friendship, something neither of us was in a hurry to fix. But time has a way of sanding down sharp edges. Eventually, we made up. I was glad we did. Life is too short for grudges, especially when it comes to friends.

Looking back, I realize how tricky it is to hire your friends. You think you're doing them a favor, but work is work, and friendships don't always survive that kind of pressure. Lesson learned. And in the end, maybe it was all for the best. If Tommy had stayed on tour with us, maybe he never would have sat behind the drum kit for The Ramones. Maybe history would have played out differently. But it didn't. He went his way, and I went mine. And somehow, we both ended up exactly where we were supposed to be.

Chapter 32

The Rock and Roll Revival

In the early 1970s, rock and roll was in a state of transformation. The countercultural explosion of the 1960s had birthed psychedelic rock, hard rock, and progressive rock, while the emergence of heavy metal and glam rock was shifting the landscape of popular music. But amid these evolving sounds, a powerful wave of nostalgia swept through the industry, bringing with it a resurgence of the pioneers who had first electrified audiences in the 1950s. This movement, known as the Rock and Roll Revival, saw legendary artists reclaim their place in the spotlight, thanks in large part to the efforts of dedicated promoters and talent agencies who recognized the lasting impact of the genre's forefathers.

Among the most influential figures behind the Rock and Roll Revival was Richard Nader, a concert promoter with a deep love for the original architects of rock and roll. Nader saw an opportunity to reintroduce audiences to the genre's golden era, and in 1969, he staged the first-ever "Rock and Roll Revival" concert at Madison Square Garden. The lineup included Bill Haley and His Comets, Chuck Berry, The Coasters, The Platters, and many other acts that had been relegated to the oldies circuit.

Nader's vision proved prophetic. The show was a massive success, igniting a renewed interest in early rock and roll. This led to a series of similar concerts across the country, where fans, both young and old, flocked to see legends perform their timeless hits.

Other notable promoters, such as Don Kirshner and the teams behind events like "Let the Good Times Roll," helped push the revival further. By the mid-1970s, these concerts had evolved from niche nostalgia acts to major arena events, demonstrating the enduring power of rock and roll's early days.

At the heart of the Rock and Roll Revival were the legendary artists themselves. For many of these musicians, the 1970s presented an opportunity to reclaim the spotlight that had dimmed as music trends shifted in the previous decade.

Chuck Berry, a true pioneer of rock and roll, had never entirely disappeared from the scene, but the revival gave him a new stage to reaffirm his status. His performances at these revival concerts, often culminating in electrifying renditions of "Johnny B. Goode" and "Roll Over Beethoven," reaffirmed his influence on the next generation of rock musicians.

Little Richard, one of the most dynamic and charismatic figures in rock history, used the revival as a platform to reassert his status as the true king of rock and roll. His high-energy shows, flamboyant persona, and powerful voice made him one of the most beloved figures in the movement.

Fats Domino, the New Orleans legend whose boogie-woogie-infused rock and roll had helped shape the genre in the 1950s, enjoyed a career resurgence during the revival, thrilling audiences with classics like "Blueberry Hill" and "Ain't That a Shame."

Bill Haley and His Comets, often credited with launching the rock and roll explosion of the 1950s with "Rock Around the Clock," confirmed Haley's status as one of the founding fathers of the movement through his participation in the revival.

Jerry Lee Lewis, an American rock and roll pioneer, earned his nickname "The Killer" for both his frenetic, piano-pounding performance style and his wild, controversial lifestyle. Lewis rose to fame in the 1950s with hits like "Whole Lotta Shakin' Goin' On" and "Great Balls of Fire," songs that showcased his energetic, boundary-pushing approach to music. As one of the first artists inducted into the Rock and Roll Hall of Fame, he helped define the genre's rebellious spirit.

The Rock and Roll Revival wasn't just about nostalgia. It was a reaffirmation of the genre's foundational influence on contemporary music. The revival directly influenced artists such as Bruce Springsteen, who famously performed with Chuck Berry and carried the torch of old-school rock and roll into the new era.

In addition to live concerts, the revival found its way into other forms of media. The success of revival concerts inspired films like "American Graffiti" and television shows such as "Happy Days," which romanticized the era and further fueled the resurgence. Even in fashion and lifestyle, elements of the 1950s began creeping back into the mainstream, with leather jackets, greased-back hair, and classic cars making a cultural comeback.

By the end of the 1970s, the Rock and Roll Revival had firmly established that the music of the 1950s was not just a relic of the past. It was an integral part of rock's DNA. Artists like The Rolling Stones, The Beatles, and Led Zeppelin had already credited the pioneers of rock and roll as their inspirations, but the revival ensured that a new generation of fans would appreciate them as well.

The legacy of the movement continues today, with artists such as Paul McCartney, Brian Setzer, and Jack White drawing from the sounds and styles of early rock and roll. The Rock and Roll Hall of Fame, established in 1983, further cemented the importance of these original artists, many of whom were inducted in its inaugural years.

Richard M. Adler

The Rock and Roll Revival of the 1970s was more than just a fleeting moment of nostalgia. It was a celebration of the genre's roots and a testament to the timeless appeal of artists who defined an era. Thanks to the efforts of promoters like Richard Nader and the enduring talent of legends like Chuck Berry, Little Richard, and Fats Domino, rock and roll's first generation was able to reclaim its place in the pantheon of music history. And in doing so, they reminded the world that rock and roll will never die.

After the Fairport Convention tour ended, I found myself unemployed and ready to start a career. My friend and former bandmate, Bob Rowland, who was a booking agent at Supreme Artists, told me that Banner Talent was looking for a booking agent. He said to go see Neal Hollander and let him know I was looking for a job. I called and set up an interview, and just like that, I got a job booking these incredible Rock and Roll Revival acts in concerts and clubs all over the country. This started my career as a booking agent, and I couldn't be happier.

I was now booking legendary artists that I had grown up listening to since I was ten years old.

The Rock and Roll Revival was more than a concert series, it was a phenomenon. Demand was soaring as fans clamored to hear the iconic sounds of Chuck Berry, Little Richard, Jerry Lee Lewis, and a rotating roster of legendary support acts. From The Drifters and The Coasters to The Shirelles, The Five Satins, Chubby Checker, and Johnny Maestro, these shows were a time capsule of music history, a night of nostalgia with a heartbeat of raw energy.

When I booked a Rock and Roll Revival show in Detroit, the headliner was none other than the Father of Rock and Roll himself: Chuck Berry. Chuck was a character like no other. He operated on his own terms, always had, always would. True to form, he arrived at the venue by mid-afternoon, carrying nothing but a suit bag slung over his shoulder and his iconic guitar case in hand. No entourage, no frills. Just Chuck.

Chuck's contract was as straightforward as his arrival: cash up front, no exceptions. Unlike most acts, who received half their fee upon signing the contract and the balance after the show, Chuck demanded his 50 percent balance in cash before stepping foot on stage. Promoters grumbled, but when you booked Chuck Berry, you knew the deal. Refuse to pay, no show. Simple as that.

Soundcheck with Chuck was a swift affair. Since Chuck refused to travel with a band, he relied on local musicians at each venue, trusting that any self-respecting rock band knew his classics inside and out. He gave the band a quick rundown, focusing only on the intros and outros of songs like "Johnny B. Goode," "Roll Over Beethoven," and "Maybellene." Within 20 minutes, soundcheck was wrapped. The rest of the evening was a waiting game until showtime.

While Chuck's no-nonsense approach may have rattled promoters, it added an air of unpredictability to his performances. No two shows were ever quite the same. That night in Detroit, as soon as Chuck hit the stage, any concerns evaporated. The crowd erupted as his fingers danced across the strings, and he reminded everyone why he was the architect of rock and roll.

Booking Ike and Tina Turner, however, was a different kind of adventure. The show was set for a theater in White Plains, New York: two performances, an early show and a late show. But a few days before the concert, ticket sales were underwhelming, only 25 percent sold for the early show and about half for the late show. I called Ike and Tina's manager to break the bad news, and we agreed to consolidate into one late show, allowing early-show ticket holders to attend.

What should have been a simple solution quickly spiraled into chaos. Reserved seating meant that many ticket holders found themselves with duplicate seats. Front-row fans from the early show were understandably outraged when they were reassigned to the back of the theater. The scramble to resolve the seating debacle delayed the show, turning the late show into what felt like the late, late show.

When the lights finally dimmed and the curtain rose, Ike and Tina Turner electrified the room. Tina's powerhouse vocals and magnetic stage presence, backed by Ike's sharp guitar work and The Ikettes' synchronized moves, made the audience forget the chaos that had preceded the performance. The energy was electric, the music infectious. Yet, the night's surprises weren't over.

After the show, I needed to discuss some business with Ike and Tina. I waited about 20 minutes before knocking on their dressing room door. A woman's voice called out, "Come in!" I stepped inside and froze. There was Tina Turner, seated casually on a chair with her legs propped up on the dressing table, stark naked and without her wig. Her hair was close-cropped.

"Don't mind me," she said with a smile and zero trace of self-consciousness. "I'm air drying."

Time seemed to slow down. My brain scrambled to decide where to look. Do I maintain eye contact? Pretend this is perfectly normal? I opted for professionalism, locking eyes with Tina and diving straight into the business discussion as if nothing were out of the ordinary. She responded with the same calm composure, her confidence as radiant as her stage presence. It was one of the more surreal moments of my career, but as they say, that's showbiz.

Another unforgettable encounter happened while working with The Platters. I had arranged for the mayor of the city to meet Tony Williams, the group's lead vocalist, backstage before the show. Tony, however, had a reputation for being a bit eccentric.

When I knocked on his dressing room door, there was no response.

"Mr. Williams?" I called. "The mayor and his wife are here to meet you."

Silence.

I knocked again, more firmly this time. Still nothing.

After a few awkward moments, the door creaked open. Tony stood there, looking less than thrilled.

"This is Mayor Thompson and his wife, Margaret," I said with a smile, trying to ease the tension.

Tony's eyes flicked to the mayor. "Got a cigarette?" he asked bluntly.

Taken aback, the mayor replied, "Sorry, I don't smoke."

Without missing a beat, Tony waved his hand dismissively. "Then get out," he said.

And just like that, the door slammed shut.

I stood there, stunned. The mayor and his wife exchanged bewildered glances. Embarrassed, I stammered an apology and suggested they enjoy the show. It was a lesson in the unpredictable nature of working with music legends. You never quite knew what you were going to get.

While working at Banner Talent, I had the privilege of collaborating with Ray Reneri, a fascinating character with a deep-rooted history in the music industry. Ray was the manager of Herman's Hermits, a band I had admired since my teenage years, and our connection added a layer of personal significance to my work. Ray's career was filled with incredible stories. He had once been the road manager for Judy Garland and had extensive experience with the Rock and Roll Revival tours. Under Ray's management, I booked numerous dates for Herman's Hermits, who seemed to be perpetually on tour across the U.S., performing everywhere from packed concert halls to intimate club venues.

At the time, Ray was locked in a legal battle with Peter Noone, the former frontman of Herman's Hermits. After Peter parted ways with the band, both he and the remaining members continued to use the name "Herman's Hermits," leading to a contentious lawsuit that captured the music industry's attention.

In 1973, the British Invasion Tour was announced, a nostalgia-fueled spectacle reminiscent of the Rock and Roll Revival, but with a distinctly British flavor. Billed as "The British Are Coming Again," the tour featured a stellar lineup: Herman's Hermits, Billy J. Kramer and the Dakotas, Gerry and the Pacemakers, The Searchers, and Wayne Fontana and the Mindbenders. This 21-date nationwide journey kicked off on the East Coast, traveled westward, and concluded in the Midwest. The bands traveled together by bus, reliving the camaraderie and chaos of their early touring days.

Peter Noone rejoined Herman's Hermits for this tour, marking a highly anticipated reunion. However, the harmony was short-lived.

Peter's wife, who accompanied him on the tour, found the raucous antics and colorful language of the musicians less than charming. Unable to endure the rowdy atmosphere, she insisted that Peter travel separately. Consequently, Peter and his wife switched to a limousine that trailed the tour bus, a move that created a rift within the band. The Hermits resented the perceived luxury and separation, feeling that Peter had distanced himself both physically and emotionally. This tension simmered throughout the tour, eventually leading to the band's decision to continue without Peter once the tour concluded.

The legal dispute over the band's name intensified. Ray Reneri argued that the band had the right to the name "Herman's Hermits," while Peter Noone contended that, as the original "Herman," he was entitled to use the name. The courtroom drama was heated, with both sides presenting compelling arguments. Ultimately, the judge ruled in favor of the band, citing a key piece of evidence: the last single had been released under the name "Peter Noone and Herman's Hermits." This phrasing implied a distinction between Peter and the band, leading the judge to conclude that the band retained ownership of the name. As a result, the remaining members of Herman's Hermits continued to perform under their original name, while Peter Noone had to be billed solely under his own name.

Despite the departure of their charismatic frontman, Herman's Hermits thrived. Karl Green, the band's talented bass player, stepped into the role of lead vocalist. His voice captured the essence of the band's signature sound, allowing them to deliver beloved hits like "I'm into Something Good" and "Mrs. Brown, You've Got a Lovely Daughter" with remarkable authenticity.

Throughout this period, I attended numerous gigs with the band, forging close friendships with the members. Backstage, the atmosphere was a blend of camaraderie and adrenaline, with moments of laughter, late-night storytelling, and spontaneous jam sessions. Watching them perform night after night, I witnessed firsthand the enduring magic of their music and the bond that connected them to their fans. Whether playing to a crowd of thousands or an intimate club audience, Herman's Hermits proved that their music transcended time, and I was proud to have played a part in their journey.

Herman's Hermits was a British rock band formed in Manchester, England in 1963. Led by singer Peter Noone, the band gained popularity in the mid-1960s with a string of hit singles and albums.

One of the things that made Herman's Hermits stand out was their ability to appeal to a wide range of audiences. Their upbeat, catchy tunes and clean-cut image made them popular with teens, while their appeal to older audiences helped them to sustain their success over the years.

One of the band's biggest hits was "I'm Into Something Good," written by Carole King and Gerry Goffin, which reached the top of the charts in the United Kingdom and the United States. Other popular Herman's Hermits songs include "Mrs. Brown, You've Got a Lovely Daughter," "I'm Henry VIII, I Am," "A Kind of Hush" and "Silhouettes."

Herman's Hermits released a number of successful albums in the 1960s, including "Mrs. Brown, You've Got a Lovely Daughter," "Both Sides of Herman's Hermits," and "Herman's Hermits on Tour." The band's popularity waned in the 1970s, but they continued to tour and perform throughout the years.

In addition to their musical success, Herman's Hermits also had a successful film career. They starred in several movies in the 1960s, including "Mrs. Brown, You've Got a Lovely Daughter" and "Hold On!"

Overall, Herman's Hermits were an influential and enduring band that left a lasting mark on the world of pop music. They will always be remembered for their catchy tunes and wholesome image that endeared them to fans of all ages.

Looking back, these moments are more than just anecdotes, they are snapshots of an era when music was raw, personalities were larger than life, and the line between chaos and brilliance was often paper-thin. From Chuck Berry's no-nonsense demands to Tina Turner's uninhibited confidence and Tony Williams' unpredictable antics, each encounter added another verse to the wild and unforgettable symphony of rock and roll history.

Richard M. Adler

Chapter 33

The Starrett City Festival

It all started with The Marvelettes at the 2001 Club in Brooklyn. That club was famous; it was where they filmed John Travolta's big dance scene in *Saturday Night Fever*. I had booked The Marvelettes, who had huge hits like *Please Mr. Postman* and *Beechwood 4-5789*. I went to the club early that night for soundcheck, just another day on the job. But I had no idea that night would lead me to one of the biggest festivals I'd ever work on.

While I was standing by the stage, a guy came up to me and asked, "Are you with the band?" I said yes, but it was too loud to talk, so he motioned for me to step outside. The second we got outside; I could tell this guy wasn't just some random concertgoer. He was one of "The Boys." He told me his name was Tony, and he got straight to the point.

"We need a guy like you," he said.

I raised an eyebrow. "For what?"

Tony explained that they were planning a huge Italian festival in Starrett City, sponsored by the Italian-American Civil Rights League. They wanted it to be something special: gambling tents, a full circus, and big-name concerts every night for ten days.

Before I could say much, he asked for my card. I handed it to him, and he said he'd call me the next day. I went back inside, still wondering what I had just walked into.

The next day, Tony called and asked me to meet him at Sparks Steakhouse in Manhattan. I met him and his partner, Phil, and they told me exactly what they wanted: ten nights of major entertainment, big-name acts like The Four Seasons, Jay and the Americans, The Four Tops, Julius La Rosa, Blood, Sweat & Tears, Jackie Mason, Enzo Stuarti, Tony Bennett, The Drifters, and The Shirelles. A full circus. A festival with food, games, and, most importantly, their gambling tents.

I told them I could book the acts, but I'd need a 50 percent deposit upfront. Tony nodded. "Don't worry about the money," he said.

"I'll bring it to you tomorrow."

Sure enough, the next day, Tony walked into my office with a briefcase full of cash. He popped it open and asked how much I needed. I gave him the number, and he counted it out right there on my desk. Then he looked at me and said, "Go book the show."

When we got to the festival site, it was just an open field, completely overgrown with weeds taller than me. Before we could build anything, we had to clear the land. I hired a crew to cut down the weeds and haul them away. Then we started putting up the stage, sound and light system, and thousands of chairs.

Every morning, a limo would show up at my house to drive me to Brooklyn. The Boys wanted to make sure I showed up every day.

Everything was coming together perfectly until the night Blood, Sweat & Tears were scheduled to play.

The weather report called for thunderstorms all night. The band's road manager pulled me aside and asked, "Want to reschedule? We'll come back tomorrow."

That wasn't my call to make. Rescheduling would cost extra, and we already had another act booked for the next night. So, I took the road manager to see Tony, who was inside a trailer guarded by two guys carrying shotguns.

I told the guards, "We need to see the boss."

They let me in, but not the road manager. Inside, Tony was sitting around a table with the heads of the Five Families, who he introduced me to.

I told Tony about the rain and the band's request for a rain date.

Tony didn't even blink. "Tell them they'll play tonight. Rain or shine."

I wasn't about to argue. So, I went back and told Blood, Sweat & Tears, "You're playing."

They went on stage after Gun Hill Road played their opening set. They made it through one song, and then, boom. The sky opened up with the worst thunderstorm I had ever seen. We had to rush the band off the stage as rain poured down. The canopy over the stage started sagging under the weight of all the water.

I grabbed a mic stand, taped a pocketknife to the end, and threw it like a spear at the bulging canvas. The moment the knife cut through, it was like a water bomb exploded. A tidal wave crashed onto the stage, drenching all of Blood, Sweat & Tears' equipment.

Now, I had a torn canopy to fix before the next night's show with Frankie Valli & The Four Seasons.

I called the stage company the next morning and told them to fix the canopy immediately. They told me they couldn't send anyone until Monday. That was three days away, and I needed it for tomorrow night's show.

I said, "You don't understand who you're dealing with. This is the Italian-American Civil Rights League you're dealing with."

Silence.

Then the guy stammered, "I'll send someone right over."

That night, Frankie Valli & The Four Seasons were set to perform, and I invited my parents to see the show. I got them great seats, and they were so proud.

The problem? Frankie Valli was stuck in traffic.

So many people came to see the free show that the Belt Parkway was shut down. Traffic was backed up for miles. By 8:00 p.m., showtime, the band wasn't even there.

I called the police for help. They sent a helicopter to find the limo and transport them to the festival.

I had to go on stage and let the crowd know that Frankie Valli & The Four Seasons were stuck in traffic. The crowd was getting rowdy.

By 9:30 p.m., the chopper landed. But when I went on stage to tell the crowd that Frankie Valli had arrived, they thought I was about to cancel the show.

People started screaming.

My father was terrified for me. But before I could say another word, Frankie Valli & The Four Seasons ran onto the stage and started playing, no introduction needed.

The crowd erupted, and just like that, the crisis was over.

Looking back, the Starrett City Italian Festival was one of the wildest experiences of my career. It had mobsters, cash-filled briefcases, helicopters, shotguns, thunderstorms, and a near-riot.

But in the end, the festival was a massive success, and nobody got whacked, including me.

And that's what I call a job well done.

Richard M. Adler

Chapter 34

The Birth of Somerset Talent

Marvelettes
'Please Mr. Postman'

Herman's Hermits
'Mrs. Brown You've Got A Lovely Daughter'

Drifters
'Up On The Roof'

Monkees
'I'm A Believer'

Cryer and Ford
'Hang On To The Good Times'

Chubby Checker
'The Twist'

The Shirelles
'Will You Love Me Tomorrow'

Tommy James
'Crimson and Clover'

Somerset Talent Assoc. INC.
200 West 57th Street
New York, N.Y. 10019

It all started after we landed a big festival booking. Ray Renier, Steve Altman, and I had been working at Banner Talent for a while, but something about that deal made us realize we were ready to strike out on our own. We had the experience, the industry connections, and most importantly, the confidence to take a leap. After some long conversations and plenty of late-night planning, we made the decision to leave Banner Talent behind and start our own agency, Somerset Talent.

Somerset Talent wasn't just another agency. We had a vision. We specialized in booking acts from the Rock and Roll Revival scene as well as some of the biggest names in disco. The music industry was changing fast in the mid-70s, and we wanted to be right in the middle of it. Before long, we were representing incredible acts like The Trammps, Shirley Alston (formerly of The Shirelles), Gloria Gaynor, and Faith, Hope & Charity, among many others.

On top of that, as a personal favor to the legendary Sid Bernstein, who was managing them at the time, I was also booking Cryer and Ford and Joe and Bing. When Sid asked me for something, I didn't say no. He was the man responsible for bringing The Beatles to America. If he believed in an artist, that was good enough for me.

I first met Sid back in the mid-70s when I was booking his acts. From the beginning, we got along well, though he had this odd little habit. Every time he came up to my office, he would pat me on the head. I never knew why he did it, and I never asked. It was just Sid being Sid.

Sid was always full of ideas. Some were brilliant, and some... not so much. One of his grand schemes was to recreate The Beatles' arrival in America, but this time with The Bay City Rollers. I told him flat out, "Sid, you can't manufacture something that happened organically." But he was determined, so I helped him give it a shot. It was an epic failure. No amount of marketing magic could replicate the sheer chaos and excitement that surrounded The Beatles when they landed in the U.S. That kind of thing only happens once.

Sid overhyped the Bay City Rollers to the point that he was calling them "The Next Beatles." That didn't go over well with the press. Sid also arranged buses to bring kids to the airports and had people make signs for them to hold.

Over the years, Sid and I attended all kinds of Beatles-related events together. One of the best was when we saw George Martin at Town Hall. That was a special night, listening to the man who shaped so much of The Beatles' sound, telling stories about working with them. You could hear the respect and admiration in his voice. It was like stepping into history for a couple of hours. Sid introduced me that night to George Martin backstage. It was a real honor to meet him.

In 2012, I was with Sid at a Fab Faux show in New Jersey. The Fab Faux, as described by Rolling Stone magazine, were "the greatest Beatles cover band – without the wigs." It was a fantastic show, and afterward, there was an exclusive after-party. I brought Sid along, and as soon as we walked in, it was like royalty had arrived. Everyone wanted to shake his hand, talk to him, and share stories. People just loved Sid. He had that effect on people. He wasn't just a music industry guy, he was a genuinely nice guy and a legend in his own right.

That night, as we sat together at the party, Sid leaned in and told me a story I'd never heard before. Back in the day, Brian Epstein, The Beatles' manager, had come to see him along with Nat Weiss, the man I worked for. They had one goal: buying the management contract for The Rascals. Brian wanted to manage them, but Sid already had them signed.

During the meeting, Brian suddenly excused himself to use the restroom. As soon as he stepped out, Nat turned to Sid and said, "Hold on to The Rascals. Don't sell them to Brian. They're going to be big."

Now, you have to understand. Nat and Brian were business partners. For Nat to go against Brian like that, even in private, was a big deal. But he saw something in The Rascals, and he wanted to make sure Sid didn't let them go.

Sid never forgot that moment. He told me, "Nat was a mensch. You know, I always respected Nat for that. He didn't have to say a word. But he did." And of course, Nat was right. The Rascals did go on to be huge.

As Sid told me the story that night, I could see the nostalgia in his eyes. He had been a part of so much music history, and he carried those memories with him like treasures. I was just glad I got to hear them straight from him.

Of course, leaving Banner Talent wasn't without its complications. When I quit, Dave Zaan, my former boss, decided he wasn't going to pay me the commission I was owed for booking the Italian Festival in Starrett City. It was a sizable amount of money, and I wasn't about to let it slide. So, I took him to court.

The courtroom was packed with other cases waiting to be heard, but when it was finally our turn, the judge wasted no time. He looked straight at Dave Zaan and asked, "Do you owe this man money?"

Dave, probably thinking he could talk his way out of it, hesitated for a moment before saying, "Yes, but…"

Before he could even finish his excuse, the judge cut him off.

"Pay him. Next case."

And just like that, it was over. The look on Dave's face was priceless. I walked out of that courtroom with my head held high, knowing I had stood my ground and won.

The day we moved into our new Somerset Talent offices on 57th Street, it felt like the beginning of something big. There was an air of excitement, a sense that we were stepping into a new chapter of our careers. But as thrilling as it was, the reality was that we were starting from scratch, literally.

We had signed the lease, picked up the keys, and now stood inside an empty office. The walls were bare, the floors echoed with every step, and we had absolutely no furniture. No desks, no chairs, no filing cabinets, nothing. The plan was simple. That afternoon, we were going to head out and buy everything we needed to turn this empty space into a real business.

But fate had other plans.

Just as we were getting settled, trying to figure out where to put everything once it arrived, we noticed some movers hauling furniture out of an office down the hall. That's when we saw Connie DeNave. If you were in the music business, you knew her name. Connie was one of the most well-known publicists in the industry, someone who had worked with some of the biggest names in entertainment. She was a true professional and had built a strong reputation over the years.

She saw us standing there, looking around at our empty office, and called out, "Hey, do you guys have office furniture yet?"

We laughed and told her, "Not yet, but we're about to go buy some."

She gave us a knowing smile and said,

"Forget it. Take all of mine, I have no use for it."

At first, we thought she was joking. Who just gives away an entire office full of furniture? But she wasn't kidding. She had no use for it because she was moving her office to her apartment, and instead of trying to sell it or move it, she simply handed it over to us.

Desks, chairs, file cabinets, everything we needed and more. We were in shock. It was a huge break, saving us thousands of dollars at a time when every penny counted. The generosity she showed us that day was rare in an industry that could be cutthroat and competitive.

So, Connie, if you're out there reading this, thank you.

With the office now fully furnished, we were ready to get to work. Somerset Talent was up and running, and we were booking some incredible acts. Everything seemed to be falling into place.

One day I came into the office, just as I was settling into my desk, ready to catch up on work, when two unexpected visitors walked into my office, Tony and Phil from the Starrett City Festival.

They were well-dressed, confident, and spoke like they had been in the music business for years. They told me they had an exciting new plan; they wanted to produce concerts at a theater in Brooklyn and needed to book the acts through my agency.

It sounded like a good opportunity. I asked them for a list of the acts they wanted to book so I could start making calls. But instead of handing me a list, Phil asked,

"Mind if I make a phone call?"

I shrugged and said, "Sure."

Then Tony asked if he could make a call too. Before I knew it, Phil was sitting at my desk, dialing away, and Tony was over at my partner Steve's desk, doing the same thing.

At first, I didn't think much of it. People used our phones all the time, it was part of the business. But after an hour passed, then two hours, then three, I started to wonder. They were still there.

By the time the workday ended, Phil and Tony were still on the phones, making calls as if this was their own office.

I figured that would be the end of it. But the next morning, they were back. And just like the day before, they sat at our desks and started making calls again. Day after day, this kept happening. Phil and Tony arrived early, took over our phones, and barely said a word to us except to ask for coffee or if we had an extra pen. Steve and I couldn't get any work done.

At first, we tried to be polite. Maybe they were working on something important. Maybe this would turn into real business for us.

But after a week of this, it became clear that they weren't booking concerts at all. In fact, I had no idea who they were talking to. They never discussed contracts, they never asked about artist fees, and they never mentioned the theater in Brooklyn again. It felt like they were running some kind of secret operation right out of our office.

Then, after about two weeks, as suddenly as they had appeared, they were gone.

One morning, I came into the office, half expecting to see them sitting at my desk. But their seats were empty. No phone calls, no sign of Tony or Phil. They never came back.

323

At first, Steve and I were relieved. It was a mystery, but at least we had our office back.

But then, a few weeks later, Ray Renieri stopped by.

He leaned against the door and gave us a look.

"Did you hear what happened to Tony and Phil?"

I shook my head. "No. Why?"

Ray sighed. "The police found them in the trunk of an abandoned car in the Meadowlands. They think it might be them. But the bodies were burned beyond recognition."

Steve and I looked at each other.

I didn't know if it was true or just a rumor, but one thing was for sure, Tony and Phil never showed up at our office again.

To this day, I have no idea what they were really up to. But whatever it was, it was something big enough to make them disappear forever.

But as with all businesses, challenges soon followed.

Not long after we settled into our new space, Ray Renieri made the difficult decision not to officially join Somerset Talent. He had a solid reason; he had a managerial contract with Herman's Hermits. If he became a booking agent, other agents might see it as a conflict of interest and refuse to book the band. It was a smart decision on his part, but we were still sorry to see him go.

A year later, another big change came when Steve Altman decided to leave as well. He had a great opportunity to work with a family member in a different industry, and he chose to take it. That left me as the sole owner of Somerset Talent.

For six months, I ran the agency alone. It was exhausting work, managing contracts, negotiating deals, handling logistics, and keeping up with an industry that was constantly shifting. I enjoyed being my own boss, but I was quickly realizing that the business of running an agency was very different from simply booking artists.

And then, just when I thought things might start to settle down, I got what I thought was my biggest break yet.

I couldn't believe it when I got the call. Somerset Talent had been recommended to The Hollies by Herman's Hermits, and we were given exclusive rights to book The Hollies' upcoming U.S. tour.

For me, this was personal. The Hollies were one of my favorite groups. They hadn't toured the U.S. in several years, and this was going to be a huge deal. Their new album was set to be released just as the tour was kicking off, and CBS Records had agreed to subsidize the entire tour, making it an even easier sell.

But nothing in the music business is ever really easy.

Because The Hollies had been away from the U.S. market for so long, promoters were skeptical. Would fans still turn out to see them? Was it worth the price the band was asking? I spent three straight months doing nothing but working on this tour, making calls, negotiating deals, and persuading promoters to take a chance.

Slowly but surely, I made it happen. I carefully routed the tour, secured every single date, and finalized the contracts. Everything was set. It was two weeks before the tour was scheduled to begin when I got the phone call that changed everything.

The Hollies' management was on the line.

"Listen," they said, "we just got word from CBS Records. They've decided not to release the album until some later date."

I was stunned.

"What? Why?"

"CBS Records had too many albums coming in the next few months. They're afraid The Hollies will get lost in the shuffle."

And just like that, the entire tour fell apart.

Without the album release, there was no promotional push, and without that, the tour didn't make sense. I was told to cancel everything and let the promoters know that once a new release date was set, we could rebook the tour.

I was crushed.

After working day and night for three months, I had nothing to show for it. I had been depending on the commissions from this tour to keep my business afloat. Now, I had no income coming in, and worse, I didn't even have enough money to pay the rent for the office.

That was it.

I knew it was time to close the doors on Somerset Talent.

I needed a job, and fast. That's when I joined Supreme Artists, a well-respected agency run by Jack Adato. Jack was an old-school booking agent who had been in the business for years. He started out booking bands for weddings and bar mitzvahs but had eventually moved into booking college concerts.

Jack had a unique way of doing business. He didn't have a fixed roster of artists. Instead, he worked directly with colleges, found out who they wanted to book, and then made it happen.

But what really set Jack apart was that he had exclusive rights to book all concerts at West Point and Annapolis. If a band wanted to play at either of those prestigious military academies, they had to go through Supreme Artists.

One of Supreme Artists' first major bookings after I joined was Art Garfunkel at West Point. After that came Elton John, and then Fleetwood Mac at Annapolis.

I went down to Annapolis to cover the Fleetwood Mac show along with my friend Bob Rowland, who also worked at Supreme Artists. The midshipmen were ecstatic to have Fleetwood Mac perform. It was one of the biggest concerts they had ever hosted.

After the show, I went backstage to check on the band and see if they needed anything before heading out. That's when Christine McVie pulled me aside.

She looked tired, clearly drained from the performance. She pointed toward the midshipmen, who had already started folding chairs and stacking them away.

With a sigh, she asked, "Could you ask them to stop that until we're ready to leave? I have a headache, and it's making it worse."

I wanted to help, but I knew I couldn't.

I looked at Christine and said, "I'd love to help, but they take orders from their commanding officer, not from the band. I'm sorry, but I can't ask them to stop."

She was not happy. She gave me a look that said she wasn't used to being told no. But there was nothing I could do. This wasn't Madison Square Garden, it was Annapolis.

In about four or five years, Christine became involved with my friend Dennis Wilson.

From Banner Talent to Somerset Talent to Supreme Artists, my journey in the music industry was a rollercoaster of highs and lows. I got to work with some of the biggest names in music.

But the biggest lesson I learned? In this business, and in life, you have to roll with the punches, take the opportunities as they come, and always stand your ground when it matters.

TALENT ROSTER

DISCO

Faith, Hope and Charity
The Trammps
Ecstacy, Passion and Pain
The Joneses
Crown Heights Affair
Touch Of Class
Gary Toms Empire
Carol Douglas
Van McCoy
Shirley and Co.
Ralph Carter
B.T. Express
Calhoon
Silver Convention
Salsoul Orchestra
First Choice
Bimbo Jet
Executive Suite

FOLK/ROCK

Cryer and Ford
Ellen McIlwaine
Jayne Olderman Band
Gunhill Road
Jae Mason
Judd
Jake and The Family Jewel
Persuasions
B. Altman
Divided We Stand

ROCK REVIVAL

Herman's Hermits
The Monkees
The Shirelles
The Drifters
The Searchers
The Crystals
The Brooklyn Bridge
Bo Diddley
Tommy James
The Capris
The Belmonts
Gary U.S. Bonds
Gary Lewis and The Playboys
Chubby Checker
Dion
Chuck Berry
Jerry Lee Lewis
The Marvelettes

Gunhill Road
Back When My Hair Was Short

Faith, Hope and Charity
'To Each His Own'

Somerset Talent Assoc. Inc.
200 West 57th Street • New York, N.Y. 10019
(212) 541-8010

Somerset Talent Roster

329

Richard M. Adler

Chapter 35

One of the Best Days of My Life

Cathy and Me 1976

June 18, 1976, stands out as one of those pivotal nights that would alter the course of my life in truly unpredictable ways. I was casually spending the evening at my friend Kenny's house when he introduced me to a man named Danny, who, as it turned out, owned a record company. The timing was almost impossibly perfect. In just a few short weeks, I was scheduled to travel to London to produce *The Best of Herman's Hermits* album because Mickey Most would not grant a license for the original recordings and was actively seeking a label to distribute the finished record. Opportunity had quite literally just walked through the door.

Danny and I settled onto Kenny's couch, leaning in close as the business negotiation commenced. Numbers, projected sales percentages, and potential album figures filled the air as I tried to stay focused on securing the most advantageous deal possible. Suddenly, our serious conversation was interrupted by the unexpected arrival of two neighborhood girls, Cathy and Patty, who were friends of Kenny's wife, Sunshine. Their laughter and animated chatter filled the room, but I valiantly attempted to remain laser-focused on the crucial business at hand.

One of the girls, Cathy, was beautiful, with an undeniably confident smile. She casually sat down right beside me. She playfully tapped my shoulder, momentarily breaking my concentration. "Hey," she teased, "it's rude to sit with your back to someone." Caught between the pressing need to seal the record deal and acknowledging her rather charming presence, I turned to her briefly and replied, "I'll talk to you when the meeting's over." Then I promptly returned to my negotiations with Danny, determined to finalize the distribution agreement.

Once the business meeting finally wrapped up, Kenny, ever the enthusiastic social instigator, immediately suggested that we all head over to Catch A Rising Star, a popular comedy club where the comedian Richard Belzer was performing that night. The spur-of-the-moment idea sounded absolutely perfect: good company, plenty of laughter, and a welcome chance to unwind after a serious business discussion. The night proved to be truly electric. Richard Belzer had us all doubled over with laughter, and the chemistry between me and Cathy, the girl from the couch, was both instant and undeniable. By the time we all stumbled back home at 4 a.m., I was completely smitten, despite the fact that she had to be at work in the city by 9 a.m.

The very next day, I simply couldn't get her out of my mind. On a hopeful whim, I picked up the phone and asked her to join me that evening to see Herman's Hermits perform at The Bitter End in New York City. Much to my initial disappointment, she politely declined, citing a headache. Undeterred and perhaps slightly emboldened, I called her again only an hour later, still hoping she might have reconsidered. Once again, she just as politely declined, saying she was now simply too tired.

Persistence is key, as they say. I waited another hour, picked up the phone one final time, and with what I hoped was a playfully charming tone, said, "This is your last chance."

Whether it was my sheer charm or just my sheer determination, she finally relented and, to my immense relief, agreed to join me. That night at The Bitter End turned out to be the very beginning of something incredibly special. The live music, the vibrant atmosphere of the club, and our shared laughter under the bright city lights created the perfect backdrop for the somewhat improbable start of what would become a lifelong love story.

Richard M. Adler

Chapter 36

London and Herman's Hermits

Just two weeks later, I boarded a flight to London, carrying with me a potent mix of excitement and professional responsibility. I had personally invested a substantial sum, $25,000, to produce *The Best of Herman's Hermits* album. It was a considerable financial risk at the time, but one I was genuinely willing to take because I believed in the musical quality of the album and the enduring appeal of the band.

The recording sessions in London were intense, filled with long and demanding days in the studio, painstakingly perfecting each track. However, the finished result was worth every single penny of my investment.

I returned home from London with the master tape of the completed album, a tangible and deeply personal reminder of my time spent in the studio. I promptly gave the tape to Danny so his record company could begin the process of cutting the vinyl records, which were intended to fulfill the anticipated customer orders we expected from a television commercial featuring Herman's Hermits promoting the album.

We decided to test market the commercials in two major media markets to gauge effectiveness. Unfortunately, the initial consumer response was not encouraging, and the distribution deal with Danny's label fell apart. Tragically, no records were ever cut, and I was left facing a $25,000 loss. To make matters worse, Danny's fledgling record company went bankrupt, and the master tape became entangled in legal proceedings.

Richard M. Adler

Fast forward to 2015. On a complete whim, I was browsing Amazon one afternoon when, to my astonishment, I stumbled upon *The Best of Herman's Hermits* album, the very same record I had helped bring to life decades earlier in London. Without hesitation, I clicked the "Buy Now" button. As I waited for the package to arrive, long-dormant memories of those intense recording sessions came rushing back.

When the album arrived, I carefully unwrapped it and held it in my hands with a mix of bittersweet nostalgia and personal pride.

Yes, I ended up paying $10.99 for a physical piece of my own convoluted personal and professional history. But as I listened to the familiar tracks, each note instantly transporting me back to that London studio, I knew it was worth every penny. Still, one question lingered, how had the album been released commercially without my knowledge or consent?

It turns out that Ray Renieri, Herman's Hermits' savvy manager, had somehow made a copy of the original master tape and had been quietly selling it to various small record labels in different countries, all without my knowledge and likely without the band's explicit consent.

I am happy to report that Cathy and I, who met that fateful day in June of 1976, got married two years later in 1978. After raising three children, we are still happily together to this very day.

Looking back, these memories and improbable anecdotes represent more than just stories from my past. They are snapshots of a truly unique and dynamic era in music history, a time when the music was raw and energetic, when the personalities were larger than life, and when the line between professional chaos and artistic brilliance was often razor-thin.

Richard M. Adler

Chapter 37

A Wedding in the Blizzard of '78

My beautiful bride and me

Richard M. Adler

It was January 21, 1978, the day I was set to marry Cathy, the love of my life. The only problem? The biggest snowstorm I could remember had just buried New York under three feet of snow. The streets were unplowed, cars were stuck, and I had no idea how I was going to get to my own wedding.

My dad and I spent the morning shoveling, trying to dig out our car, but it was no use. We were stranded in Forest Hills with no way to get to Leonard's in Great Neck, where Cathy was already waiting for me. We didn't have cell phones back then, so I couldn't even call to tell her I might be late.

Then, Cathy called me with a plan. Her family friend, George O'Neill, had rented a bus to get our guests to the wedding. The bus would stop first at O'Neill's in Maspeth, where Cathy's guests would board, then head to my parents' apartment in Forest Hills to pick me up along with my guests. Anyone who could make it to either location would have a ride to the wedding.

To help offset the cost, George asked each person to chip in five dollars for the ride. I asked my best man, Roy, to collect the money, but he was not happy about it. He thought it was cheap and embarrassing, but I didn't care, we had a wedding to get to!

The bus arrived at O'Neill's as planned, and guests piled in. Just as it was about to pull away, though, it got stuck in the snow. It took what felt like forever to get a tow truck to pull the bus free. By the time we were finally on our way, I was already late to my own wedding.

Cathy, waiting at Leonard's with no way to contact me, was worried sick. But when I finally arrived, she was just relieved to see me. The ceremony went on, and despite the chaos, it was a beautiful night.

Roy, on the other hand, was so embarrassed about collecting money from our guests that he never spoke to me again. To this day, I wonder if he ever forgave me!

Fast forward to May 1979. Cathy and I had been married for over a year, and we were expecting our first child, Jennifer, in late June. Life was about to change in a big way.

At the time, I was working at Supreme Artists, booking concerts for musicians. I had booked some big acts, but I was barely making a decent salary. The music business was unpredictable. It felt like gambling on horses, if you picked the right one, you were rich; if you didn't, you were broke.

I needed stability. I needed a job where I could support my growing family.

That's when I decided to learn about computers.

NYU was offering a six-week course in computer programming, and I signed up immediately. I had no background in technology, but I was determined to succeed.

The course was intense. We had to submit programming projects, and the grading system was strict. If you turned it in on time and it was correct, you got an A. If you were even one day late, your grade dropped to B. Two days late, C...

I practically lived in the computer lab. While my classmates went home, I stayed late, making sure my projects were perfect.

Then, in June 1979, one of the biggest moments of my life happened, Jennifer was born.

I was over the moon. Seeing my daughter for the first time filled me with an unstoppable determination. I had to get an A in this course. I had to find a good job. I had to create a better future for my family.

On the last day of class, the instructor called out four names, including mine, and asked us to stay after class. He told us, "You are the only students in the class who got an A."

Then, he said something that changed my life forever: "I got you all job interviews with Teacher's Insurance. Your interviews are on Monday."

That Monday, I walked into Teacher's Insurance for my first-ever IT job interview. By the end of the day, I was hired.

Just like that, my time in the music industry was over, and my journey in Information Technology had begun.

From 1979 to 1983, I worked for different companies, learning everything I could about computers and IT. But deep down, I always had an entrepreneurial spirit.

In 1981, Cathy and I had another child, Ryan was born on June 15, 1981. I now had a son and a daughter, and I couldn't be happier.

In 1983, I took the biggest leap of my career. Along with my two business partners, Arthur Goldstein and Lou DiGregorio, I started my own IT consulting firm, Decision Support Inc.

Starting a company wasn't easy, but it was the best decision I ever made. Over the years, we built Decision Support into a successful business, and to this day, I am still the President of the company.

It's amazing to think how much my life changed between 1978 and 1983. I got married in the middle of a blizzard. I became a father and realized I needed a better career. I left the music business behind and took a chance on a new industry. I became an expert in IT and started my own company.

In 1986, Jonathan was born. I now had a daughter and two sons, and our family was complete. Jonathan is an incredible drummer and loves music as much as I do. Jennifer has already claimed my record collection for when I no longer need it.

Sometimes, life takes you in unexpected directions. If you had told me in 1978 that I would leave the music industry and become the president of an IT firm, I never would have believed you.

But looking back, I wouldn't change a thing.

I learned that success isn't just about luck. It's about determination, hard work, and knowing when to take a leap of faith.

Fast forward to July 24, 1986. The summer air buzzed with excitement at the Orange County Fairgrounds in Middletown, New York. Crowds gathered from all over, eagerly anticipating The Monkees' 20th Anniversary Reunion Tour with Herman's Hermits, Gary Puckett and the Union Gap, and The Grass Roots.

The fairgrounds were alive with the aroma of popcorn and cotton candy, the distant hum of carnival rides, and the electric energy of a night filled with music and memories.

Amidst the bustling crowd, my wife Cathy and I made our way toward the backstage entrance, hand in hand with our two children, Jennifer, seven years old, and Ryan, five. Their eyes sparkled with anticipation as they clutched their ticket stubs, not fully understanding the unique experience that awaited them. But I knew this night would be something special. Thanks to my history with both The Monkees and Herman's Hermits through my talent agency, Somerset Talent, getting on the guest list was a breeze. After all, Somerset Talent had booked shows for The Monkees, Dolenz, Jones, Boyce, and Hart (featuring Micky Dolenz and Davy Jones), and Herman's Hermits over the years. This connection opened the backstage doors for us, and tonight, those doors led to a once-in-a-lifetime experience.

As we passed security and stepped backstage, the atmosphere shifted from the lively chaos of the fairgrounds to the buzzing camaraderie of performers preparing for the stage. Roadies hustled about, tuning instruments and adjusting lights, while distant sound checks echoed through the air. The kids clung to our hands, their eyes darting from one scene to the next as they absorbed the magic behind the curtain of a world usually hidden from view.

Suddenly, a familiar voice called out. "Hey, Richard! Long time no see!" It was Micky Dolenz himself, striding toward us with that signature smile. Before I could reply, Davy Jones appeared beside him, both of them radiating the same youthful energy that had made them famous. My kids froze in awe, their gazes bouncing between the two Monkees as they tried to process the moment.

"And who do we have here?" Davy asked, crouching to meet Jennifer and Ryan at eye level. "Are these your little rock stars?"

Jennifer giggled shyly, clutching Cathy's hand, while Ryan puffed out his chest, determined to make a good impression.

"I'm Ryan!" he declared proudly.

Micky chuckled and ruffled Ryan's hair. "Well, Ryan, it's a pleasure to meet you. And you too, Jennifer. You both picked a great night to come backstage."

As if on cue, Karl Greene from Herman's Hermits joined the group, extending his hand with a warm smile. "Richard! Great to see you again. And these must be your little VIPs for the night!"

From that moment on, Jennifer and Ryan became the evening's unofficial stars. The bands treated them like royalty, inviting them to explore the tour buses, mobile sanctuaries filled with guitars, costumes, and memorabilia from years on the road. The kids marveled at the rows of bunks and shelves stocked with snacks, wide-eyed as they discovered this hidden world of traveling musicians.

"Look at this!" Jennifer gasped as she found a shelf of colorful sunglasses, trying on a pair far too big for her small face. The musicians laughed good-naturedly, and Karl snapped a photo with a disposable camera to capture the moment.

Ryan, meanwhile, was captivated by a drum tucked into a corner of the bus. Lek, the lead guitarist of Herman's Hermits, noticing his fascination, picked up a pair of drumsticks and knelt beside him. "Want to give it a try?" he asked. Ryan's eyes lit up as he nodded eagerly. With Lek guiding his hands, he tapped out a simple beat, the rhythmic thumps echoing through the bus. The musicians clapped and cheered as if he had just performed a sold-out concert.

Before long, it was time for the bands to take the stage. We found our seats and enjoyed the show.

The lights dimmed, and a wave of cheers swept through the fairgrounds as the show began. Jennifer and Ryan clapped and

345

danced, their laughter mingling with the music as if they were part of the show itself.

Years later, Jennifer and Ryan remember only fragments of that night, flashes of stage lights, the warmth of friendly musicians, and the rhythmic thump of drums echoing through a tour bus. Yet for Cathy and me, the memory remains crystal clear: a night when the magic of music bridged generations, and our children became part of rock and roll history, if only for one unforgettable summer night.

Chapter 38

Surf's Up - The Beach Party Musical

It was the summer of 2002, and I was deep in the world of computers. I was busy running my IT consulting business, Decisions Support Inc. But that wasn't my only passion. I had an idea, one that had been bouncing around in my head for a while. What if we took the fun, over-the-top energy of those 1960s beach movies and turned it into a musical?

Richard M. Adler

My son Ryan was bitten by the acting bug, and I wanted to help him. We were sitting on the beach at the Atlantis Hotel in Paradise Island when it hit me. I would write a musical about the beach. Why not write a spoof on the 60s beach party movies and write a part specifically for Ryan?

I had thought about using the songs of the Beach Boys and building a story around them, but it was not to be. I could not secure licenses for most of the Beach Boys' songs.

I had always loved those old films, the kind where teenagers surfed all day, danced all night, and somehow found time to fall in love, outsmart villains, or get tangled up in some ridiculous plot involving spies, monsters, or mad scientists. They were silly, they were fun, and most importantly, they had great music.

So, I started working on it. I teamed up with Eric Kornfeld, a New York comedy writer suggested to me by one of the writers on Saturday Night Live. Together, we started shaping the show. We wanted it to be a parody, but also a tribute, something that would make people laugh while celebrating the music and spirit of those classic films. I didn't know it at the time, but we were actually ahead of the curve. We had started working on this before *Mamma Mia!* became a global sensation using the same concept of plugging well-known pop songs into a completely new story, a jukebox musical.

But once *Mamma Mia!* took off, suddenly everyone thought we were jumping on the bandwagon. The truth was, we had been working on *Surf's Up* long before ABBA's music took over Broadway. And now, we were finally ready to give people a taste of what we had created.

Rather than writing original songs, we decided to use the greatest hits of the 1960s, the music that defined the beach movie era. We carefully selected a mix of classic surf songs and pop hits, including:

• "Surfin' USA" – The Beach Boys

• "Surf City" – Jan & Dean

• "The End of the World" – Skeeter Davis

• "Little Old Lady From Pasadena" – Jan & Dean

• "Calendar Girl" – Neil Sedaka

• "Secret Agent Man" – Johnny Rivers

• "Soldier Boy" – The Shirelles

• "I Will Follow Him" – Little Peggy March

• "Beach Baby" – The First Class

• "Sloop John B" – The Beach Boys

• "Barbara Ann" – The Beach Boys

• "Do You Wanna Dance" – The Beach Boys

The songs weren't just there for nostalgia. They were woven into the story, just like in *Mamma Mia!* or *Jersey Boys*. The challenge was making sure they fit naturally while keeping that breezy, fun-loving beach vibe.

Of course, we needed characters who felt like they stepped right out of a 1960s beach movie. If you've ever seen one of those films, you know the types:• the cool surfer dude, the nerdy scientist, the mysterious stranger, the wild sidekick, the all-American girl next door, and of course, the villainous adult trying to ruin all the fun.

We played up those stereotypes, making sure everything felt lighthearted and a little ridiculous. That's why we gave the characters names like:

• Hot Dog (probably the best surfer on the beach, or at least, he thinks he is)

• Derek Von Dusseldorf (the head of a motorcycle gang?)

• The Professor (every beach movie needs one)

• Bongo (for comic relief and because someone's always playing the bongos)

• Big Mo (owner of Big Mo's Soda Shop, the beach hangout spot)

• Barbara Ann, Whitey, and Skip (because every surf movie needs a fun-loving crew)

My producing partner, Roger Gindi, called the show a parody/tribute, and he was right. It was our way of saying, "Yeah, these movies were goofy, but weren't they also a blast?"

Bringing Surf's Up to the Stage

Now, here's the thing about creating a musical, you don't just wake up one day and book a Broadway theater. You have to test the waters first.

That's why, on June 25, 2002, we held a private industry reading in New York City. The goal was to present the show to people who could help make it a reality, investors, producers, and decision-makers.

We wanted to see if they laughed at the right moments, if the music got them moving, and if they could see *Surf's Up* becoming a full-scale production.

It wasn't the first time we had read the script out loud, but earlier versions were bare-bones, just a group of people reading lines while playing the original recordings of the songs. This time, we had 16 live performers, and if the show made it to a full production, it would have at least 24 cast members plus a band.

Our cast was filled with incredible talent, including:

• Stuart Marland

• Leslie Denniston

• Andy Karl

• Jessica Grove

• Brian Duguay

• Andrew Wright

• Anne Kittredge

• Lou Martini

• Ryan Adler

• Darren Richie

• Jason Jones

• Diane Phelan

• John Jeffrey Martin

Richard M. Adler

• Eric Harper

• Joanna Wasick

• And Eric Kornfeld

With Danny Kosarin as our music director and Ray Roderick as our director, we had everything lined up for a great first showing.

Would *Surf's Up* make it to Broadway?

That was the big question. We knew that shows like *Grease* and *Mamma Mia!* had proven nostalgia was a goldmine, but getting *Surf's Up* to the next level would take a lot of things coming together, the right investors, the right theater, and the right timing.

We believed in the show. We knew it was fun; we knew the music was great, and we knew audiences would love the over-the-top beach movie energy. But in the world of theater, you don't always know what's going to stick.

At the end of the day, whether *Surf's Up* became the next big musical or not, I was proud of what we created. We had taken a piece of pop culture history, added a fresh spin, and brought it to life on stage.

And who knows? Maybe one day, *Surf's Up* will ride the wave again.

Back in the early 2000s, I had a dream, bringing *Surf's Up*, a musical featuring the unforgettable songs of The Beach Boys, to Broadway. I had the vision, the team, and the passion to make it happen. But there was one major problem: securing the rights to The Beach Boys' music. Without those songs, there was no show.

At first, it seemed simple. I reached out to the music publisher, expecting to negotiate a deal. That's when I found out that the rights to the songs had already been promised, verbally, not in writing, to another producer. The catch? This producer was dragging her feet, taking forever to move forward with her production. Meanwhile, I was ready to go.

I wasn't about to give up. I called the publisher repeatedly, making my case. My attorney sent letter after letter, arguing that if the other producer wasn't moving forward, the rights should be given to us. I even got Brian Wilson involved, hoping he could help. But there was a heartbreaking truth, Brian didn't even own his own songs anymore. Years earlier, his father had sold them without his knowledge, leaving him powerless over his own music.

Despite the roadblocks, my persistence paid off. Eventually, the publisher saw that my team was serious about *Surf's Up*. We had everything in place, ready to launch a Broadway production. Seeing this, the publisher gave the other producer a strict deadline. She had until January 27, 2005, to open her show on Broadway. If she failed to meet that deadline, the rights to The Beach Boys' songs would be awarded to *Surf's Up*.

That producer was working on a show called *Good Vibrations*. But there was a problem, her production wasn't ready. It still needed time to develop, to refine the story, to get everything right. But now, with the publisher's deadline looming, she had no choice. She rushed the show into previews on January 27, 2005, just in time to meet the requirement and secure the rights to the songs.

And just like that, my dream was crushed. The songs were locked into *Good Vibrations*, and *Surf's Up* was dead in the water.

But here's the ironic part. *Good Vibrations* was a disaster. Because it was rushed to the stage, the show was messy and unpolished. The critics tore it apart, calling it uninspired and poorly written.

Audiences didn't connect with it either, and ticket sales plummeted. After just 94 performances, the show closed on April 24, 2005. Investors lost $10 million.

And here's what stung the most. I later found out that the producer of *Good Vibrations* had attended my reading of *Surf's Up* before their own script was even written. Their show ended up being too similar to mine, which meant that once it flopped, there was no room for another Beach Boys musical on Broadway. The failure of *Good Vibrations* didn't just end their show. It killed *Surf's Up* before it ever had a chance.

It was a tough pill to swallow. I had fought so hard, done everything right, and still lost. But that's show business. Sometimes, even the best ideas get swept away by forces beyond your control.

Surf's Up: A Beach Party Musical Adventure

The cast of Surf's Up with the Producers Richard Adler and Peter Fill. My son Ryan is on the bottom holding the surfboard.

In 2006, I had the pleasure of producing *Surf's Up*, a lively musical that I co-wrote with Eric Kornfeld. This production, staged at the Hackensack Cultural Arts Center (HCAC) in New Jersey, was a nostalgic yet comedic tribute to the beach movies of the 1960s, complete with catchy tunes, quirky characters, and a lot of surfboard swagger. One of the highlights of the production was seeing my son, Ryan Adler, take the stage as Bongo, a laid-back surfer dude with a knack for rhythm and fun.

355

Richard M. Adler

The musical was brought to life by Teaneck New Theatre (TNT) under the expert direction of Marilyn Schilkie, with music direction by Dennis Schaefer and choreography by Carrie Nagy. My co-producer, Peter Fill, and I were excited to see our creation come to life during its run from February 17 to March 5, with performances every Friday and Saturday night and Sunday matinees.

The story of *Surf's Up* was a playful spoof of classic beach flicks but delivered with a loving, tongue-in-cheek humor that celebrated the era. The plot revolved around Barbara Ann, a 17-year-old misfit and high school valedictorian who dreams of becoming a surfer. Her journey to ride the waves leads her into the orbit of Hotdog, the king of the surf, and a colorful cast of characters, including Derrick Von Dusseldorf, the eccentric leader of a motorcycle gang; a mysterious professor with oddball inventions; and Fifi LeClique, a seductive French photographer whose motives are as intriguing as her accent.

Set against a backdrop of sand, sun, and surfboards, the show was packed with beloved songs from the 1960s that had audiences tapping their feet and singing along. Classics like *Do You Wanna Dance, Surfin' USA, Barbara Ann, Surfer Girl, Beach Baby*, and *Surfin' Safari* transported theatergoers back to the carefree days of summer, making them forget the winter chill outside.

Adding to the beach-themed fun, the Pottery Barn Kids mail-order catalog generously donated "Surf's Up" beach towels, which were given away as door prizes during the run of the show. It was a small touch that added to the immersive, sun-soaked atmosphere we wanted to create.

The cast, a talented ensemble of performers from across New Jersey and New York, brought energy, humor, and heart to the production. Brandon Ruckdashel from Jersey City starred as Hotdog, the charming 20-year-old ladies' man with a surfboard in one hand and a smile for every girl on the beach. Caity Olenowski of Denville portrayed Barbara Ann, capturing both her awkward charm and her determination to conquer the waves.

Adding a touch of nostalgia, Robert Hernest from Hewitt and Mary-Ann L. Barranger from Bound Brook played Bob and Barb McCreedy, the older versions of Hotdog and Barbara Ann, offering a glimpse into their future lives. Oscar Flores of Ridgewood, New York, delivered a scene-stealing performance as the wild and wacky Derrick Von Dusseldorf, while Chris Mavrick of North Plainfield brought laughs as the eccentric professor whose inventions often caused more chaos than convenience. Lisa Garrabrant from Little Falls added a dose of international intrigue as the sultry Fifi LeClique, while Joshua David Bishop of Brooklyn played Whitey, the brainy surfer who proved that you can ride the waves and still hit the books. Robert Lascar brought youthful energy as Junior, the youngest surfer of the bunch.

Of course, one of the proudest moments for me personally was watching my son, Ryan Adler, light up the stage as Bongo, the easygoing surfer dude with a heart of gold and a talent for drumming on anything that stood still long enough. His performance brought both humor and warmth to the show, and seeing him take center stage in a production I helped create was an unforgettable experience.

Rounding out the ensemble were Kristina Diakos from Lyndhurst and Carrie Nagy from Clifton, whose vibrant dancing and energetic performances added to the lively beach party atmosphere that defined the show.

The production was a true labor of love, from the initial writing process with Eric Kornfeld to the collaborative efforts of the entire creative team and cast. Seeing *Surf's Up* come to life on stage, with its mix of nostalgic music, comedic twists, and heartfelt moments, was a dream come true. And hearing the audience laugh, cheer, and sing along was the ultimate reward.

Even now, years later, I still smile when I think of those performances, the sound of surf music filling the theater, the sight of brightly colored beach costumes, and the joy of seeing my son Ryan shine on stage. *Surf's Up* was more than just a musical; it was a celebration of a simpler time, a loving tribute to the beach movies of the past, and a reminder that sometimes, all you need is a surfboard, a sunny day, and a good song to make life feel like a beach party.

Chapter 39

The Smartest (and Greediest) Man in Showbiz

I'm grateful to my friend Robert Rowland for gifting me this framed autographed poster. Thank you so much, Robert!

Richard M. Adler

A few years before he passed away, I had the chance to hang out with Mike Smith, the legendary lead singer and keyboardist of the Dave Clark Five. My friend Robert Rowland had booked Mike to perform at the Wolf Den in Mohegan Sun, and after the show, we went backstage to see him. I had no idea that night would turn into a deep dive into one of the most fascinating and, honestly, shocking stories I'd ever heard about the music business.

Mike was in a great mood after the show. His voice was still strong, and he still had that charm that made the Dave Clark Five such a force during the British Invasion. As we sat around talking, laughing, and reminiscing about the old days, the conversation somehow drifted toward Dave Clark himself. And that's when Mike started telling us things that made my jaw drop.

"You know Dave didn't actually play drums on the records, right?" Mike said, shaking his head with a grin.

I blinked. "Wait, what? He was the drummer!"

Mike chuckled. "Not on the records, he wasn't. He hired a session drummer to do the studio work."

That was just the beginning. As the stories kept coming, I realized that Dave Clark wasn't just the leader of the band, he was the boss in every possible way. Unlike other British bands of the time, where members shared in the profits of records, tours, and merchandise, Dave owned the entire operation. The rest of the band? They were employees. They got a paycheck, but they never saw a share of the massive profits the band was pulling in.

And the profits were enormous. The Dave Clark Five sold over 100 million records. They had more appearances on *The Ed Sullivan Show* than The Beatles. They starred in movies, played to screaming crowds worldwide, and were part of the soundtrack of the 1960s. But all of it, the records, the tours, the publishing rights, the merchandise, belonged to Dave Clark.

Then Mike told us something even crazier.

"If we wrote a song and the band recorded it, we had to give Dave a co-writing credit, and he took all the publishing rights."

I was stunned. "He didn't even write the songs?"

Mike shook his head. "Nope. But if you wanted your song on a Dave Clark Five record, you had to give him a cut."

I had been in the music business for a long time, and I had seen my share of greedy managers, unfair record deals, and artists who got ripped off. But this was something different. Dave Clark didn't just sign a bad contract, he controlled the entire system.

And it didn't stop there. Unlike most artists at the time, Clark owned the master recordings of all their records. Instead of signing them away to a record label, he leased them to the companies, keeping full control and making 100 percent of the profits.

Think about that for a second. In the early 1960s, when bands were signing away their futures for pennies on the dollar, Dave Clark figured out how to own everything. He was the producer of the records, he controlled the business side, and he made sure every dollar flowed back to him.

"So let me get this straight," I said, trying to process it all. "He made money off the records, the concerts, the TV shows, the movies, the publishing, the merchandise, and the songwriting credits, even when he didn't write the songs?"

Mike nodded. "That's right. Every penny."

I sat back, shaking my head. "That's either the smartest or the greediest move I've ever heard of."

Mike laughed. "Probably both. But I'll give him credit, he was ahead of his time. No one else in the business had that kind of deal."

By the end of the night, I had a whole new understanding of the Dave Clark Five, and a new appreciation for just how ruthless and brilliant Dave Clark really was. He may not have been the best drummer, the best songwriter, or even the best businessman, but he knew how to control an empire. And when all was said and done, he walked away with a fortune.

The rest of the band? Well, they got a paycheck. Not too shabby, but nowhere near what they could have made.

I left that night shaking my head, thinking about how different music history might have been if the other band members had shared in the success. But one thing was certain, Dave Clark played the business game better than anyone.

Chapter 40

Boy Scouts of America

Looking back on my Rock and Roll Fantasy life, it might surprise some readers to learn that long before I stood behind a camera capturing rock legends or shared stages with future Ramones, I proudly wore the uniform of the Boy Scouts of America.

It all started when I was just eight years old, a kid from Bethpage with a buzz cut and a boundless curiosity for the outdoors. I joined the Cub Scouts mostly because my friends were doing it, but something clicked. I wasn't just showing up for badges or merit pins. I believed in what the Scouts stood for: self-reliance, community, integrity. When I turned eleven and bridged into the Boy Scouts, those ideals only deepened. The knot-tying, the campfires, the service projects, they weren't just skills or activities, they became part of how I saw the world.

One of the best parts of Scouting was the friendships. In fact, one of my closest friends to this day, Kenny, entered my life through our local troop. There's something about building a lean-to in the rain or hiking ten miles with thirty pounds of gear on your back that bonds people for life. Every summer, except the two years I was tangled up in Tangerine Puppets gigs, I spent a full month at Ten Mile River Scout Camps, especially at Camp Kernochan. That place was a second home. When I turned eighteen, I worked there as a staff member, giving back to a program that had shaped me.

And yes, I wore the uniform. Proudly. Even during the rebellious teen years, when conformity was out and long hair was in, I never once felt ashamed. Oddly enough, no one ever gave me grief about

363

it, not even the kids in the neighborhood who might have rolled their eyes at anything "square." Maybe they sensed I wasn't trying to prove anything. I was just being me.

I went all in on Scouting. I earned every Cub Scout badge and then every merit badge required for Eagle, plus quite a few more. I was determined to finish the journey, and just one week before my eighteenth birthday, the absolute deadline, I was awarded the rank of Eagle Scout. That moment remains one of my proudest achievements.

But it didn't come easy.

To become an Eagle Scout, you need more than just badges. You need to plan and execute a service project that benefits your community and demonstrates leadership. I had already fulfilled all the academic and skills requirements. Now it was time to lead. I was seventeen, staring down that final challenge, and I wanted to do something meaningful.

Even though I opposed the Vietnam War, I had tremendous empathy for the young men who had been drafted, guys just a few years older than me, pulled from their homes and shipped halfway across the world into chaos. So, I created a project to help them, to bring them some small comforts from home.

I organized my troop to collect basic necessities for soldiers: soap, razors, shaving cream, deodorant, socks, toothpaste, even underwear. We created flyers, and I assigned each Scout a set of apartment buildings to post them in. The flyers announced that on a specific Saturday, we would come back to collect donations. And people responded, big time. The generosity of our neighbors blew me away. Boxes piled up in my parents' living room, packed with supplies and handwritten notes of support. I arranged for Catholic Charities to handle the shipping and distribution to troops stationed in Vietnam.

The project was a success by every measurable standard. I wrote a full report detailing the planning, logistics, execution, and leadership involved. I walked into my Board of Review, the final interview with Scout leaders before earning the Eagle rank, feeling confident and proud.

And I failed.

They told me my Eagle Project didn't meet the standard. When I asked why, their answer stunned me. It wasn't the leadership, or the organization, or even the results. It was the subject. They didn't like that I had helped American soldiers. The Board members, it turned out, were vocally anti-war, and they saw my project as supporting a cause they opposed.

To say I was blindsided is an understatement. I wasn't supporting the war, I was supporting people. Young guys, some of whom probably didn't even believe in what they were fighting for, trying to stay clean and sane in the middle of a jungle. Toothpaste and socks weren't weapons. They were reminders that someone back home cared. I refused to accept their decision.

So, I wrote a letter to the Boy Scout Council, laying out my case. I requested a new Board of Review. Thankfully, my appeal was granted. I went before a new panel, presented the exact same project, and this time, just one week before I aged out, I passed.

I received my Eagle Award in a small ceremony attended by my Scout troop, friends, family, and one unexpected guest: Senator Alfonse D'Amato. He had heard about my project and came to present the award personally. After the ceremony, he pulled me aside and told me he was recommending me for admission to West Point. I was floored. It was a tremendous honor, but one I ultimately declined. As proud as I was of my service and my accomplishment, I couldn't reconcile my opposition to the war with a future in the military.

Still, the moment stuck with me. Not just the honor, but the principle. You can believe in your country without supporting every policy. You can help people without backing the politics that put them in harm's way.

Becoming an Eagle Scout wasn't about the badge. It was about grit, conviction, and standing your ground when it would've been easier to give in. It was about living the values I'd been taught as a kid: leadership, service, and loyalty, not to institutions, but to people.

When my son Ryan became a Tiger Cub in the Cub Scouts, I went to every meeting and event with him. When Ryan became a Wolf, we heard that the Cubmaster was leaving to move on to Boy Scouts with his son and that the Pack was looking for a new Cubmaster. This was my chance to give back to Scouting, so I volunteered and became the new Cubmaster of our Pack. I went to Ten Mile River with my son Ryan, and then when my son Jon became a Cub Scout, I also went to camp with him. One year, Ryan as a Boy Scout and Jon as a Cub Scout were at Ten Mile River Scout Camp with me. This was a dream come true, my boys enjoying Scout camp as much as I did.

And that legacy didn't end with me.

When my son Ryan became a Tiger Cub in the Cub Scouts, I was right there beside him at every meeting and every event. I knew this was my chance to give back to Scouting in a new way. When Ryan moved up to Wolf rank, we heard that the Cubmaster was stepping down to move on with his own son into the Boy Scouts. The Pack needed a new leader, and I raised my hand. I became Cubmaster of the Pack, guiding not just Ryan but dozens of other boys through their first steps in Scouting.

I took Ryan to Ten Mile River, something I never got to experience with my dad. Then, when my younger son Jon joined the Cubs, I did the same with him. One summer, both of my boys were at Ten Mile River at the same time, Ryan as a Boy Scout, Jon as a Cub Scout, and I was there with them. That was a dream come true. My sons were experiencing the same joy, camaraderie, and sense of adventure that I had cherished decades earlier.

It was full circle. From a boy with a handbook and a tent to a father watching his kids fall in love with the same trail. Scouting wasn't just a chapter in my life; it was a thread that tied generations together.

Today, my grandson Aiden recently moved up from Cub Scouts to Boy Scouts, and my son Ryan is a Scout Leader. I am very proud of both of them.

And that, as much as anything in my so-called rock and roll fantasy life, shaped the man I became.

Richard M. Adler